WHO KNOWS WHAT ADVENTURES WAIT for us in the years to come? Only a short time ago, manned flights to the moon were far-off dreams. Today, they make headlines. The ten stories in this collection are only dreams today, guesses about man's probable future. But read them carefully—you may be in the midst of these adventures tomorrow.

BEYOND TOMORROW

edited by DAMON KNIGHT

A FAWCETT GOLD MEDAL BOOK
Fawcett Publications, Inc., Greenwich, Conn.
Member of American Book Publishers Council, Inc.

ACKNOWLEDGMENTS

For permission to use the stories in this volume, grateful acknowledgment is made to the following:

David McKay Company, Inc., for "Brightside Crossing," by Alan E. Nourse, copyright © 1956 by Galaxy Publishing Corp., 1961 by Alan E. Nourse.

Arthur C. Clarke and Scott Meredith Literary Agency, Inc., for "The Deep Range," copyright 1954 by Ballantine Books, Inc.

Robert A. Heinlein and Lurton Blassingame for "Coventry," copyright 1940 by Street & Smith Publications, Inc., 1953 by Robert A. Heinlein.

Kate Wilhelm for "The Mile-long Spaceship," copyright © 1957 by Street & Smith Publications, Inc.

A. E. van Vogt and Forrest J. Ackerman for "The Seesaw," copyright 1941 by Street & Smith Publications, Inc.

Isaac Asimov for "Nightfall," copyright 1941 by Street & Smith Publications, Inc. Copyright © renewed 1968 by Isaac Asimov.

Ray Bradbury and Harold Matson Company, Inc., for "The Million-Year Picnic," copyright 1946 by Love Romances Publishing Co., Inc., 1950 by Ray Bradbury.

Clifford D. Simak and Robert P. Mills for "Desertion," copyright 1944 by Street & Smith Publications, Inc., 1952 by Clifford D. Simak.

John W. Campbell for "Twilight," copyright 1934 by Street & Smith Publications, Inc., 1951 by John W. Campbell, Jr.

Catherine Kuttner Reggie and Harold Matson Company, Inc., for "Happy Ending," copyright 1948 by Standard Magazines, Inc.

Printed through special arrangement with Harper & Row, Publishers, Inc.

Library of Congress Catalog Card Number: 65-20251

Printed in the United States of America

CONTENTS

INTRODUCTION

TIME TRAVEL IS POSSIBLE, OF COURSE: ALL YOU HAVE
to do is keep on living. By this means I have reached
the present, and (as a traveler from 1922) I can report that the future is an even more surprising place
than I expected. The other day, for example, I picked
up a high-school literature book belonging to a fifteen-
year-old boy I know, and found it full of science fiction.
Such a thing could never have happened when I was in
high school. In those days science fiction was a pulp
magazine that you had to smuggle home under your
sweater to hide its embarrassingly gaudy cover. As for
literature textbooks, the only fiction in them was by
authors who had been dead at least since 1890.

My notion is that some of the kids who smuggled
those magazines home under their sweaters have now
grown up and become editors of English literature textbooks. (The magazines are now collectors' items.) *Your*
children will be doing things you cannot foresee and
would not approve of, thirty or fifty years from now;
furthermore, if I knew what some of these things were
and could tell you, you would not believe me.

This one simple idea—that the future will be different—used to make science fiction unacceptable to
most people. The small-town people among whom I
grew up didn't *want* to believe that the world was changing, could change. Most adults are like that even today,
and most adult fiction is written under the invisible
dunce cap of a tacit agreement to pretend that (*a*) tech-
nological change does not happen; (*b*) if it does happen, it is not important; or (*c*) if it is important, it is
incomprehensible and frightening.

I take this to be a temporary state of affairs, though
it has been going on for about a century; you can't make

7

change go away by turning your back on it, and sooner or later, as a culture, we must find that out. I think the increased number of science fiction readers, especially among young people, is a sign that we are finding it out.

With all its faults, and it has many, science fiction is one of the few open lines of communication between C. P. Snow's "two cultures"—the scientists and the liberal-arts people. It is a going concern; it works. That is about all that can be said for man himself, but it is enough. Members of our species invented agriculture and mathematics, rounded the Horn, discovered America, painted the first picture and cooked the first stew, climbed Everest, reached the North Pole. Our probing into space and into the ocean is no more than a logical continuation of a process which has been going on without interruption ever since man discovered that he could think.

Of course there are still people who do not care about Mars, just as there were once people who did not care about Coromandel; but they are being left behind.

Man, after all, is the animal who wants to know. What was the origin of the universe? Are there intelligent beings in space—or in the depths of our own oceans? Can we survive on other planets? Can we find a way to live together without fear? This is the sort of thing that science fiction is about; and all these questions are dealt with in the stories collected here. We are all traveling into the future, like it or not . . . and the future is a fascinating place.

Damon Knight

BRIGHTSIDE CROSSING

by Alan E. Nourse

"Brightside Crossing" is a tale of adventure, in
the great tradition of the "Explorers' Club"
stories written by H. F. Heard, Lord Dunsany,
Lawrence Manning, and many others. But it
goes a little beyond any such story that I have
ever read before. Although it takes place on
Mercury, a planet man has not yet reached, it
is so plausibly written, so well researched, that
it might almost be an article from a future issue
of *National Geographic*.

JAMES BARON WAS NOT PLEASED TO HEAR THAT HE
had had a visitor when he reached the Red Lion that
evening. He had no stomach for mysteries, vast or
trifling, and there were pressing things to think about
at this time. Yet the doorman had flagged him as he
came in from the street: "A thousand pardons, Mr.
Baron. The gentleman—he would leave no name. He
said you'd want to see him. He will be back by eight."

Baron drummed his fingers on the tabletop, staring
about the quiet lounge. Street trade was discouraged at
the Red Lion, gently but persuasively; the patrons
were few in number. Across to the right was a group
that Baron knew vaguely—Andean climbers, or at
least two of them were. Over near the door he recog-

nized old Balmer, who had mapped the first passage to the core of Vulcan Crater on Venus. Baron returned his smile with a nod. Then he settled back and waited impatiently for the intruder who demanded his time without justifying it.

Presently a small, grizzled man crossed the room and sat down at Baron's table. He was short and wiry. His face held no key to his age—he might have been thirty or a thousand—but he looked weary and immensely ugly. His cheeks and forehead were twisted and brown, with scars that were still healing.

The stranger said, "I'm glad you waited. I've heard you're planning to attempt the Brightside."

Baron stared at the man for a moment. "I see you can read telecasts," he said coldly. "The news was correct. We are going to make a Brightside Crossing."

"At perihelion?"

"Of course. When else?"

The grizzled man searched Baron's face for a moment without expression. Then he said slowly, "No, I'm afraid you're not going to make the Crossing."

"Say, who are you, if you don't mind?" Baron demanded.

"The name is Claney," said the stranger.

There was a silence. Then: "Claney? *Peter* Claney?"

"That's right."

Baron's eyes were wide with excitement, all trace of anger gone. "My God, man—*where have you been hiding?* We've been trying to contact you for months!"

"I know. I was hoping you'd quit looking and chuck the whole idea."

"Quit looking!" Baron bent forward over the table. "My friend, we'd given up hope, but we've never quit looking. Here, have a drink. There's so much you can tell us." His fingers were trembling.

Peter Claney shook his head. "I can't tell you anything you want to hear."

"But you've *got* to. You're the only man on Earth who's attempted a Brightside Crossing and lived through it! And the story you cleared for the news—it was nothing. We need *details*. Where did your equipment fall down? Where did you miscalculate? What were the trouble spots?" Baron jabbed a finger at Claney's face. "That, for instance—epithelioma? Why? What was wrong with your glass? Your filters? We've got to know those things. If you can tell us, we can make it across where your attempt failed—"

"You want to know why we failed?" asked Claney.

"Of course we want to know. We *have* to know."

"It's simple. We failed because it can't be done. We couldn't do it and neither can you. No human beings will ever cross the Brightside alive, not if they try for centuries."

"Nonsense," Baron declared. "We will."

Claney shrugged. "I was there. I know what I'm saying. You can blame the equipment or the men— there were flaws in both quarters—but we just didn't know what we were fighting. It was the *planet* that whipped us, that and the *Sun*. They'll whip you, too, if you try it."

"Never," said Baron.

"Let me tell you," Peter Claney said.

I'd been interested in the Brightside for almost as long as I can remember (Claney said). I guess I was about ten when Wyatt and Carpenter made the last attempt—that was in 2082, I think. I followed the news stories like a tri-V serial, and then I was heartbroken when they just disappeared.

I know now that they were a pair of idiots, starting off without proper equipment, with practically no knowledge of surface conditions, without any charts— but I didn't know that then and it was a terrible tragedy. After that, I followed Sanderson's work in the Twilight Lab up there and began to get Brightside into my blood.

But it was Mikuta's idea to attempt a Crossing. Did you ever know Tom Mikuta? I don't suppose you did.

No, not Japanese—Polish-American. He was a major in the Interplanetary Service for some years and hung onto the title after he gave up his commission.

He was with Armstrong on Mars during his Service days, with a good deal of the original mapping and surveying for the colony to his credit. I first met him on Venus; we spent five years together up there doing some of the nastiest exploring since the Matto Grosso. Then he made the attempt on Vulcan Crater that paved the way for Balmer a few years later.

I'd always liked the Major—he was big and quiet and cool, the sort of guy who always had things figured a little further ahead than anyone else and always knew what to do in a tight place. Too many men in this game are all nerve and luck, with no judgment. The Major had both. He also had the kind of personality that could take a crew of wild men and make them work like a well-oiled machine across a thousand miles of Venus jungle. I liked him and I trusted him.

He contacted me in New York, and he was very casual at first. We spent an evening here at the Red Lion, talking about old times; he told me about the Vulcan business, and how he'd been out to see Sanderson and the Twilight Lab on Mercury, and how he preferred a hot trek to a cold one any day of the year —and then he wanted to know what I'd been doing since Venus and what my plans were.

"No particular plans," I told him. "Why?"

He looked me over. "How much do you weigh, Peter?"

I told him one thirty-five.

"That much!" he said. "Be damned. Well, there can't be much fat on you, at any rate. How do you take heat?"

"You should know," I said. "Venus was no ice-box."

"No, I mean *real* heat."

Then I began to get it. "You're planning a trip."

"That's right. A hot trip." He grinned at me. "Might be dangerous, too."

"What trip?"

"Brightside of Mercury," the Major said.

I whistled cautiously. "Aphelion?"

He threw his head back. "Why try a Crossing at aphelion? What have you done then? Four thousand miles of butcherous heat, just to have some joker come along, use your data, and drum you out of the glory by crossing at perihelion forty-four days later? No, thanks. I want the Brightside without any nonsense about it." He leaned toward me eagerly. "I want to make a Crossing at perihelion and I want to cross on the surface. If a man can do that, he's got Mercury. Until then, *nobody's* got Mercury. I want Mercury—but I'll need help getting it."

I'd thought of it a thousand times and never dared consider it. Nobody had, since Wyatt and Carpenter disappeared. Mercury turns on its axis in the same time that it wheels around the Sun, which means that the Brightside is always facing in. That makes the Brightside of Mercury at perihelion the hottest place in the Solar System, with one single exception: the surface of the Sun itself.

It would be a hellish trek. Only a few men had ever learned just *how* hellish and they never came back to tell about it. It was a real Hell's Crossing, but someday somebody would cross it.

I wanted to be along.

The Twilight Lab, near the northern pole of Mercury, was the obvious jumping-off place. The setup there wasn't very extensive—a rocket landing, the labs and quarters for Sanderson's crew sunk deep into the crust, and the tower that housed the Solar 'scope that Sanderson had built up there ten years before.

Twilight Lab wasn't particularly interested in the Brightside, of course—the Sun was Sanderson's baby and he'd picked Mercury as the closest chunk of rock to the Sun that could hold his observatory. He'd chosen a good location, too. On Mercury, the Brightside temperature hits 770° F. at perihelion and the Darkside runs pretty constant at —410° F. No permanent installation with a human crew could survive at either extreme. But with Mercury's wobble, the twilight zone between Brightside and Darkside offers something closer to survival temperatures.

Sanderson built the Lab up near the pole, where the zone is about 5 miles wide, so the temperature only varies 50 to 60 degrees with the libration. The Solar 'scope could take that much change, and they'd get good clear observation of the Sun for about 70 out of the 88 days it takes the planet to wheel around.

The Major was counting on Sanderson knowing something about Mercury as well as the Sun when we camped at the Lab to make final preparations.

Sanderson did. He thought we'd lost our minds and he said so, but he gave us all the help he could. He spent a week briefing Jack Stone, the third member of our party, who had arrived with the supplies and equipment a few days earlier. Poor Jack met us at the rocket landing almost bawling, Sanderson had given him such a gloomy picture of what Brightside was like.

Stone was a youngster—hardly twenty-five, I'd say —but he'd been with the Major at Vulcan and had begged to join this trek. I had a funny feeling that Jack really didn't care for exploring too much, but he thought Mikuta was God, followed him around like a puppy.

It didn't matter to me as long as he knew what he was getting in for. You don't go asking people in this game why they do it—they're liable to get awfully uneasy, and none of them can ever give you an answer that makes sense. Anyway, Stone had borrowed three men from the Lab and had the supplies and equipment all lined up when we got there, ready to check and test.

We dug right in. With plenty of funds—tri-V money and some government cash the Major had talked his way around—our equipment was new and good. Mikuta had done the designing and testing himself, with a big assist from Sanderson. We had four Bugs, three of them the light pillow-tire models, with special lead-cooled cut-in engines when the heat set in, and one heavy-duty tractor model for pulling the sledges.

The Major went over them like a kid at the circus. Then he said, "Have you heard anything from McIvers?"

"Who's he?" Stone wanted to know.

"He'll be joining us. He's a good man—got quite a name for climbing, back home." The Major turned to me. "You've probably heard of him."

I'd heard plenty of stories about Ted McIvers and I wasn't too happy to hear that he was joining us. "Kind of a daredevil, isn't he?"

"Maybe. He's lucky and skillful. Where do you draw the line? We'll need plenty of both."

"Have you ever worked with him?" I asked.

"No. Are you worried?"

"Not exactly. But Brightside is no place to count on luck."

The Major laughed. "I don't think we need to worry about McIvers. We understood each other when I talked up the trip to him, and we're going to need each other too much to do any fooling around." He turned back to the supply list. "Meanwhile, let's get this stuff listed and packed. We'll need to cut weight sharply and our time is short. Sanderson says we should leave in three days."

Two days later, McIvers hadn't arrived. The Major didn't say much about it: Stone was getting edgy and so was I. We spent the second day studying charts of the Brightside, such as they were. The best available were pretty poor, taken from so far out that the detail dissolved into blurs on blowup. They showed the biggest ranges of peaks and craters and faults, and that was all. Still, we could use them to plan a broad outline of our course.

"This range here," the Major said as we crowded around the board, "is largely inactive, according to

Sanderson. But these to the south and west *could* be active. Seismograph tracings suggest a lot of activity in that region, getting worse down toward the equator—not only volcanic, but sub-surface shifting."

Stone nodded. "Sanderson told me there was probably constant surface activity."

The Major shrugged. "Well, it's treacherous, there's no doubt of it. But the only way to avoid it is to travel over the Pole, which would lose us days and offer us no guarantee of less activity to the west. Now we might avoid some if we could find a pass through this range and cut sharp east—"

It seemed that the more we considered the problem, the further we got from a solution. We knew there were active volcanoes on the Brightside— even on the Darkside, though surface activity there was pretty much slowed down and localized.

But there were problems of atmosphere on Brightside, as well. There *was* an atmosphere and a constant atmospheric flow from Brightside to Darkside. Not much—the lighter gases had reached escape velocity and disappeared from Brightside millennia ago—but there was CO_2, and nitrogen, and traces of other heavier gases. There was also an abundance of sulfur vapor, as well as carbon disulfide and sulfur dioxide.

The atmospheric tide moved toward the Darkside, where it condensed, carrying enough volcanic ash with it for Sanderson to estimate the depth and nature of the surface upheavals on Brightside from his samplings. The trick was to find a passage that avoided those upheavals as far as possible. But in the final analysis, we were barely scraping the surface. The only way we would find out what was happening where was to be there.

Finally, on the third day, McIvers blew in on a freight rocket from Venus. He'd missed by a few hours the ship that the Major and I had taken and conned his way to Venus in hopes of getting a hop from there. He didn't seem too upset about it, as though this were his usual way of doing things, and he couldn't see why everyone should get so excited.

He was a tall, rangy man with long, wavy hair prematurely gray, and the sort of eyes that looked like a climber's—half closed, sleepy, almost indolent, but capable of abrupt alertness. And he never stood still; he was always moving, always doing something with his hands, or talking, or pacing about.

Evidently the Major decided not to press the issue of his arrival. There was still work to do, and an hour later we were running the final tests on the pressure suits. That evening, Stone and McIvers were thick as thieves, and everything was set for an early departure.

"And that," said Baron, finishing his drink and signaling the waiter for another pair, "was your first big mistake."

Peter Claney raised his eyebrows. "McIvers?"

"Of course."

Claney shrugged, glanced at the small quiet tables around them. "There are lots of bizarre personalities around a place like this, and some of the best wouldn't seem to be the most reliable at first glance. Anyway, personality problems weren't our big problem right then. *Equipment* worried us first and *route* next."

Baron nodded in agreement. "What kind of suits did you have?"

"The best insulating suits ever made," said Claney. "Each one had an inner lining of a fiberglas modification, to avoid the clumsiness of asbestos, and carried the refrigerating unit and oxygen storage which we recharged from the sledges every eight hours. Outer layer carried a monomolecular chrome-reflecting surface that made us glitter like Christmas trees. And we had a half-inch dead-air space under positive pressure between the two layers. Warning thermocouples, of course—at 770 degrees, it wouldn't take much time to fry us to cinders if the suits failed somewhere."

"How about the Bugs?"

"They were insulated, too, but we weren't counting on them too much for protection."

"You weren't!" Baron exclaimed. "Why not?"

"We'd be in and out of them too much. They gave us mobility and storage, but we knew we'd have to do a lot of forward work on foot." Claney smiled bitterly. "Which meant that we had an inch of fiberglas and a half-inch of dead air between us and a surface temperature where lead flowed like water and zinc was almost at melting point and the pools of sulfur in the shadows were boiling like oatmeal over a campfire."

Baron licked his lips. His fingers stroked the cool, wet glass.

"Go on," he said tautly. "You started on schedule?"

"Oh, yes," said Claney, "we started on schedule, all right. We just didn't quite end on schedule, that was all. But I'm getting to that."

He settled back in his chair and continued.

We jumped off from Twilight on a course due southeast, with thirty days to make it to the Center of Brightside. If we could cross an average of seventy miles a day, we could hit Center exactly at perihelion, the point of Mercury's closest approach to the Sun— which made Center the hottest part of the planet at the hottest it ever gets.

The Sun was already huge and yellow over the horizon when we started, twice the size it appears on Earth. Every day that Sun would grow bigger and whiter, and every day the surface would get hotter. But once we reached Center, the job was only half done— we would still have to travel another 2,000 miles to the opposite twilight zone. Sanderson was to meet us on the other side in the Laboratory's scout ship, approximately sixty days from the time we jumped off.

That was the plan, in outline. It was up to us to cross those seventy miles a day, no matter how hot it became, no matter what terrain we had to cross. Detours would be dangerous and time-consuming. Delays could cost us our lives. We all knew that.

The Major briefed us on details an hour before we left. "Peter, you'll take the lead Bug, the small one we stripped down for you. Stone and I will flank you on either side, giving you a hundred-yard lead. McIvers, you'll have the job of dragging the sledges, so we'll have to direct your course pretty closely. Peter's job is to pick the passage at any given point. If there's any doubt of safe passage, we'll all explore ahead on foot before we risk the Bugs. Got that?"

McIvers and Stone exchanged glances. McIvers said: "Jack and I were planning to change around. We figured he could take the sledges. That would give me a little more mobility."

The Major looked up sharply at Stone. "Do you buy that, Jack?"

Stone shrugged. "I don't mind. Mac wanted—"

McIvers made an impatient gesture with his hands. "It doesn't matter. I just feel better when I'm on the move. Does it make any difference?"

"I guess it doesn't," said the Major. "Then you'll flank Peter along with me. Right?"

"Sure, sure." McIvers pulled at his lower lip. "Who's going to do the advance scouting?"

"It sounds like I am," I cut in. "We want to keep the lead Bug as light as possible."

Mikuta nodded. "That's right. Peter's Bug is stripped down to the frame and wheels."

McIvers shook his head. "No, I mean the *advance* work. You need somebody out ahead—four or five miles, at least—to pick up the big flaws and active surface changes, don't you?" He stared at the Major. "I mean, how can we tell what sort of a hole we may be moving into, unless we have a scout up ahead?"

"That's what we have the charts for," the Major said sharply.

"Charts! I'm talking about *detail* work. We don't

need to worry about the major topography. It's the little faults you can't see on the pictures that can kill us."
He tossed the charts down excitedly. "Look, let me
take a Bug out ahead and work reconnaissance, keep
five, maybe ten miles ahead of the column. I can stay
on good solid ground, of course, but scan the area
closely and radio back to Peter where to avoid the
flaws. Then—"

"No dice," the Major broke in.

"But why not? We could save ourselves days!"

"I don't care what we could save. We stay together.
When we get to the Center, I want live men along with
me. That means we stay within easy sight of each
other at all times. Any climber knows that everybody
is safer in a party than one man alone—anytime, anyplace."

McIvers stared at him, his cheeks an angry red. Finally he gave a sullen nod. "Okay. If you say so."

"Well, I say so and I mean it. I don't want any
fancy stuff. We're going to hit Center together, and
finish the Crossing together. Got that?"

McIvers nodded. Mikuta then looked at Stone and
me and we nodded, too.

"All right," he said slowly. "Now that we've got it
straight, let's go."

It was hot. If I forget everything else about that
trek, I'll never forget that huge yellow Sun glaring
down, without a break, hotter and hotter with every
mile. We knew that the first few days would be the
easiest, and we were rested and fresh when we started
down the long ragged gorge southeast of the Twilight
Lab.

I moved out first; back over my shoulder, I could
see the Major and McIvers crawling out behind me,
their pillow tires taking the rugged floor of the gorge
smoothly. Behind them, Stone dragged the sledges.

Even at only 30 percent Earth gravity they were a
strain on the big tractor, until the ski-blades bit into

the fluffy volcanic ash blanketing the valley. We even had a path to follow for the first twenty miles.

I kept my eyes pasted to the big polaroid binocs, picking out the track the early research teams had made out into the edge of Brightside. But in a couple of hours we rumbled past Sanderson's little outpost observatory and the tracks stopped. We were in virgin territory and already the Sun was beginning to bite.

We didn't *feel* that heat so much those first days out. We *saw* it. The refrig units kept our skins at a nice comfortable 75° F. inside our suits, but our eyes watched that glaring Sun and the baked yellow rocks going past, and some nerve pathways got twisted up, somehow. We poured sweat as if we were in a super-heated furnace.

We drove eight hours and slept five. When a sleep period came due, we pulled the Bugs together into a square, threw up a light aluminum sun-shield and lay out in the dust and rocks. The sun-shield cut the temperature down sixty or seventy degrees, for whatever help that was. And then we ate from the forward sledge—sucking through tubes—protein, carbohydrates, bulk gelatin, vitamins.

The Major measured water out with an iron hand, because we'd have drunk ourselves into nephritis in a week otherwise. We were constantly, unceasingly thirsty. Ask the physiologists and psychiatrists why—they can give you half a dozen interesting reasons—but all we knew, or cared about, was that it happened to be so.

We didn't sleep the first few stops, as a consequence. Our eyes burned in spite of the filters and we had roaring headaches, but we couldn't sleep them off. We sat around looking at each other. Then McIvers would say how good a beer would taste, and off we'd go. We'd have butchered our grandmothers for one ice-cold bottle of beer.

After a few driving periods, I began to get my bearings at the wheel. We were moving down into desolation that made Earth's old Death Valley look like a Japanese rose garden. Huge sun-baked cracks opened up in the floor of the gorge, with black cliffs jutting up on either side; the air was filled with a barely visible yellowish mist of sulfur and sulfurous gases.

It was a hot, barren hell-hole, no place for any man to go, but the challenge was so powerful you could almost feel it. No one had ever crossed this land before and escaped. Those who had tried it had been cruelly punished, but the land was still there, so it had to be crossed. Not the easy way. It had to be crossed the hardest way possible: overland, through anything the land could throw up to us, at the most difficult time possible.

Yet we knew that even the land might have been conquered before, except for that Sun. We'd fought absolute cold before and won. We'd never fought heat like this and won. The only worse heat in the Solar System was the surface of the Sun itself.

Brightside was worth trying for. We would get it or it would get us. That was the bargain.

I learned a lot about Mercury those first few driving periods. The gorge petered out after a hundred miles and we moved onto the slope of a range of ragged craters that ran south and east. This range had shown no activity since the first landing on Mercury forty years before, but beyond it there were active cones. Yellow fumes rose from the craters constantly; their sides were shrouded with heavy ash.

We couldn't detect a wind, but we knew there was a hot, sulfurous breeze sweeping in great continental tides across the face of the planet. Not enough for erosion, though. The craters rose up out of jagged gorges, huge towering spears of rock and rubble. Below were the vast yellow flatlands, smoking and hissing from the gases beneath the crust. Over everything was gray dust —silicates and salts, pumice and limestone and granite ash, filling crevices and declivities—offering a soft, treacherous surface for the Bug's pillow tires.

I learned to read the ground, to tell a covered fault by the sag of the dust; I learned to spot a passable crack, and tell it from an impassable cut. Time after time the Bugs ground to a halt while we explored a passage on foot, tied together with light copper cable, digging, advancing, digging some more until we were sure the surface would carry the machines. It was cruel work; we slept in exhaustion. But it went smoothly, at first.

Too smoothly, it seemed to me, and the others seemed to think so, too.

McIvers' restlessness was beginning to grate on our nerves. He talked too much, while we were resting or while we were driving: wisecracks, witticisms, unfunny jokes that wore thin with repetition. He took to making side trips from the route now and then, never far, but a little farther each time.

Jack Stone reacted quite the opposite; he grew quieter with each stop, more reserved and apprehensive. I didn't like it, but I figured that it would pass off after a while. I was apprehensive enough myself; I just managed to hide it better.

And every mile the Sun got bigger and whiter and higher in the sky and hotter. Without our ultraviolet screens and glare filters we would have been blinded; as it was our eyes ached constantly, and the skin on our faces itched and tingled at the end of an eight-hour trek.

But it took one of those side trips of McIvers' to deliver the penultimate blow to our already fraying nerves. He had driven down a side branch of a long canyon running off west of our route and was almost out of sight in a cloud of ash when we heard a sharp cry through our earphones.

I wheeled my Bug around with my heart in my throat and spotted him through the binocs, waving frantically from the top of his machine. The Major and I took off, lumbering down the gulch after him as fast as the Bugs could go, with a thousand horrible pictures racing through our minds. . . .

We found him standing stock-still, pointing down the gorge and, for once, he didn't have anything to say. It was the wreck of a Bug, an old-fashioned half-track model of the sort that hadn't been in use for years. It was wedged tight in a cut in the rock, an axle broken, its casing split wide open up the middle, half buried in a rock slide. A dozen feet away were two insulated suits with the white bones gleaming through the fiberglas helmets.

This was as far as Wyatt and Carpenter had gotten on *their* Brightside Crossing.

On the fifth driving period out, the terrain began to change. It looked the same, but every now and then it *felt* different. On two occasions I felt my wheels spin, with a howl of protest from my engine. Then, quite suddenly, the Bug gave a lurch; I gunned my motor and nothing happened.

I could see the dull-gray stuff seeping up around the hubs, thick and tenacious, splattering around in steaming gobs as the wheels spun. I knew what had happened the moment the wheels gave and, a few minutes later, they chained me to the tractor and dragged me back out of the mire. It looked for all the world like thick gray mud, but it was a pit of molten lead, steaming under a soft layer of concealing ash.

I picked my way more cautiously then. We were getting into an area of recent surface activity; the surface was really treacherous. I caught myself wishing that the Major had okayed McIvers' scheme for an advance scout; more dangerous for the individual, maybe, but I was driving blind now and I didn't like it.

One error in judgment could sink us all, but I wasn't thinking much about the others. I was worried about *me,* plenty worried. I kept thinking, better McIvers should go than me. It wasn't healthy thinking and I knew it, but I couldn't get the thought out of my mind.

It was a grueling eight hours, and we slept poorly. Back in the Bugs again, we moved still more slowly— edging out on a broad flat plateau, dodging a network of gaping surface cracks—winding back and forth in an effort to keep the machines on solid rock. I couldn't see far ahead, because of the yellow haze rising from the cracks, so I was almost on top of it when I saw a sharp cut ahead where the surface dropped six feet beyond a deep crack.

I let out a shout to halt the others; then I edged my Bug forward, peering at the cleft. It was deep and wide. I moved fifty yards to the left, then back to the right.

There was only one place that looked like a possible crossing: a long, narrow ledge of gray stuff that lay down across a section of the fault like a ramp. Even as I watched it, I could feel the surface crust under the Bug trembling and saw the ledge shift over a few feet.

The Major's voice sounded in my ears. "How about it, Peter?"

"I don't know. This crust is on roller skates," I called back.

"How about that ledge?"

I hesitated. "I'm scared of it, Major. Let's backtrack and try to find a way around."

There was a roar of disgust in my earphones and McIvers' Bug suddenly lurched forward. It rolled down past me, picked up speed, with McIvers hunched behind the wheel like a race driver. He was heading past me straight for the gray ledge.

My shout caught in my throat; I heard the Major take a huge breath and roar: "My God, Mac, *stop that thing,* you fool!" and then McIvers' Bug was out on the ledge, lumbering across like a juggernaut.

The ledge jolted as the tires struck it; for a horrible moment, it seemed to be sliding out from under the machine. And then the Bug was across in a cloud of dust, and I heard McIvers' voice in my ears, shouting in glee, "Come on, you slowpokes. It'll hold you!"

Something unprintable came through the earphones as the Major drew up alongside me and moved his Bug out on the ledge slowly and over to the other side. Then he said, "Take it slow, Peter. Then give Jack a hand with the sledges." His voice sounded tight as a wire.

Ten minutes later, we were on the other side of the cleft. The Major checked the whole column; then he turned on McIvers angrily. "One more trick like that," he said, "and I'll strap you to a rock and leave you. Do you understand me? *One more time—*"

McIvers' voice was heavy with protest. "Good Lord, if we leave it up to Claney, he'll have us out here forever! Any blind fool could see that that ledge would hold."

"I saw it moving," I shot back at him.

"All right, all right, so you've got good eyes. Why all the fuss? We got across, didn't we? But I say we've got to have a little nerve and use it once in a while if we're ever going to get across this lousy hotbox."

"We need to use a little judgment, too," the Major snapped. "All right, let's roll. But if you think I was joking, you just try me out once." He let it soak in for a minute. Then he geared his Bug on around to my flank again.

At the stopover, the incident wasn't mentioned again, but the Major drew me aside just as I was settling down for sleep. "Peter, I'm worried," he said slowly.

"McIvers? Don't worry. He's not as reckless as he seems—just impatient. We are over a hundred miles behind schedule, and we're moving awfully slow. We only made forty miles this last drive."

The Major shook his head. "I don't mean McIvers. I mean the kid."

"Jack? What about him?"

"Take a look."

Stone was shaking. He was over near the tractor—away from the rest of us—and he was lying on his back, but he wasn't asleep. His whole body was shaking, convulsively. I saw him grip an outcropping of rock hard.

I walked over and sat down beside him. "Get your water all right?" I said.

He didn't answer. He just kept on shaking.

"Hey, boy," I said. "What's the trouble?"

"It's hot," he said, choking out the words.

"Sure it's hot, but don't let it throw you. We're in really good shape."

"We're not," he snapped. "We're in rotten shape, if you ask me. *We're not going to make it,* do you know that? That crazy fool's going to kill us for sure—" All of a sudden, he was bawling like a baby. "I'm scared—I shouldn't be here—I'm *scared*. What am I trying to prove by coming out here, for God's sake? I'm some kind of hero or something? I tell you I'm scared—"

"Look," I said. "Mikuta's scared, *I'm* scared. So what? We'll make it, don't worry. And nobody's trying to be a hero."

"Nobody but Hero Stone," he said bitterly. He shook himself and gave a tight little laugh. "Some hero, eh?"

"We'll make it," I said.

"Sure," he said finally. "Sorry. I'll be okay."

I rolled over, but waited until he was good and quiet. Then I tried to sleep, but I didn't sleep too well. I kept thinking about that ledge. I'd known from the look of it what it was; a zinc slough of the sort Sanderson had warned us about, a wide sheet of almost pure zinc that had been thrown up white-hot from below, quite recently, just waiting for oxygen or sulfur to rot it through.

I knew enough about zinc to know that at these temperatures it gets brittle as glass. Take a chance like

McIvers had taken and the whole sheet could snap like a dry pine board. But it wasn't McIvers' fault that it hadn't.

Five hours later, we were back at the wheel. We were hardly moving at all. The ragged surface was almost impassable—great jutting rocks peppered the plateau; ledges crumbled the moment my tires touched them; long, open canyons turned into lead-mires or sulfur pits.

A dozen times I climbed out of the Bug to prod out an uncertain area with my boots and pikestaff. Whenever I did, McIvers piled out behind me, running ahead like a schoolboy at the fair, then climbing back again, red-faced and panting, while we moved the machines ahead another mile or two.

Time was pressing us now, and McIvers wouldn't let me forget it. We had made only about 320 miles in six driving periods, so we were about a hundred miles or even more behind schedule.

"We're not going to make it," McIvers would complain angrily. "That Sun's going to be out to aphelion by the time we hit the Center—"

"Sorry, but I can't take it any faster," I told him. I was getting good and mad. I knew what he wanted but didn't dare let him have it. I was scared enough pushing the Bug out on those ledges, even knowing that at least *I* was making the decisions. Put him in the lead and we wouldn't last for eight hours. Our nerves wouldn't take it, at any rate, even if the machines did.

Jack Stone looked up from the aluminum chart sheets. "Another hundred miles and we should hit a good stretch," he said. "Maybe we can make up distance there for a couple of days."

The Major agreed, but McIvers couldn't hold his impatience. He kept staring up at the Sun as if he had a personal grudge against it, and stamped back and forth under the sun-shield. "That'll be just fine," he said. *"If* we ever get that far, that is."

We dropped it there, but the Major stopped me as

we climbed aboard for the next run. "That guy's going to blow wide open if we don't move faster, Peter. I don't want him in the lead, no matter what happens. He's right, though, about the need to make better time. Keep your head, but crowd your luck a little, okay?"

"I'll try," I said. It was asking the impossible and Mikuta knew it. We were on a long downward slope that shifted and buckled all around us, as though there was a molten underlay beneath the crust; the slope was broken by huge crevasses, partly covered with dust and zinc sheeting, like a vast glacier of stone and metal. The outside temperature registered 547° F. and getting hotter. It was no place to start rushing ahead.

I tried it anyway. I took half a dozen shaky passages, edging slowly out on flat zinc ledges, then toppling over and across. It seemed easy for a while and we made progress. We hit an even stretch and raced ahead. And then I quickly jumped on my brakes and jerked the Bug to a halt in a cloud of dust.

I'd gone too far. We were out on a wide, flat sheet of gray stuff, apparently solid—until I'd suddenly caught sight of the crevasse beneath in the corner of my eye. It was an overhanging shelf that trembled under me as I stopped. McIvers' voice was in my ear. "What's the trouble now, Claney?"

"Move back!" I shouted. "It can't hold us!"

"Looks solid from here."

"You want to argue about it? It's too thin, it'll snap. Move back!"

I started edging back down the ledge. I heard McIvers swear; then I saw his Bug start to creep *outward* on the shelf. Not fast or reckless, this time, but slowly, churning up dust in a gentle cloud behind him.

I just stared and felt the blood rush to my head. It seemed so hot I could hardly breathe as he edged out beyond me, farther and farther—

I think I felt it snap before I saw it. My own machine gave a sickening lurch and a long black crack appeared across the shelf—and widened. Then the ledge began to upend. I heard a scream as McIvers' Bug rose up and up and then crashed down into the crevasse in a thundering slide of rock and shattered metal.

I just stared for a full minute, I think. I couldn't move until I heard Jack Stone groan and the Major shouting, "Claney! I couldn't see—*what happened?*"

"It snapped on him, that's what happened," I roared. I gunned my motor, edged forward toward the fresh-broken edge of the shelf. The crevasse gaped; I couldn't see any sign of the machine. Dust was still billowing up blindingly from below.

We stood staring down, the three of us. I caught a glimpse of Jack Stone's face through his helmet. It wasn't pretty.

"Well," said the Major heavily, "that's that."

"I guess so." I felt the way Stone looked.

"Wait," said Stone. "I heard something."

He had. It was a cry in the earphones—faint, but unmistakable.

"Mac!" the Major called. "Mac, can you hear me?"

"Yeah, yeah. I can hear you." The voice was very weak.

"Are you all right?"

"I don't know. Broken leg, I think. It's—hot." There was a long pause. Then: "I think my cooler's gone out."

The Major shot me a glance, then turned to Stone. "Get a cable from the second sledge fast. He'll fry alive if we don't get him out of there. Peter, I need you to lower me. Use the tractor winch."

I lowered him: he stayed down only a few moments. When I hauled him up, his face was drawn. "Still alive," he panted. "He won't be very long, though." He hesitated for just an instant. "We've got to make a try."

"I don't like this ledge," I said. "It's moved twice

since I got out. Why not back off and lower him a cable?"

"No good. The Bug is smashed and he's inside it. We'll need torches and I'll need one of you to help." He looked at me and then gave Stone a long look. "Peter, you'd better come."

"Wait," said Stone. His face was very white. "Let me go down with you."

"Peter is lighter."

"I'm not so heavy. Let me go down."

"Okay, if that's the way you want it." The Major tossed him a torch. "Peter, check these hitches and lower us slowly. If you see any kind of trouble, *anything,* cast yourself free and back off this thing, do you understand? This whole ledge may go."

I nodded. "Good luck."

They went over the ledge. I let the cable down bit by bit until it hit two hundred feet and slacked off.

"How does it look?" I shouted.

"Bad," said the Major. "We'll have to work fast. This whole side of the crevasse is ready to crumble. Down a little more."

Minutes passed without a sound. I tried to relax, but I couldn't. Then I felt the ground shift, and the tractor lurched to the side.

The Major shouted, *"It's going, Peter—pull back!"* and I threw the tractor into reverse, jerked the controls as the tractor rumbled off the shelf. The cable snapped, coiled up in front like a broken clock-spring. The whole surface under me was shaking wildly now; ash rose in huge gray clouds. Then, with a roar, the whole shelf lurched and slid sideways. It teetered on the edge for seconds before it crashed into the crevasse, tearing the side wall down with it in a mammoth slide. I jerked the tractor to a halt as the dust and flame billowed up.

They were gone—all three of them, McIvers and the Major and Jack Stone—buried under thousands of tons of rock and zinc and molten lead. There wasn't any danger of anybody ever finding their bones.

Peter Claney leaned back, finishing his drink, rubbing his scarred face as he looked across at Baron.

Slowly, Baron's grip relaxed on the chair arm. *"You got back."*

Claney nodded. "I got back, sure. I had the tractor and the sledges. I had seven days to drive back under that yellow Sun. I had plenty of time to think."

"You took the wrong man along," Baron said. "That was your mistake. Without him you would have made it."

"Never." Claney shook his head. "That's what I was thinking the first day or so—that it was *McIvers'* fault, that *he* was to blame. But that isn't true. He was wild, reckless, and had lots of nerve."

"But his judgment was bad!"

"It couldn't have been sounder. We had to keep to our schedule even if it killed us, because it would positively kill us if we didn't."

"But a man like that—"

"A man like McIvers was necessary. Can't you see that? It was the Sun that beat us, that surface. Perhaps we were licked the very day we started." Claney leaned across the table, his eyes pleading. "We didn't realize that, but it was *true*. There are places that men can't go, conditions men can't tolerate. The others had to die to learn that. I was lucky, I came back. But I'm trying to tell you what I found out—that *nobody* will ever make a Brightside Crossing."

"We will," said Baron. "It won't be a picnic, but we'll make it."

"But suppose you do," said Claney, suddenly. "Suppose I'm all wrong, suppose you *do* make it. Then what? *What comes next?*"

"The Sun," said Baron.

Claney nodded slowly. "Yes. That would be it,

wouldn't it?" He laughed. "Good-by, Baron. Jolly talk and all that. Thanks for listening."

Baron caught his wrist as he started to rise. "Just one question more, Claney. Why did you come here?"

"To try to talk you out of killing yourself," said Claney.

"You're a liar," said Baron.

Claney stared down at him for a long moment. Then he crumpled in the chair. There was defeat in his pale blue eyes and something else.

"Well?"

Peter Claney spread his hands, a helpless gesture. "When do you leave, Baron? I want you to take me along."

THE DEEP RANGE

by Arthur C. Clarke

Here is another story that scores very high in plausibility. Arthur C. Clarke, an undersea explorer himself (and a former president of the British Interplanetary Society), often seems to live more in the future than in our present time. If anybody now knows what the world of 1980 is going to be like, it is probably Clarke, and he makes it sound like an exciting place to live.

THERE WAS A KILLER LOOSE ON THE RANGE. A COPTER patrol, five hundred miles off Greenland, had seen the great corpse staining the sea crimson as it wallowed in the waves. Within seconds, the intricate warning system had been alerted: men were plotting circles and moving counters on the North Atlantic chart—and Don Burley was still rubbing the sleep from his eyes as he dropped silently down to the twenty-fathom line.

The pattern of green lights on the telltale was a glowing symbol of security. As long as that pattern was unchanged, as long as none of those emerald stars winked to red, all was well with Don and his tiny craft. Air—fuel—power—this was the triumvirate which ruled his life. If any of them failed, he would be sink-

34

ing in a steel coffin down toward the pelagic ooze, as Johnnie Tyndall had done the season before last. But there was no reason why they should fail; the accidents one foresaw, Don told himself reassuringly, were never the ones that happened.

He leaned across the tiny control board and spoke into the mike. Sub 5 was still close enough to the mother ship for radio to work, but before long he'd have to switch to the sonics.

"Setting course 255, speed 50 knots, depth 20 fathoms, full sonar coverage. . . . Estimated time to target area, 70 minutes. . . . Will report at 10-minute intervals. That is all. . . . Out."

"Message received and understood. Good hunting. What about the hounds?"

Don chewed his lower lip thoughtfully. This might be a job he'd have to handle alone. He had no idea, to within fifty miles either way, where Benj and Susan were at the moment. They'd certainly follow if he signaled for them, but they couldn't maintain his speed and would soon have to drop behind. Besides, he might be heading for a pack of killers, and the last thing he wanted to do was to lead his carefully trained porpoises into trouble. That was common sense and good business. He was also very fond of Susan and Benj.

"It's too far, and I don't know what I'm running into," he replied. "If they're in the interception area when I get there, I may whistle them up."

The acknowledgment from the mother ship was barely audible, and Don switched off the set. It was time to look around.

He dimmed the cabin lights so that he could see the scanner screen more clearly, pulled the polaroid glasses down over his eyes, and peered into the depths. This was the moment when Don felt like a god, able to hold within his hands a circle of the Atlantic twenty miles across, and to see clear down to the still-unexplored deeps, three thousand fathoms below. The slowly rotating beam of inaudible sound was searching the world in which he floated, seeking out friend and foe in the eternal darkness where light could never penetrate. The pattern of soundless shrieks, too shrill even for the hearing of the bats who had invented sonar a million years before man, pulsed out into the watery night: the faint echoes came tingling back as floating, blue-green flecks on the screen.

Through long practice, Don could read their message with effortless ease. A thousand feet below, stretching out to his submerged horizon, was the scattering layer—the blanket of life that covered half the world. The sunken meadow of the sea, it rose and fell with the passage of the sun, hovering always at the edge of darkness. But the ultimate depths were no concern of his. The flocks he guarded, and the enemies who ravaged them, belonged to the upper levels of the sea.

Don flicked the switch of the depth-selector, and his sonar beam concentrated itself into the horizontal plane. The glimmering echoes from the abyss vanished, but he could see more clearly what lay around him here in the ocean's stratospheric heights. That glowing cloud two miles ahead was a school of fish; he wondered if Base knew about it, and made an entry in his log. There were some larger, isolated blips at the edge of the school—the carnivores pursuing the cattle, insuring that the endlessly turning wheel of life and death would never lose momentum. But this conflict was no affair of Don's; he was after bigger game.

Sub 5 drove on toward the west, a steel needle swifter and more deadly than any other creature that roamed the seas. The tiny cabin, lit only by the flicker of lights from the instrument board, pulsed with power as the spinning turbines thrust the water aside. Don glanced at the chart and wondered how the enemy had broken through this time. There were still many weak points, for fencing the oceans of the world had been a gigantic task. The tenuous electric fields, fanning out between generators many miles apart, could not always hold at bay the starving monsters of the deep. They were learning, too. When the fences were opened, they would sometimes slip through with the whales and wreak havoc before they were discovered.

The long-range receiver bleeped plaintively, and Don switched over to TRANSCRIBE. It wasn't practical to send speech any distance over an ultrasonic beam, and code had come back into its own. Don had never learned to read it by ear, but the ribbon of paper emerging from the slot saved him the trouble.

COPTER REPORTS SCHOOL 50—100 WHALES HEADING 95 DEGREES GRID REF x186475 y43804. STOP. MOVING AT SPEED. STOP. MELVILLE. OUT.

Don started to set the coordinates on the plotting grid, then saw that it was no longer necessary. At the extreme edge of his screen, a flotilla of faint stars had appeared. He altered course slightly, and drove head-on toward the approaching herd.

The copter was right: they were moving fast. Don felt a mounting excitement, for this could mean that they were on the run and luring the killers toward him. At the rate at which they were traveling he would be among them in five minutes. He cut the motors and felt the backward tug of water bringing him swiftly to rest.

Don Burley, a knight in armor, sat in his tiny dim-lit room fifty feet below the bright Atlantic waves, testing his weapons for the conflict that lay ahead. In these moments of poised suspense, before action began, his racing brain often explored such fantasies. He felt a kinship with all shepherds who had guarded their flocks back to the dawn of time. He was David, among ancient Palestinian hills, alert for the mountain lions that would prey upon his father's sheep. But far nearer in time, and far closer in spirit, were the men who had marshaled the great herds of cattle on the American plains, only a few lifetimes ago. They would have understood his work, though his implements would have been magic to them. The pattern was the same; only the scale had altered. It made no fundamental difference that the beasts Don herded weighed almost a hundred tons, and browsed on the endless savannahs of the sea.

The school was now less than two miles away, and Don checked his scanner's continuous circling to concentrate on the sector ahead. The picture on the screen altered to a fan-shaped wedge as the sonar beam started to flick from side to side; now he could count every whale in the school, and even make a good estimate of its size. With a practiced eye, he began to look for stragglers.

Don could never have explained what drew him at once toward those four echoes at the southern fringe of the school. It was true that they were a little apart from the rest, but others had fallen as far behind. There is some sixth sense that a man acquires when he has stared long enough into a sonar screen—some hunch which enables him to extract more from the moving flecks than he has any right to do. Without conscious thought, Don reached for the control which would start the turbines whirling into life. Sub 5 was just getting under way when three leaden thuds reverberated through the hull, as if someone was knocking on the front door and wanted to come in.

"Well I'm damned," said Don. "How did *you* get here?" He did not bother to switch on the TV; he'd know Benj's signal anywhere. The porpoises must have been in the neighborhood and had spotted him before he'd even switched on the hunting call. For the thousandth time, he marveled at their intelligence and loyalty. It was strange that Nature had played the same trick twice—on land with the dog, in the ocean with the porpoise. Why were these graceful sea-beasts so fond of man, to whom they owed so little? It made one feel that the human race was worth something after all, if it could inspire such unselfish devotion.

It had been known for centuries that the porpoise was at least as intelligent as the dog, and could obey quite complex verbal commands. The experiment was still in progress, but if it succeeded then the ancient partnership between shepherd and sheep-dog would have a new lease on life.

Don switched on the speakers recessed into the sub's hull and began to talk to his escorts. Most of the sounds he uttered would have been meaningless to other human ears; they were the product of long research by the animal psychologists of the World Food Administration. He gave his orders twice to make sure that they were understood, then checked with the sonar screen to see that Benj and Susan were following astern as he had told them to.

The four echoes that had attracted his attention were clearer and closer now, and the main body of the whale pack had swept past him to the east. He had no fear of a collision; the great animals, even in their panic, could sense his presence as easily as he could detect theirs, and by similar means. Don wondered if he should switch on his beacon. They might recognize its sound pattern and it would reassure them. But the still unknown enemy might recognize it too.

He closed for an interception, and hunched low over the screen as if to drag from it by sheer will power every scrap of information the scanner could give. There were two large echoes, some distance apart, and one was accompanied by a pair of smaller satellites. Don wondered if he was already too late. In his mind's eye, he could picture the death struggle taking place in the water less than a mile ahead. Those two fainter blips would be the enemy—either shark or grampus —worrying a whale while one of its companions stood by in helpless terror, with no weapons of defense except its mighty flukes.

Now he was almost close enough for vision. The TV camera in Sub 5's prow strained through the gloom, but at first could show nothing but the fog of plankton. Then a vast shadowy shape began to form in the center of the screen, with two smaller companions below it. Don was seeing, with the greater precision but hopelessly limited range of ordinary light, what the sonar scanners had already told him.

Almost at once he saw his mistake. The two satellites were calves, not sharks. It was the first time he had ever met a whale with twins; although multiple births were not unknown, a cow could suckle only two young at once and usually only the stronger would survive. He choked down his disappointment; this error had cost him many minutes and he must begin the search again.

Then came the frantic tattoo on the hull that meant danger. It wasn't easy to scare Benj, and Don shouted his reassurance as he swung Sub 5 round so that the camera could search the turgid waters. Automatically, he had turned toward the fourth blip on the sonar screen—the echo he had assumed from its size to be another adult whale. And he saw that, after all, he had come to the right place.

"Jesus!" he said softly. "I didn't know they came that big." He'd seen larger sharks before, but they had all been harmless vegetarians. This, he could tell at a glance, was a Greenland shark, the killer of the northern seas. It was supposed to grow up to thirty feet long, but this specimen was bigger than Sub 5. It was every inch of forty feet from snout to tail, and when he spotted it, it was already turning in toward the kill. Like the coward it was, it had launched its attack at one of the calves.

Don yelled to Benj and Susan, and saw them racing ahead into his field of vision. He wondered fleetingly why porpoises had such an overwhelming hatred of sharks; then he loosed his hands from the controls as the autopilot locked on to the target. Twisting and turning as agilely as any other sea-creature of its size,

Sub 5 began to close in upon the shark, leaving Don free to concentrate on his armament.

The killer had been so intent upon his prey that Benj caught him completely unawares, ramming him just behind the left eye. It must have been a painful blow: an iron-hard snout, backed by a quarter-ton of muscle moving at fifty miles an hour is something not to be laughed at even by the largest fish. The shark jerked round in an impossibly tight curve, and Don was almost jolted out of his seat as the sub snapped onto a new course. If this kept up, he'd find it hard to use his Sting. But at least the killer was too busy now to bother about his intended victims.

Benj and Susan were worrying the giant like dogs snapping at the heels of an angry bear. They were too agile to be caught in those ferocious jaws, and Don marveled at the coordination with which they worked. When either had to surface for air, the other would hold off for a minute until the attack could be resumed in strength.

There was no evidence that the shark realized that a far more dangerous adversary was closing in upon it, and that the porpoises were merely a distraction. That suited Don very nicely; the next operation was going to be difficult unless he could hold a steady course for at least fifteen seconds. At a pinch he could use the tiny rocket torps to make a kill. If he'd been alone and faced with a pack of sharks, he would certainly have done so. But it was messy, and there was a better way. He preferred the technique of the rapier to that of the hand-grenade.

Now he was only fifty feet away, and closing rapidly. There might never be a better chance. He punched the launching stud.

From beneath the belly of the sub, something that looked like a sting-ray hurtled forward. Don had checked the speed of his own craft; there was no need to come any closer now. The tiny, arrow-shaped hy-

drofoil, only a couple of feet across, could move far
faster than his vessel and would close the gap in seconds. As it raced forward, it spun out the thin line of
the control wire, like some underwater spider laying its
thread. Along that wire passed the energy that powered the Sting, and the signals that steered it to its
goal. Don had completely ignored his own larger craft
in the effect of guiding this underwater missile. It re-
sponded to his touch so swiftly that he felt he was
controlling some sensitive high-spirited steed.

The shark saw the danger less than a second before
impact. The resemblance of the Sting to an ordinary
ray confused it, as the designers had intended. Before
the tiny brain could realize that no ray behaved like
this, the missile had struck. The steel hypodermic,
rammed forward by an exploding cartridge, drove
through the shark's horny skin, and the great fish
erupted in a frenzy of terror. Don backed rapidly
away, for a blow from that tail would rattle him
around like a pea in a can and might even cause damage to the sub. There was nothing more for him to do,
except to speak into the microphone and call off his
hounds.

The doomed killer was trying to arch its body so
that it could snap at the poisoned dart. Don had now
reeled the Sting back into its hiding place, pleased that
he had been able to retrieve the missile undamaged.
He watched without pity as the great fish succumbed
to its paralysis.

Its struggles were weakening. It was swimming aim-
lessly back and forth, and once Don had to sidestep
smartly to avoid a collision. As it lost control of buoy-
ancy, the dying shark drifted up to the surface. Don
did not bother to follow; that could wait until he had
attended to more important business.

He found the cow and her two calves less than a
mile away, and inspected them carefully. They were
uninjured, so there was no need to call the vet in his
highly specialized two-man sub which could handle

any cetological crisis from a stomach-ache to a Caesarian. Don made a note of the mother's number, stenciled just behind the flippers. The calves, as was obvious from their size, were this season's and had not yet been branded.

Don watched for a little while. They were no longer in the least alarmed, and a check on the sonar had shown that the whole school had ceased its panicky flight. He wondered how they knew what had happened; much had been learned about communication among whales, but much was still a mystery.

"I hope you appreciate what I've done for you, old lady," he muttered. Then, reflecting that fifty tons of mother love was a slightly awe-inspiring sight, he blew his tanks and surfaced.

It was calm, so he cracked the airlock and popped his head out of the tiny conning tower. The water was only inches below his chin, and from time to time a wave made a determined effort to swamp him. There was little danger of this happening, for he fitted the hatch so closely that he was quite an effective plug.

Fifty feet away, a long slate-colored mound, like an overturned boat, was rolling on the surface. Don looked at it thoughtfully and did some mental calculations. A brute this size should be valuable; with any luck, there was a chance of a double bonus. In a few minutes he'd radio his report, but for the moment it was pleasant to drink the fresh Atlantic air and to feel the open sky above his head.

A gray thunderbolt shot up out of the depths and smashed back onto the surface of the water, smothering Don with spray. It was just Benj's modest way of drawing attention to himself; a moment later the porpoise had swum up to the conning tower, so that Don could reach down and tickle its head. The great, intelligent eyes stared back into his; was it pure imagination, or did an almost human sense of fun also lurk in their depths?

Susan, as usual, circled shyly at a distance until jealousy overpowered her and she butted Benj out of the way. Don distributed caresses impartially and apologized because he had nothing to give them. He undertook to make up for the omission as soon as he returned to the *Herman Melville*.

"I'll go for another swim with you, too," he promised, "as long as you behave yourselves next time." He rubbed thoughtfully at a large bruise caused by Benj's playfulness, and wondered if he was not getting a little too old for rough games like this.

"Time to go home," Don said firmly, sliding down into the cabin and slamming the hatch. He suddenly realized that he was very hungry, and had better do something about the breakfast he had missed. There were not many men on earth who had earned a better right to eat their morning meal. He had saved for humanity more tons of meat, oil and milk than could easily be estimated.

Don Burley was the happy warrior, coming home from one battle that man would always have to fight. He was holding at bay the specter of famine which had confronted all earlier ages, but which would never threaten the world again while the great plankton farms harvested their millions of tons of protein, and the whale herds obeyed their new masters. Man had come back to the sea after aeons of exile; until the oceans froze, he would never be hungry again. . . .

Don glanced at the scanner as he set his course. He smiled as he saw the two echoes keeping pace with the central splash of light that marked his vessel. "Hang around," he said. "We mammals must stick together." Then, as the autopilot took over, he lay back in his chair.

And presently Benj and Susan heard a most peculiar noise, rising and falling against the drone of the turbines. It had filtered faintly through the thick walls of Sub 5, and only the sensitive ears of the porpoises could have detected it. But intelligent beasts though they were, they could hardly be expected to understand why Don Burley was announcing, in a highly unmusical voice, that he was Heading for the Last Round-up. . . .

COVENTRY

by Robert A. Heinlein

"Coventry," although it can be read by itself,
is a companion piece to Robert A. Heinlein's
novel *If This Goes On . . . ,* in which he de-
scribes the overthrow of a religious dictatorship in the United States. Here, in a story which
takes place about fifty years later, Heinlein
deals with the question of the "good society."
How would it work? Would it be a society in
which everyone agrees not to use force? Then
how would it deal with lawbreakers?

HAVE YOU ANYTHING TO SAY BEFORE SENTENCE IS
pronounced on you?" The mild eyes of the senior judge
studied the face of the accused. His sympathetic regard
was answered by a sullen silence.

"Very well—the jury has determined the fact that
you have violated a basic custom agreed to under the
Covenant, and that through that act you did damage
another free citizen. It is the opinion of the jury and of
the court that you did so knowingly, and aware of the
probability of damage to a free citizen. Therefore you
are sentenced to choose between the Two Alternatives."

A trained observer might have detected a momentary
trace of dismay breaking through the mask of stoical in-

difference with which the young man had faced his trial. Dismay at the sentence was unreasonable; in view of his offense, the sentence was inevitable—but reasonable men do not receive the sentence.

After waiting a decent interval, the judge turned to the bailiff. "Take him away."

Before that official could reach him he stood up, knocking over his chair with the violence of his movement. He glared wildly around at the little company assembled about the long table and burst into speech.

"Hold on!" he cried. "I've got something to say first!" In spite of his rough manner there was about him, somehow, the noble dignity of a strong and untamed beast at bay. He stared at those around him, breathing heavily, as if they were, in fact, a circle of hunting dogs waiting to drag him down.

"Well?" he demanded. "Well? Do I get to talk or don't I? It'd be the best joke of this whole damned comedy if a condemned man couldn't speak his mind at the last!"

"You may speak," the senior judge told him in the same even, unhurried tones with which he had pronounced sentence, "David MacKinnon, as long as you like, and in any manner that you like. There is no limit to that freedom, even for those who have broken the Covenant. Please speak into the recorder."

MacKinnon glanced with distaste at the tiny microphone hanging near his face. The knowledge that any word spoken in its range would be broken down into typed phonetic symbols by a recording voder somewhere in the Hall of Archives inhibited his speech. "I don't ask for records," he snapped.

"But we must have them," the judge replied patiently, "in order that others may determine whether or not we have dealt with you fairly, and according to the Covenant. Oblige us, please."

"Oh, very well!" He ungraciously conceded the requirement and directed his voice toward the instrument. "There's no damn sense in me talking at all—but, just

the same, I'm going to talk and you're going to listen.
You talk about your precious 'Covenant' as if it were
something holy. I don't agree to it, and I don't accept it.
You act as if it had been sent down from heaven in a
burst of light. My grandfathers fought in the Second
Revolution—but they fought to abolish superstition,
not to let sheep-minded fools set up new ones.

"There were men in those days!" He looked with
aversion around the ring of faces. "What is there left
today? Cautious, compromising, 'safe' weaklings with
water in their veins. You've planned your whole world
so carefully that you've planned the fun and zest right
out of it. Nobody is ever hungry, nobody ever gets
hurt. Your ships can't crack up and your crops can't
fail. You even have the weather tamed so it rains polite-
ly—after midnight. Why wait till midnight, I don't
know—you all go to bed at nine o'clock!

"If one of you safe little people *should* have an unpleasant emotion—perish the thought!—you'd trot
right over to the nearest psychodynamics clinic and get
your soft little minds readjusted. Thank God I never
succumbed to that dope habit. I'll keep my own feelings, thanks, no matter how bad they taste.

"You won't even make love without consulting a
psychotechnician! Is her mind as flat and insipid as
mine? Is there any emotional instability in her family?
It's enough to make a man gag. As for fighting over a
woman—if anyone had the guts to do that he'd find a
proctor at his elbow in two minutes, looking for the
most convenient place to paralyze him, and inquiring
with sickening humility, 'May I do you a service, sir?' "

The bailiff edged closer to MacKinnon. He turned on
the official. "Stand back, you. I'm not through yet."
Then, resuming, "You've told me to choose between
the Two Alternatives. Well, it's no hard choice for me.
Before I'd submit to treatment, before I'd enter one of
your neat little, safe little, pleasant little reorientation
homes and let my mind be pried into by a lot of soft-
fingered doctors—before I did anything like that I'd

choose a nice, clean death. Oh, no—there is just one choice for me, not two. I take the choice of going to Coventry—and damned glad to. I hope I never hear of the United States again!

"But there is just one thing I want to ask you before I go—why do you bother to live, anyhow? I would think that any one of you would welcome an end to your silly, futile lives just from sheer boredom. That's all." He turned back to the bailiff. "Come on, you."

"One moment, David MacKinnon." The senior judge held up a restraining hand. "We have listened to you. Although custom does not compel it, I am minded to answer some of your statements. Will you listen?"

Unwilling, but less willing to appear loutish in the face of a request so obviously reasonable, the younger man consented.

The judge commenced to speak in gentle, scholarly words appropriate to a lecture room. "David MacKinnon, you have spoken in a fashion that doubtless seems wise to you. Nevertheless, your words were wild, and spoken in haste. I am moved to correct your obvious misstatements of fact. The Covenant is not a superstition, but a simple temporal contract entered into by those same revolutionists for pragmatic reasons. They wished to insure the maximum possible liberty for every person.

"You yourself have enjoyed that liberty. No possible act, nor mode of conduct, was forbidden to you as long as your action did not damage another. Even an act specifically prohibited by law could not be held against you unless the State were able to prove that your particular act damaged, or caused evident danger of damage to a particular individual.

"Even if one should willfully and knowingly damage another—as you have done—the State does not attempt to sit in moral judgment, nor to punish. We have not the wisdom to do that, and the chain of injustices that have always followed such moralistic coercion endanger the liberty of all. Instead, the convicted is given

the choice of submitting to psychological readjustment
to correct his tendency to wish to damage others, or of
having the State withdraw itself from him—of sending
him to Coventry!

"You complain that our way of living is dull and un-
romantic, and imply that we have deprived you of excitement to which you feel entitled. You are free to hold
and express your aesthetic opinion of our way of living,
but you must not expect us to live to suit your tastes.
You are free to seek danger and adventure if you wish
—there is danger still in experimental laboratories;
there is hardship in the mountains of the Moon, and
death in the jungles of Venus—but you are not free to
expose us to the violence of your nature."

"Why make so much of it?" MacKinnon protested
contemptuously. "You talk as if I had committed a
murder. I simply punched a man in the nose for offend-
ing me outrageously!"

"I agree with your aesthetic judgment of that individual," the judge continued calmly, "and am not dis-
pleased at his misfortune, but your psychometrical tests
show that you believe yourself capable of judging mor-
ally your fellow citizens and feel justified in personally
correcting and punishing their lapses. You are a dangerous individual, David MacKinnon, a danger to all of
us, for we cannot predict what damage you may do
next. From a social standpoint, your delusion makes
you as mad as the March Hare.

"You refuse treatment—therefore we withdraw our
society from you, we cast you out, we divorce you.
To Coventry with you." He turned to the bailiff. "Take
him away."

MacKinnon peered out of a forward port of the big
transport helicopter with repressed excitement in his
heart. There! That must be it—that black band in the
distance. The helicopter drew closer, and he became
certain that he was seeing the Barrier—the mysterious,

impenetrable wall that divided the United States from the reservation known as Coventry.

His guard looked up from the magazine he was reading and followed his gaze. "Nearly there, I see," he said pleasantly. "Well, it won't be long now."

"It can't be any too soon for me!"

The guard looked at him quizzically, but with tolerance. "Pretty anxious to get on with it, eh?"

MacKinnon held his head high. "You've never brought a man to the gateway that was more anxious to pass through!"

"Hm-m-m—maybe. They all say that, you know. Nobody goes through the gate against his own will."

"I mean it!"

"They all do. Some of them come back, just the same."

"Say—maybe you can give me some dope as to conditions inside."

"Sorry," the guard said, shaking his head, "but that is no concern of the United States, nor any of its employees. You'll know soon enough."

MacKinnon frowned a little. "It seems strange. I tried inquiring, but found no one who would admit that they had any notion about the inside. And yet you say that some come out. Surely some of them must talk—"

"That's simple," smiled the guard, "part of their reorientation is a subconscious compulsion not to discuss their experiences."

"That's a pretty scabby trick. Why should the government deliberately conspire to prevent me, and people like me, from knowing what we are going up against?"

"Listen, buddy," the guard answered, with mild exasperation, "you've told the rest of us to go to the devil. You've told us that you could get along without us. You are being given plenty of living room in some of the best land on this continent, and you are being allowed to take with you everything that you own, or your credit could buy. What the deuce else do you expect?"

MacKinnon's face settled in obstinate lines. "What assurance have I that there will be any land left for me?"

"That's your problem. The government sees to it that there is plenty of land for the population. The divvy-up is something you rugged individualists have to settle among yourselves. You've turned down our type of social cooperation; why the hell should you expect the safeguards of our organization?" The guard turned back to his reading and ignored him.

They landed on a small field which lay close under the blank black wall. No gate was apparent, but a guardhouse was located at the side of the field. MacKinnon was the only passenger. While his escort went over to the guardhouse, he descended from the passenger compartment and went around to the freight hold.

Two members of the crew were letting down a ramp from the cargo port. When MacKinnon drew near, one of them eyed him and said, "O.K., there's your stuff. Help yourself."

He sized up the job and said, "It's quite a lot, isn't it? I'll need some help. Will you give me a hand with it?"

The crew member addressed paused to light a cigarette before replying. "It's your stuff. If you want it, get it out. We take off in ten minutes." The two walked around him and re-entered the ship.

"Why, you—" MacKinnon shut up and kept the rest of his anger to himself. The surly louts! Gone was the faintest trace of regret at leaving civilization. He'd show them! He could get along without them.

But it was twenty minutes and more before he stood beside his heaped-up belongings and watched the ship rise. Fortunately the skipper had not been adamant about the time limit. MacKinnon turned and commenced loading his steel tortoise. Under the romantic influence of the classic literature of a bygone day he had considered using a string of burros, but had been unable to find a zoo that would sell them to him. It was just as well—he was completely ignorant of the limits, foibles, habits, vices, illnesses, and care of those useful little beasts, and unaware of his own ignorance. Master and servant would have vied in making each other unhappy.

The vehicle he had chosen was not an unreasonable substitute for burros. It was extremely rugged, easy to operate, and almost foolproof. It drew its power from six square yards of sun-power screens on its low curved roof. These drove a constant-load motor, or, when halted, replenished the storage battery against cloudy weather, or night travel. The bearings were "everlasting," and every moving part, other than the caterpillar treads and the controls, was sealed up, secure from inexpert tinkering.

It could maintain a steady six miles per hour on smooth, level pavement. When confronted by hills, or rough terrain, it did not stop, but simply slowed until the task demanded equaled its steady power output.

The steel tortoise gave MacKinnon a feeling of Crusoe-like independence. It did not occur to him that his chattel was the end product of the cumulative effort and intelligent cooperation of hundreds of thousands of men, living and dead. He had been accustomed all his life to the unfailing service of much more intricate machinery, and honestly regarded the tortoise as a piece of equipment of the same primitive level as a woodsman's ax, or a hunting knife. His talents had been devoted in the past to literary criticism rather than engineering, but that did not prevent him from believing that his native intelligence and the aid of a few reference books would be all that he would really need to duplicate the tortoise, if necessary.

His goods filled every compartment of the compact little freighter. He checked the last item from his inventory and ran a satisfied eye down the list. Any explorer, or adventurer of the past might well be pleased with such equipment, he thought. He could imagine showing Jack London his knock-down cabin. "See, Jack," he would say, "it's proof against any kind of weather—perfectly insulated walls and floor, and can't rust. It's so light that you can set it up in five minutes by yourself, yet it's so strong that you can sleep sound with the biggest grizzly in the world snuffling right outside your door."

And London would scratch his head and say, "Dave, you're a wonder. If I'd had that in the Yukon it would have been a cinch!"

He checked over the list again. Enough concentrated and dessicated food and vitamin concentrates to last six months. That would give him time enough to build hothouses for hydroponics and get his seeds started. Medical supplies—he did not expect to need those, but foresight was always best. Reference books of all sorts. A light sporting rifle—vintage: last century. His face clouded a little at this. The War Department had positively refused to sell him a portable blaster. When he had claimed the right of common social heritage, they had grudgingly provided him with the plans and specifications and told him to build his own. Well, he would, the first spare time he got.

Everything else was in order. MacKinnon climbed into the cockpit, grasped the two hand controls and swung the nose of the tortoise toward the guardhouse. He had been ignored since the ship had landed; he wanted to have the gate opened and to leave.

Several soldiers were gathered around the guardhouse. He picked out a legate by the silver stripe down the side of his kilt and spoke to him. "I'm ready to leave. Will you kindly open the gate?"

"O.K.," the officer answered him, and turned to a soldier who wore the plain gray kilt of a private's field uniform. "Jenkins, tell the powerhouse to dilate—about a number three opening, tell them," he added, sizing up the dimensions of the tortoise.

He turned to MacKinnon. "It is my duty to tell you that you may return to civilization, even now, by agreeing to be hospitalized for your neurosis."

"I have no neurosis!"

"Very well. If you change your mind at any future time, return to the place where you entered. There is an alarm there with which you may signal to the guard that you wish the gate opened."

"I can't imagine needing to know that."

The legate shrugged. "Perhaps not—we send refugees to quarantine all the time. If I were making the rules, it might be harder to get out again." He was cut off by the ringing of an alarm. The soldiers near them double-timed away, drawing their blasters from their belts as they ran. The ugly snout of a fixed blaster poked out over the top of the guardhouse and pointed toward the Barrier.

The legate answered the question on MacKinnon's face. "The powerhouse is ready to open up." He waved smartly toward that building and turned back. "Drive straight through the center of the opening. It takes a lot of power to suspend the stasis; if you touch the edge we'll have to pick up the pieces."

A tiny, bright dot appeared in the foot of the Barrier opposite where they waited. It spread into a half circle across the lampblack nothingness. Now it was large enough for MacKinnon to see the brown countryside beyond through the arch it had formed. He peered eagerly.

The opening grew until it was twenty feet wide, then stopped. It framed a scene of rugged, barren hills. He took this in and turned angrily on the legate. "I've been tricked!" he exclaimed. "That's not fit land to support a man."

"Don't be hasty," the legate told MacKinnon. "There's good land beyond. Besides, you don't have to enter. But if you are going, go!"

MacKinnon flushed and pulled back on both hand

controls. The treads bit in and the tortoise lumbered away, straight for the gateway to Coventry.

MacKinnon glanced back when he was several yards beyond the gate. The Barrier loomed behind him, with nothing to show where the opening had been. There was a little sheet-metal shed adjacent to the point where he had passed through. He supposed that it contained the alarm the legate had mentioned, but he was not interested, and turned his eyes back to his driving.

Stretching before him, twisting between the rocky hills, was a road of sorts. It was not paved, and the surface had not been repaired recently, but the grade averaged downhill, and the tortoise was able to maintain a respectable speed. He continued down it, not because he fancied it, but because it was the only road which led out of surroundings obviously unsuited to his needs.

The road was untraveled. This suited him; he had no wish to encounter other human beings until he had located desirable land to settle on and had staked out his claim. But the hills were not devoid of life; several times he caught glimpses of little dark shapes scurrying among the rocks, and occasionally bright, beady eyes stared back into his.

It did not occur to him at first that these timid little animals, streaking for cover at his coming, could replenish his larder—he was simply amused and warmed by their presence. When he did happen to consider that they might be used as food, the thought was at first repugnant to him— the practice of killing for "sport" had ceased to be customary long before his time; and inasmuch as the development of cheap synthetic proteins in the latter half of the preceding century had spelled the economic ruin of the business of breeding animals for slaughter, it is doubtful if he had ever tasted animal tissue in his life.

But once considered, it was logical to act. He expected to live off the country; although he had plenty of food on hand for the immediate future, it would be wise to conserve it. He suppressed his aesthetic distaste and ethical misgivings, and determined to shoot one of the little animals at the first opportunity.

Accordingly, he dug out the rifle, loaded it, and placed it handy. With the usual perversity of the world as it is, no game was evident for the next half-hour. He was passing a little shoulder of rocky outcropping when he saw his prey. It peeked at him from behind a small boulder, its sober eyes wary but unperturbed. He stopped the tortoise and took careful aim, resting and steadying the rifle on the side of the cockpit. His quarry accommodated him by hopping out into full view.

He pulled the trigger, involuntarily tensing his muscles and squinting his eyes as he did so. Naturally, the shot went high and to the right.

But he was much too busy just then to be aware of it. It seemed that the whole world had exploded. His right shoulder was numb, his mouth stung as if he had been kicked there, and his ears rang in a strange and unpleasant fashion. He was surprised to find the gun still intact in his hands and apparently none the worse for the incident.

He put it down, clambered out of the car, and rushed up to where the small creature had been. There was no sign of it anywhere. He searched the immediate neighborhood but did not find it. Mystified, he returned to his conveyance, having decided that the rifle was in some way defective, and that he should inspect it carefully before attempting to fire it again.

His recent target watched his actions cautiously from a vantage point many yards away, to which it had stampeded at the sound of the explosion. It was equally mystified, being no more used to firearms than MacKinnon.

Before he started the tortoise again, MacKinnon had to see to his upper lip, which was swollen and tender, and bleeding from a deep scratch. This increased his

conviction that the gun was defective. Nowhere in the
romantic literature of the nineteenth and twentieth
centuries, to which he was addicted, had there been a
warning that, when firing a gun heavy enough to drop
a man in his tracks, it is well not to hold the right hand
in such a manner that the recoil will cause the right
thumb and thumbnail to strike the mouth.

He applied an antiseptic and a dressing of sorts and
went on his way, somewhat subdued. The little arroyo
by which he had entered the hills had widened out,
and the hills were greener. He passed around one particularly sharp turn in the road and found a broad, fer-
tile valley spread out before him. It stretched away
until it was lost in the warm day's haze.

Much of the valley floor was cultivated, and he
could make out human habitations. He continued toward it with mixed feelings. People meant fewer hard-
ships, but it did not look as if staking out a claim
would be as simple as he had hoped. However, Coventry was a big place.

He had reached the point where the road gave onto
the floor of the valley, when two men stepped out into
his path. They were carrying weapons of some sort at
the ready. One of them called out to him: "Halt!"

MacKinnon did so, and answered him as they came
abreast. "What do you want?"

"Customs inspection. Pull over there by the office."
He indicated a small building set back a few feet from
the road, which MacKinnon had not previously noticed. He looked from it back to the spokesman and
felt a slow, unreasoning heat spread up from his vis-
cera. It colored his point of view and rendered his
none-too-stable judgment still more unsound.

"What the deuce are you talking about?" he
snapped. "Stand aside and let me pass."

The one who had remained silent raised his weapon
and aimed it at MacKinnon's chest. The other grabbed
his arm and pulled the weapon out of line. "Don't
shoot the dumb fool, Joe," he said testily. "You're al-

ways too anxious." Then, to MacKinnon, "You're resisting the law. Come on—be quick about it!"

"The law?" MacKinnon gave a short, bitter laugh,
and snatched his rifle up from the seat beside him. It
never reached his shoulder—the man who had done all
the talking fired casually, without apparently taking
time to aim. The rifle was smacked from MacKinnon's
grasp, and flew into the air, landing some forty feet
away in the roadside ditch behind the tortoise.

The member of the pair who had remained silent
followed the flight of the gun with detached interest
and remarked, "Nice shot, Blackie. Never touched
him."

"Oh, just luck," the other demurred, but grinned his
pleasure at the compliment. "Glad I didn't nick him,
though—saves writing out a report." He returned his
stubby, curiously convoluted weapon to his belt, reas-
sumed a crisp, official manner, and spoke again to
MacKinnon, who had been sitting in dumfounded silence, rubbing his painfully smarting hands. "Well,
tough guy? Do you behave, or do we come up there
and get you?"

MacKinnon gave in. He drove the tortoise to the
designated spot and waited sullenly for orders. "Get
out and start unloading," he was told.

He obeyed, under compulsion. As he piled his precious possessions on the ground, the one addressed as
Blackie separated each item into two piles, while Joe
listed them on a printed form. He noticed presently
that Joe listed only the items that went into the first
pile. But he did not understand that he was being
robbed until Blackie told him to reload the tortoise
with the items from that pile, and commenced himself
to carry goods from the other pile into the building.
MacKinnon started to protest—

Joe punched him in the mouth, coolly and without
rancor. MacKinnon went down, but got up again, fighting. He was in such a blind rage that he would have
tackled a charging rhino just as readily. Joe timed his

rush and clipped him again. This time he could not get up at once.

Blackie stepped over to the washstand in one corner of the office. Presently he came back with a wet towel and chucked it at MacKinnon. "Wipe your face on that, bud, and get back into the buggy. We got to get going."

MacKinnon had time to do a lot of serious thinking as he drove Blackie into town. Beyond a terse answer of "Prize court" to MacKinnon's inquiry as to their destination, Blackie did not converse, nor did MacKinnon press him to, anxious as he was to have information. His mouth pained him from the repeated punishment it had taken, his head ached, and he was no longer tempted to precipitate action by hasty speech.

Evidently Coventry was not quite the frontier anarchy he had expected it to be. There was a government of sorts, evidently, but it resembled nothing that he had ever been used to. He had visualized a land of noble, independent spirits who gave each other wide berth and practiced mutual respect. There would be villains, of course, but they would be treated to summary, and probably lethal, justice as soon as they demonstrated their ugly natures. He had a strong, though subconscious, assumption that virtue is necessarily triumphant.

But having found government, he expected it to follow the general pattern that he had been used to all his life—honest, conscientious, reasonably efficient, and invariably careful of a citizen's rights and liberties. He was aware that government had not always been like that, but he had never experienced it—the idea was as remote and implausible as cannibalism, or chattel slavery.

Had he stopped to think about it, he might have realized that public servants in Coventry would never have been examined psychologically to determine their temperamental fitness for their duties, and that, since every inhabitant of Coventry was there—as he was—for violating a basic custom and refusing treatment thereafter, it was a foregone conclusion that most of them would be erratic and arbitrary.

He pinned his hope on the knowledge that they were going to court. All he asked was a chance to tell his story to the judge.

His immediate dependence on judicial procedure may appear inconsistent in view of how recently he had renounced all reliance on organized government, but it was only superficially so. He could renounce government verbally, but he could not do away with a lifetime of environmental conditioning. His cortex was canalized, whether he wished it or not, into certain evaluating habits. He could curse the court that had humiliated him by condemning him to the Two Alternatives, but he expected courts to dispense justice. He could assert his own rugged independence, but he expected persons he encountered to behave as if they were bound by the Covenant—he had met no other sort. He was no more able to discard his past history than he would have been to discard his accustomed body.

But he did not know it yet.

MacKinnon failed to stand up when the judge entered the courtroom. Court attendants quickly set him right, but not before he had provoked a glare from the bench. The judge's appearance and manner were not reassuring. He was a well-fed man, of ruddy complexion, whose sadistic temper was evident in face and voice. They waited while he dealt drastically with several petty offenders. It seemed to MacKinnon, as he listened, that almost everything was against the law.

Nevertheless, he was relieved when his name was called. He stepped up and undertook at once to tell his story. The judge's gavel cut him short.

"What is this case?" the judge demanded, staring at MacKinnon's damaged features, his face set in grim, intolerant lines. "Drunk and disorderly, apparently. I shall put a stop to this slackness among the young if it takes the last ounce of strength in my body!" He turned to the clerk. "Any previous offenses?"

The clerk whispered in his ear. The judge threw MacKinnon a look of mixed annoyance and suspicion, then told the customs guard to come forward. Blackie told a clear, straightforward tale with the ease of a man used to giving testimony. MacKinnon's condition was attributed to resisting an officer in the execution of his duty. He submitted the inventory his colleague had prepared, but failed to mention the large quantity of goods which had been abstracted before the inventory was made.

The judge turned to MacKinnon. "Do you have anything to say for yourself?"

"I certainly have, Doctor," he began eagerly. "There isn't a word of—"

Bang! The gavel cut him short. A court attendant hurried to MacKinnon's side and attempted to explain to him the proper form to use in addressing the court. The explanation confused him. In his experience, "judge" naturally implied a medical man—a psychologist skilled in social problems. Nor had he heard of any special speech forms appropriate to a courtroom. But he amended his language as instructed.

"May it please the honorable court, this man is lying. He and his companion assaulted and robbed me. I was simply—"

"Smugglers generally think they are being robbed when customs officials catch them," the judge sneered. "Do you deny that you attempted to resist inspection?"

"No, Your Honor, but—"

"That will do. Penalty of fifty per cent is added to the established scale of duty. Pay the clerk."

"But, Your Honor, I can't—"

"Can't you pay it?"

"I haven't any money. I have only my possessions."

"So?" He turned to the clerk. "Condemnation proceedings. Impound his goods. Ten days for vagrancy. The community can't have these immigrant paupers roaming at large, and preying on law-abiding citizens. Next case!"

They hustled him quickly away. It took the sound of the key grating in the barred door behind him to make him realize the extent of his predicament.

"Hi, pal, how's the weather outside?" The detention cell had a prior inmate, a small, well-knit man who looked up from a game of solitaire to address Mac-Kinnon. He sat astraddle a wooden bench on which he had spread his cards, and studied the newcomer with unworried, bright, beady eyes.

"Clear enough outside—but stormy in the court-room," MacKinnon answered, trying to adopt the same bantering tone and not succeeding very well. His mouth hurt him and spoiled his grin.

The other swung a leg over the bench and approached him with a light, silent step. "Say, pal, you must 'a caught that in a gear box," he commented, inspecting MacKinnon's mouth. "Does it hurt?"

"Like the devil," MacKinnon admitted.

"We'll have to do something about that." He went to the cell door and rattled it, filling the building with the din. "Hey! Lefty! The house is on fire! Come a-runnin'!"

The guard sauntered down and stood opposite their cell door. "Wha' d'yuh want, Fader?" he said noncommittally.

"My old school chum has been slapped in the face with a wrench, and the pain is inordinate. Here's a chance for you to get right with heaven by oozing down to the dispensary and snagging a dressing and about five grains of neoanodyne."

The guard's expression was not encouraging. The prisoner looked grieved. "Why, Lefty," he said, "I thought you would jump at a chance to do a little pure charity like that." He waited for a moment, then added, "Tell you what—you do it and I'll show you how to work that puzzle about 'How old is Ann?' Is it a go?"

"Show me first."

"It would take too long. I'll write it out and give it to you."

When the guard returned, MacKinnon's cellmate dressed his wounds with gentle deftness, talking the while. "They call me Fader Magee. What's your name, pal?"

"David MacKinnon. I'm sorry, but I didn't quite catch your first name."

"Fader. It isn't," he explained with a grin, "the name my mother gave me. It's more a professional tribute to my shy and unobtrusive nature."

MacKinnon looked puzzled. "Professional tribute? What is your profession?"

Magee looked pained. "Why, Dave," he said, "I didn't ask you that. However," he went on, "it's probably the same as yours—self-preservation."

Magee was a sympathetic listener, and MacKinnon welcomed the chance to tell someone about his troubles. He related the story of how he had decided to enter Coventry rather than submit to the sentence of the court, and how he had hardly arrived when he was hijacked and hauled into court.

Magee nodded. "I'm not surprised," he observed. "A man has to have larceny in his heart or he wouldn't be a customs guard."

"But what happens to my belongings?"

"They auction them off to pay the duty."

"I wonder how much there will be left for me."

Magee stared at him. "Left over? There won't be anything left over. You'll probably have to pay a deficiency judgment."

"Huh? What's that?"

"It's a device whereby the condemned pays for the execution," Magee explained succinctly, if somewhat obscurely. "What it means to you is that when your ten days are up you'll still be in debt to the court. Then it's the chain gang for you, my lad. You'll work it off at a dollar a day."

"Fader—you're kidding me."

"Wait and see. You've got a lot to learn, Dave."

Coventry was an even more complex place than Dave had gathered up to this time. Magee explained to him that there were actually three sovereign, independent jurisdictions. The jail where they were prisoners lay in the so-called New America. It had the forms of democratic government, but the treatment he had already received was a fair sample of the fashion in which it was administered.

"This place is heaven itself compared with the Free State," Magee maintained. "I've been there."

The Free State was an absolute dictatorship; the head man of the ruling clique was designated the "Liberator." Their watchwords were duty and obedience; an arbitrary discipline was enforced with a severity that left no room for any freedom of opinion. Governmental theory was vaguely derived from the old functionalist doctrines. The State was thought of as a single organism with a single head, a single brain, and a single purpose. Anything not compulsory was forbidden.

"Honest, so help me," claimed Magee, "you can't go to bed in that place without finding one of their damned secret police between the sheets.

"But at that," he continued, "it's an easier place to live than with the Angels."

"The Angels?"

"Sure. We still got 'em. Must've been two or three thousand diehards that chose to go to Coventry after the Revolution—you know that. There's still a colony up in the hills to the north, complete with Prophet Incarnate and the works. They aren't bad hombres, but they'll pray you into heaven even if it kills you."

All three States had one curious characteristic in common—each one claimed to be the only legal government of the entire United States, and looked forward to some future day when they would reclaim the "unredeemed" portion; i.e., outside Coventry. To the Angels this was an event which would occur when the First Prophet returned to Earth to lead them again. In New America it was hardly more than a convenient campaign plank, to be forgotten after each election. But in the Free State it was a fixed policy.

Pursuant to this purpose there had been a whole series of wars between the Free State and New America. The Liberator held, quite logically, that New America was an unredeemed section, and that it was necessary to bring it under the rule of the Free State before the advantages of their culture could be extended to the outside.

Magee's words demolished MacKinnon's dream of finding an anarchistic Utopia within the Barrier, but he could not let his fond illusion die without a protest. "But see here, Fader," he persisted, "isn't there some place where a man can live quietly by himself without all this insufferable interference?"

"No—" considered Fader. "No, not unless you took to the hills and hid. Then you'd be all right, as long as you steered clear of the Angels. But it would be pretty slim pickin's, living off the country. Ever tried it?"

"No, not exactly. But I've read all the classics: Zane Grey, and Emerson Hough, and so forth."

"Well—maybe you could do it. But if you really want to go off and be a hermit you'd do better to try it on the Outside, where there aren't so many objections to it."

"No"—MacKinnon's backbone stiffened at once—"no, I'll never do that. I'll never submit to psychological reorientation just to have a chance to be let alone. If I could go back to where I was a couple of months ago, before I was arrested, it might be all right to go off to the Rockies, or look up an abandoned farm somewhere. But with that diagnosis staring me in the face—after being told I wasn't fit for human society until I had had my emotions retailored to fit a cautious little pattern—I couldn't face it. Not if it meant going to a sanitarium—"

"I see," agreed Fader, nodding, "you want to go to Coventry, but you don't want the Barrier to shut you off from the rest of the world."

"No, that's not quite fair— Well, maybe, in a way. Say, you don't think I'm not fit to associate with, do you?"

"You look all right to me," Magee reassured him with a grin, "but I'm in Coventry, too, remember. Maybe I'm no judge."

"You don't talk as if you liked it much. Why are you here?"

Magee held up a gently admonishing finger. "Tut! Tut! That is the one question you must never ask a man here. You must assume that he came here because he knew how swell everything is here."

"Still—you don't seem to like it."

"I didn't say I didn't like it. I do like it; it has flavor. Its little incongruities are a source of innocent merriment. And any time they turn on the heat I can always go back through the gate and rest up for a while in a nice quiet hospital until things quiet down."

MacKinnon was puzzled again. "Turn on the heat? Do they supply too hot weather here?"

"Huh? Oh, I didn't mean weather control—there isn't any of that here except what leaks over from Outside. I was just using an old figure of speech."

"What does it mean?"

Magee smiled to himself. "You'll find out."

After supper—bread, stew in a metal dish, a small apple—Magee introduced MacKinnon to the mysteries of cribbage. Fortunately MacKinnon had no cash to lose. Presently Magee put the cards down without shuffling them. "Dave," he said, "are you enjoying the hospitality offered by this institution?"

"Hardly. Why?"

"I suggest that we check out."

"A good idea, but how?"

"That's what I've been thinking about. Do you suppose you could take another poke on that battered
phiz of yours in a good cause?"

MacKinnon cautiously fingered his face. "I suppose
so—if necessary. It can't do me much more harm,
anyhow."

"That's mother's little man! Now listen. This guard,
Lefty, in addition to being kind o' unbright, is sensitive
about his appearance. When they turn out the lights,
you just—"

"Let me out of here! Let me out of here!" Mac-
Kinnon beat on the bars and screamed. No answer
came. He renewed the racket, his voice a hysterical
falsetto. Lefty arrived to investigate, grumbling.

"What the hell's eating on you?" he demanded,
peering through the bars.

MacKinnon changed to tearful petition. "Oh, Lefty,
please let me out of here. Please! I can't stand the
dark. It's dark in here—please don't leave me alone."
He flung himself, sobbing, on the bars.

The guard cursed to himself. "Another slug-nutty.
Listen, you—shut up and go to sleep or I'll come in
there and give you something to yelp for!" He started
to leave.

MacKinnon changed instantly to the vindictive, un-
predictable anger of the irresponsible. "You big, ugly
baboon! You rat-faced idiot! Where'd ja get that
nose?"

Lefty turned back, fury in his face. He started to
speak. MacKinnon cut him short. "Yah! Yah! Yah!"
he gloated like a nasty little boy. "Lefty's mother was
scared by a warthog—"

The guard swung at the spot where MacKinnon's
face was pressed between the bars of the door. Mac-
Kinnon ducked and grabbed simultaneously. Off balance at meeting no resistance, the guard rocked forward, thrusting his forearm between the bars. Mac-

Kinnon's fingers slid along his arm and got a firm purchase on Lefty's wrist.

He threw himself backward, dragging the guard with him, until Lefty was jammed up against the outside of the barred door, with one arm inside, to the wrist of which MacKinnon clung as if welded.

The yell which formed in Lefty's face miscarried; Magee had already acted. Out of the darkness, silent as death, his slim hands had snaked between the bars and embedded themselves in the guard's fleshy neck. Lefty heaved and almost broke free, but MacKinnon threw his weight to the right and twisted the arm he gripped in an agonizing, bone-breaking leverage.

It seemed to MacKinnon that they remained thus, like some grotesque game of statues, for an endless period. His pulse pounded in his ears until he feared that it must be heard by others, and bring rescue to Lefty.

Magee spoke at last. "That's enough," he whispered. "Go through his pockets."

He made an awkward job of it, for his hands were numb and trembling from the strain, and it was anything but convenient to work between the bars. But the keys were there, in the last pocket he tried. He passed them to Magee, who let the guard slip to the floor and accepted them.

Magee made a quick job of it. The door swung open with a distressing creak. Dave stepped over Lefty's body, but Magee kneeled down, unhooked a truncheon from the guard's belt, and cracked him behind the ear with it.

MacKinnon paused. "Did you kill him?" he asked.

"Cripes, no," Magee answered softly. "Lefty is a friend of mine. Let's go."

They hurried down the dimly lighted passageway between the cells toward the door leading to the administrative offices—their only outlet. Lefty had carelessly left it ajar, and light shone through the crack, but as they silently approached it they heard ponderous footsteps from the far side. Dave looked hurriedly

for cover, but the best he could manage was to slink
back into the corner formed by the cell block and the
wall. He glanced around for Magee, but he had disappeared completely.

The door swung open; a man stepped through,
paused, and looked around. MacKinnon saw that he
was carrying a black light and wearing its complement
—rectifying spectacles. He realized then that the darkness gave him no cover. The black light swung his
way; he tensed to spring—

He heard a dull *clank!* The guard sighed, swayed
gently, then collapsed into a loose pile. Magee stood
over him, poised on the balls of his feet, and surveyed
his work while caressing the business end of the truncheon with the cupped fingers of his left hand.

"That will do," he decided. "Shall we go, Dave?"

Magee eased through the door without waiting for
an answer. MacKinnon was close behind him. The
lighted corridor led away to the right and ended in a
large double door to the street. On the left wall, near
the street door, a smaller office door stood open.

Magee drew MacKinnon to him. "It's a cinch," he
whispered. "There'll be nobody in there now but the
desk sergeant. We get past him, then out that door and
into the ozone—" He motioned Dave to keep behind
him and crept silently up to the office door. After
drawing a small mirror from a pocket in his belt, he
lay down on the floor, placed his head near the door
frame, and cautiously extended the tiny mirror an inch
or two past the edge.

Apparently he was satisfied with the reconnaissance
the improvised periscope afforded him, for he drew
himself back onto his knees and turned his head so
that MacKinnon could see the words shaped by his silent lips. "It's all right," he breathed, "there's only—"

Two hundred pounds of uniformed Nemesis landed
on his shoulders. A clanging alarm sounded through
the corridor. Magee went down fighting, but he was

outclassed and caught off guard. He jerked his head free and shouted, "Run for it, kid!"

MacKinnon could hear running feet from somewhere, but could see nothing but the struggling figures before him. He shook his head and shoulders like a dazed animal, then kicked the larger of the two contestants in a fashion forbidden by sportsmanship. The man screamed and let go his hold. MacKinnon grasped his small companion by the scruff of the neck and hauled him roughly to his feet.

Magee's eyes were still merry. "Well played, my lad," he commended in clipped syllables, as they burst out the street door, "if hardly cricket! Where did you learn *la Savate*?"

MacKinnon had no time to answer, being fully occupied in keeping up with Magee's weaving, deceptively rapid progress. They ducked across the street, down an alley, and between two buildings.

The succeeding minutes, or hours, were confusion to MacKinnon. He remembered afterward crawling along a rooftop and letting himself down to crouch in the blackness of an interior court, but he could not remember how they had gotten on the roof. He also recalled spending an interminable period alone, compressed inside a most unsavory refuse bin, and his terror when footsteps approached the bin and a light flashed through a crack.

A crash and the sound of footsteps in flight immediately thereafter led him to guess that Fader had drawn the pursuit away from him. But when Fader did return and opened the top of the bin, MacKinnon almost throttled him before identification was established.

When the active pursuit had been taken off, Magee guided him across town, showing a sophisticated knowledge of back ways and short cuts, and a genius for taking full advantage of cover. They reached the outskirts of the town in a dilapidated quarter, far from the civic center. Magee stopped. "I guess this is the end of the line, kid," he told Dave. "If you follow this street you'll come to the open country shortly. That's what you wanted, wasn't it?"

"I suppose so," MacKinnon replied uneasily, and peered down the street. Then he turned back to speak again to Magee.

But Magee was gone. He had faded away into the shadows. There was neither sight nor sound of him.

MacKinnon started in the suggested direction with a heavy heart. There was no possible reason to expect Magee to stay with him; the service Dave had done him with a lucky kick had been repaid with interest—yet he had lost the only friendly companionship he had found in a strange place. He felt lonely and depressed.

He continued along, keeping to the shadows and watching carefully for shapes that might be patrolmen. He had gone a few hundred yards and was beginning to worry about how far it might be to open countryside when he was startled into gooseflesh by a hiss from a dark doorway.

He did his best to repress the unreasoning panic that beset him, and was telling himself that policemen never hiss, when a shadow detached itself from the blackness and touched him on the arm.

"Dave," it said softly.

MacKinnon felt a childlike sense of relief and well-being. "Fader!"

"I changed my mind, Dave. The gendarmes would have you in tow before morning. You don't know the ropes—so I came back."

Dave was both pleased and crestfallen. "Hell's bells, Fader," he protested, "you shouldn't worry about me. I'll get along."

Magee shook him roughly by the arm. "Don't be a chump. Green as you are, you'd start to holler about your civil rights, or something, and get clipped in the mouth again.

"Now see here," he went on, "I'm going to take you to some friends of mine who will hide you until you're smartened up to the tricks around here. But they're on the wrong side of the law, see? You'll have to be all three of the three sacred monkeys—see no evil, hear no evil, tell no evil. Think you can do it?"

"Yes, but—"

"No 'buts' about it. Come along!"

The entrance was in the rear of an old warehouse. Steps led down into a little sunken court. From this open areaway—foul with accumulated refuse—a door let into the back wall of the building. Magee tapped lightly but systematically, waited and listened. Presently he whispered, *"Ps-s-st!* It's the Fader."

The door opened quickly and Magee was encircled by two great, fat arms. He was lifted off his feet, while the owner of those arms planted a resounding buss on his cheek. "Fader!" she exclaimed. "Are you all right, lad? We've missed you."

"Now that's a proper welcome, Mother," he answered when he was back on his own feet, "but I want you to meet a friend of mine. Mother Johnston, this is David MacKinnon."

"May I do you a service?" David acknowledged with automatic formality, but Mother Johnston's eyes tightened with instant suspicion.

"Is he stooled?" she snapped.

"No, Mother, he's a new immigrant—but I vouch for him. He's on the dodge, and I've brought him here to cool."

She softened a little under his sweetly persuasive tones. "Well—"

Magee pinched her cheek. "That's a good girl! When are you going to marry me?"

She slapped his hand away. "Even if I were forty years younger I'd not marry such a scamp as you! Come along, then," she continued to MacKinnon, "as long as you're a friend of the Fader—though it's no credit to you!" She waddled quickly ahead of them down a flight of stairs while calling out for someone to open the door at its foot.

The room was poorly lighted with a few obsolete glow tubes and was furnished principally with a long table and some chairs, at which an odd dozen people were seated, drinking and talking. It reminded Mac-Kinnon of prints he had seen of old English pubs in the days before the Collapse.

Magee was greeted with a babble of boisterous welcome. "Fader!" "It's the kid himself!" "How'd ja do it this time, Fader? Crawl down the drains?" "Set 'em up, Mother—the Fader's back!"

He accepted the ovation with a wave of his hand and a shout of inclusive greeting, then turned to MacKinnon. "Folks," he said, his voice cutting the confusion, "I want you to know Dave—the best pal that ever kicked a jailer at the right moment. If it hadn't been for Dave I wouldn't be here."

MacKinnon found himself seated between two others at the table and a stein of beer was thrust into his hand by a not uncomely young woman. He started to thank her, but she had hurried off to help Mother Johnston take care of the sudden influx of orders. Seated opposite him was a rather surly young man who had taken little part in the greeting to Magee. He looked MacKinnon over with a face expressionless except for a recurrent tic which caused his right eye to wink spasmodically every few seconds.

"What's your line?" he demanded.

"Leave him alone, Alec," Magee cut in swiftly but in a friendly tone. "He's just arrived inside; I told you that. But he's all right," he continued, raising his voice to include the others present. "He's been here less than twenty-four hours, but he's broken jail, beat up two customs busies, and sassed old Judge Fleishacker right to his face. How's that for a busy day?"

Dave was the center of approving interest, but the party with the tic persisted. "That's all very well, but I asked him a fair question: What's his line? If it's the same as mine, I won't stand for it—it's too crowded now."

"That cheap racket you're in is always crowded, but he's not in it. Forget about his line."

"Why don't he answer for himself?" Alec countered suspiciously. He half stood up. "I don't believe he's stooled—"

It appeared that Magee was cleaning his nails with the point of a slender knife. "Put your nose back in your glass, Alec," he remarked in a conversational tone, without looking up, "or must I cut it off and put it there?"

The other fingered something nervously in his hand. Magee seemed not to notice it, but nevertheless told him, "If you think you can use a vibrator on me faster than I use steel, go ahead—it will be an interesting experiment."

The man facing him stood uncertainly for a moment longer, his tic working incessantly. Mother Johnston came up behind him and pushed him down by the shoulders, saying, "Boys! Boys! Is that any way to behave—and in front of a guest, too! Fader, put that toad sticker away. I'm ashamed of you."

The knife was gone from his hands. "You're right, as always, Mother." He grinned. "Ask Molly to fill up my glass again."

An old chap sitting on MacKinnon's right had followed these events with alcoholic uncertainty, but he seemed to have gathered something of the gist of it, for now he fixed Dave with a serum-filled eye and inquired, "Boy, are you stooled to the rogue?" His sweetly sour breath reached MacKinnon as the old man leaned toward him and emphasized his question with a trembling, joint-swollen finger.

Dave looked to Magee for advice and enlightenment. Magee answered for him. "No, he's not— Mother Johnston knew that when she let him in. He's here for sanctuary—as our customs provide!"

An uneasy stir ran around the room. Molly paused in her serving and listened openly. But the old man seemed satisfied. "True—true enough," he agreed, and took another pull at his drink. "Sanctuary may be given when needed, if—" His words were lost in a mumble.

The nervous tension slackened. Most of those present were subconsciously glad to follow the lead of the old man and excuse the intrusion on the score of necessity. Magee turned back to Dave. "I thought that what you didn't know couldn't hurt you—or us—but the matter has been opened."

"But what did he mean?"

"Gramps asked you if you had been stooled to the rogue—whether or not you were a member of the ancient and honorable fraternity of thieves, cutthroats, and pickpockets!"

Magee stared into Dave's face with a look of saturnine amusement. Dave looked uncertainly from Magee to the others, saw them exchange glances, and wondered what answer was expected of him.

Alec broke the pause. "Well," he sneered, "what are you waiting for? Go ahead and put the question to him —or are the great Fader's friends free to use this club without so much as a by-your-leave?"

"I thought I told you to quiet down, Alec," the Fader replied evenly. "Besides, you're skipping a requirement. All the comrades present must first decide whether or not to put the question at all."

A quiet little man with a chronic worried look in his eyes answered him. "I don't think that quite applies, Fader. If he had come himself, or fallen into our hands — In that case, yes. But you brought him here. I think I speak for all when I say he should answer the question. Unless someone objects, I will ask him myself." He allowed an interval to pass. No one spoke up. "Very well, then. Dave, you have seen too much and heard too much. Will you leave us now—or will you stay and take the oath of our guild? I must warn you that once stooled you are stooled for life—and there is but one punishment for betraying the rogue."

He drew his thumb across his throat in an age-old

deadly gesture. Gramps made an appropriate sound effect by sucking air wetly through his teeth, and chuckled.

Dave looked around. Magee's face gave him no help. "What is it that I have to swear to?" he temporized.

The parley was brought to an abrupt ending by the sound of pounding outside. There was a shout, muffled by two closed doors and a stairway, of "Open up down there!" Magee got lightly to his feet and beckoned to Dave.

"That's for us, kid," he said. "Come along."

He stepped over to a ponderous old-fashioned radio-phonograph which stood against the wall, reached under it, fiddled for a moment, then swung out one side panel of it. Dave saw that the mechanism had been cunningly rearranged in such a fashion that a man could squeeze inside it. Magee urged him into it, slammed the panel closed and left him.

MacKinnon's face was pressed up close to the slotted grille which was intended to cover the sound box. Molly had cleared off the two extra glasses from the table and was dumping one drink so that it spread along the table top and erased the rings their glasses had made.

MacKinnon saw the Fader slide under the table and reach up. Then he was gone. Apparently he had, in some fashion, attached himself to the underside of the table.

Mother Johnston made a great to-do of opening up. The lower door she opened at once, with much noise. Then she clumped slowly up the steps, pausing, wheezing, and complaining aloud. MacKinnon heard her unlock the outer door.

"A fine time to be waking honest people up!" she protested. "It's hard enough to get the work done and make both ends meet without dropping what I'm doing every five minutes and—"

"Enough of that, old girl," a man's voice answered,

"just get along downstairs. We have business with you."

"What sort of business?" she demanded.

"It might be selling liquor without a license, but it's not—this time."

"I don't. This is a private club. The members own the liquor; I simply serve it to them."

"That's as may be. It's those members I want to talk to. Get out of the way now, and be spry about it."

They came pushing into the room, Mother Johnston, still voluble, carried along by the van. The speaker was a sergeant of police. He was accompanied by a patrolman. Following them were two other uniformed men, but they were soldiers. MacKinnon judged by the markings on their kilts that they were corporal and private—provided the insignia in New America were similar to those used by the United States Army.

The sergeant paid no more attention to Mother Johnston. "All right, you men," he called out, "line up!"

They did so, ungraciously but promptly. Molly and Mother Johnston watched them and moved closer to each other.

"All right, Corporal—take charge!"

The boy who washed up in the kitchen had been staring round-eyed. He dropped a glass. It bounced around on the hard floor, giving out bell-like sounds in the silence.

The man who had questioned Dave spoke up. "What's all this?"

The sergeant answered with a pleased grin. "Conscription—that's what it is. You are all enlisted in the army for the duration."

"Press gang!" It was an involuntary gasp that came from no particular source.

The corporal stepped briskly forward. "Form a column of twos," he directed. But the little man with the worried eyes was not done.

"I don't understand this," he objected. "We signed an armistice with the Free State three weeks ago."

"That's not your worry," countered the sergeant, "nor mine. We are picking up every able-bodied man not in essential industry. Come along."

"Then you can't take me."

"Why not?"

He held up the stump of a missing hand. The sergeant glanced from it to the corporal, who nodded grudgingly and said, "O.K.—but report to the office in the morning and register."

He started to march them out, when Alec broke ranks and backed up to the wall, screaming, "You can't do this to me! I won't go!" His deadly little vibrator was exposed in his hand, and the right side of his face was drawn up in a spastic wink that left his teeth bare.

"Get him, Steeves," ordered the corporal. The private stepped forward, but stopped when Alec brandished the vibrator at him. He had no desire to have a vibroblade between his ribs, and there was no doubt as to the uncontrolled dangerousness of his hysterical opponent.

The corporal, looking phlegmatic, almost bored, leveled a small tube at a spot on the wall over Alec's head. Dave heard a soft *pop!* and a thin tinkle. Alec stood motionless for a few seconds, his face even more strained, as if he were exerting the limit of his will against some unseen force, then slid quietly to the floor. The tonic spasm in his face relaxed, and his features smoothed into those of a tired and petulant, and rather bewildered, little boy.

"Two of you birds carry him," directed the corporal. "Let's get going."

The sergeant was the last to leave. He turned at the door and spoke to Mother Johnston. "Have you seen the Fader lately?"

"The Fader?" She seemed puzzled. "Why, he's in jail."

"Ah, yes—so he is." He went out.

Magee refused the drink that Mother Johnston offered him. Dave was surprised to see that he appeared worried for the first time. "I don't understand it," Magee muttered, half to himself, then addressed the one-handed man. "Ed, bring me up to date."

"Not much news since they tagged you, Fader. The armistice was before that. I thought from the papers that things were going to be straightened out for once."

"So did I. But the government must expect war if they are going in for general conscription." He stood up. "I've got to have more data. Al!" The kitchen boy stuck his head into the room.

"Whatcha want, Fader?"

"Go out and make palaver with five or six of the beggars. Look up their king. You know where he makes his pitch?"

"Sure. Over by the auditorium."

"Find out what's stirring, but don't let them know I sent you."

"Right, Fader. It's in the bag." The boy swaggered out.

"Molly."

"Yes, Fader?"

"Will you go out and do the same things with some of the business girls? I want to know what they hear from their customers." She nodded agreement. He went on, "Better look up that little redhead that has her beat up on Union Square. She can get secrets out of a dead man. Here"—he pulled a wad of bills out of his pocket and handed her several—"You better take this grease. You might have to pay off a cop to get back out of the district."

Magee was not disposed to talk and insisted that Dave get some sleep. He was easily persuaded, not having slept since he entered Coventry. That seemed like a lifetime past; he was exhausted. Mother Johnston fixed him a shakedown in a dark, stuffy room on the same underground level. It had none of the hygienic comforts to which he was accustomed—air-conditioning, restful music, hydraulic mattress, nor sound-proofing—and he missed his usual relaxing soak and auto-massage, but he was too tired to care. He slept in clothing and under covers for the first time in his life.

He woke up with a headache, a taste in his mouth like tired sin, and a sense of impending disaster. At first he could not remember where he was—he thought he was still in dentention Outside. His surroundings were inexplicably sordid; he was about to ring for the attendant and complain when his memory pieced in the events of the day before. Then he got up and discovered that his bones and muscles were painfully stiff, and—which was worse—that he was, by his standards, filthy dirty. He itched.

MacKinnon entered the common room and found Magee sitting at the table. He greeted Dave. "Hi, kid. I was about to wake you. You've slept almost all day. We've got a lot to talk about."

"O.K.—shortly. Where's the 'fresher?"

"Over there."

It was not Dave's idea of a refreshing chamber, but he managed to take a sketchy shower in spite of the slimy floor. Then he discovered that there was no air blast installed, and he was forced to dry himself unsatisfactorily with his handkerchief. He had no choice in clothes. He must put back on the ones he had taken off or go naked. He recalled that he had seen no nudity anywhere in Coventry, even at sports—a difference in customs, no doubt.

He put his clothes back on, though his skin crawled at the touch of the once-used linen.

Mother Johnston had thrown together an appetizing breakfast for him. He let coffee restore his courage as Magee talked. It was, according to Fader, a serious situation. New America and the Free State had compromised their differences and had formed an alliance.

They quite seriously proposed to break out of Coventry and attack the United States.

MacKinnon looked up at this. "That's ridiculous, isn't it? They'd be outnumbered enormously. Besides, how about the Barrier?"

"I don't know—yet. But they have some reason to think that they can break through the Barrier—and there are rumors that whatever it is can be used as a weapon, too, so that a small army might be able to whip the whole United States."

MacKinnon looked puzzled. "Well," he observed, "I haven't any opinion of a weapon I know nothing about, but as to the Barrier—I'm not a mathematical physicist, but I was always told that it was theoretically impossible to break the Barrier—that it was just a nothingness that there was no way to touch. Of course, you can fly over it, but even that is supposed to be deadly to life."

"Suppose they had found some way to shield from the effects of the Barrier's field," suggested Magee. "Anyhow, that's not the point for us. The point is: They've made this combine; the Free State supplies the techniques and most of the officers; and New America, with its bigger population, supplies most of the men. And that means to us that we don't dare show our faces anyplace, or we are in the army before you can blink.

"Which brings me to what I was going to suggest. I'm going to duck out of here as soon as it gets dark and light out for the gateway before they send somebody after me who is bright enough to look under a table. I thought maybe you might want to come along."

"Back to the psychologists?" MacKinnon was honestly aghast.

"Sure—why not? What have you got to lose? This whole damn place is going to be just like the Free State in a couple of days—and a joe of your temperament would be in hot water all the time. What's so bad about a nice quiet hospital room as a place to hide out until things quiet down? You don't have to pay any attention to the psychiatrists—just make animal noises at 'em every time one sticks his nose into your room, until they get discouraged."

Dave shook his head. "No," he said slowly, "I can't do that."

"Then what will you do?"

"I don't know yet. Take to the hills, I guess. Go live with the Angels if it came to a showdown. I wouldn't mind them praying for my soul as long as they left my mind alone."

They were each silent for a while. Magee was mildly annoyed at MacKinnon's bullheaded stubbornness in the face of what seemed to him a reasonable offer. Dave continued busily to stow away grilled ham while considering his position. He cut off another bite. "My, but this is good," he remarked, to break the awkward silence. "I don't know when I've had anything taste so good. Say—"

"What?" inquired Magee, looking up and seeing the concern written on MacKinnon's face.

"This ham—is it synthetic, or is it *real meat?*"

"Why, it's real. What about it?"

Dave did not answer. He managed to reach the refreshing room before that which he had eaten departed from him.

Before he left, Magee gave Dave some money with which he could have purchased for him things that he would need in order to take to the hills. MacKinnon protested, but the Fader cut him short. "Quit being a damn fool, Dave. I can't use New American money on the Outside, and you can't stay alive in the hills without proper equipment. You lie doggo here for a few days while Al or Molly picks up what you need, and you'll stand a chance—unless you'll change your mind and come with me?"

Dave shook his head at this and accepted the money.

It was lonely after Magee left. Mother Johnston and Dave were alone in the club, and the empty chairs reminded him depressingly of the men who had been conscripted. He wished that Gramps or the one-handed man would show up. Even Alec, with his nasty temper, would have been company—he wondered if Alec had been punished for resisting the draft.

Mother Johnston inveigled him into playing checkers in an attempt to relieve his evident low spirits. He felt obligated to agree to her gentle conspiracy, but his mind wandered. It was all very well for the senior judge to tell him to seek adventure in interplanetary exploration, but only engineers and technicians were eligible for such billets. Perhaps he should have gone in for science, or engineering, instead of literature; then he might now be on Venus, contending against the forces of nature in high adventure instead of hiding from uniformed bullies. It wasn't fair. No—he must not kid himself; there was no room for an expert in literary history on the raw frontier of the planets; that was not human injustice, that was a hard fact of nature, and he might as well face it.

He thought bitterly of the man whose nose he had broken and thereby landed himself in Coventry. Maybe he was an "upholstered parasite," after all— but the recollection of the phrase brought back the same unreasoning anger that had gotten him into trouble. Involuntarily he let his cortex drop out of his circuit of consciousness, and he let himself be dominated by his throbbing, emotional thalamus—the "old brain" of his prehistoric, tooth-and-claw ancestors, with its undelayed reactions and unreasoned evaluations. He was glad that he had socked that so-and-so! What right had he to go around sneering and calling people things like that.

A faint knock caused them to put away the checkerboard in a hurry. Mother Johnston paused before answering. "That's not our knock," she considered, "but it's not loud enough to be the nosies. Be ready to hide."

MacKinnon waited by the foxhole where he had hidden the night before, while Mother Johnston went to investigate. He heard her unbar and unlock the upper door, then she called out to him in a low but urgent voice, "Dave! Come here, Dave—hurry!"

It was Fader, unconscious, with his own bloody trail behind him.

Mother Johnston was attempting to pick up the limp form. MacKinnon crowded in, and between the two of them they managed to get him downstairs and lay him on the long table. He came to for a moment as they straightened his limbs. "Hi, Dave," he whispered, managing to achieve the ghost of his debonair grin. "Somebody trumped my ace."

"You keep quiet!" Mother Johnston snapped at him, then in a lower voice to Dave, "Oh, the poor darling—Dave, we must get him to the doctor."

"Can't . . . do . . . that," muttered the Fader. "Got . . . to get to the . . . gate—" His voice trailed off. Mother Johnston's fingers had been busy all the while, as if activated by some separate intelligence. A small pair of scissors, drawn from some hiding place about her large person, clipped away at his clothing, exposing the superficial extent of the damage. She examined the trauma critically.

"This is no job for me," she decided, "and he must sleep while we move him. Dave, get that hypodermic kit out of the medicine chest in the 'fresher."

"No, Mother!" It was Magee, his voice strong and vibrant. "Get me a pepper pill. There's—"

"But, Fader—"

He cut her short. "I've got to get to the doctor, all right, but how the devil will I get there if I don't walk?"

"We would carry you."

"Thanks, Mother," he told her, his voice softened, "I know you would—but the police would be curious. Get me that pill."

Dave followed her into the 'fresher and questioned her while she rummaged through the medicine chest. "Why don't we just send for a doctor?"

"There is only one doctor we can trust, and that's *the* doctor. Besides, none of the others are worth the power to blast them."

Magee was out again when they came back into the room. Mother Johnson slapped his face until he came around, blinking and cursing. Then she fed him the pill.

The powerful stimulant, esoteric offspring of common coal tar, took hold almost at once. To all surface appearance Magee was a well man. He sat up and tried his own pulse, searching it out in his left wrist with steady, sensitive fingers. "Steady as a metronome," he announced. "The old ticker can stand that dosage, all right."

Magee waited while Mother Johnston applied sterile packs to his wounds, and then said good-by. MacKinnon looked at Mother Johnston. She nodded.

"I'm going with you," he told the Fader.

"What for? It will just double the risk."

"You're in no shape to travel alone—stimulant or no stimulant."

"Nuts. *I'd* have to look after *you*."

"I'm going with you."

Magee shrugged his shoulders and capitulated.

Mother Johnston wiped her perspiring face and kissed both of them.

Until they were well out of town, their progress reminded MacKinnon of their nightmare flight of the previous evening. Thereafter they continued to the north-northwest by a highway which ran toward the foothills, and left the highway only when necessary to avoid the sparse traffic. Once they were almost surprised by a police patrol car, equipped with black light and almost invisible, but the Fader sensed it in time, and they crouched behind a low wall which separated the adjacent field from the road.

Dave inquired how he had known the patrol was near. Magee chuckled. "Damned if I know," he said, "but I believe I could smell a cop staked out in a herd of goats."

The Fader talked less and less as the night progressed. His usually untroubled countenance became lined and old as the effect of the drug wore off. It seemed to Dave as if this unaccustomed expression gave him a clearer insight into the man's character— that the mask of pain was his true face rather than the unworried features Magee habitually showed the world. He wondered for the nth time what the Fader had done to cause a court to adjudge him socially insane.

This question was uppermost in his mind with respect to every person he met in Coventry. The answer was fairly obvious in most cases; their types of instability were gross and showed up at once. Mother Johnston had been an enigma until she had explained it herself. She had followed her husband into Coventry. Now that she was a widow she preferred to remain with the friends she knew and the customs and conditions she was adjusted to, rather than change for another and possibly less pleasing environment.

Magee sat down beside the road. "It's no use, kid," he admitted. "I can't make it."

"The hell we can't. I'll carry you."

Magee grinned faintly.

"No, I mean it," Dave persisted. "How much farther is it?"

"Matter of two or three miles, maybe."

"Climb aboard." He took him pickaback and started on.

The first few hundred yards were not too difficult; Magee was forty pounds lighter than Dave. After that the strain of the additional load began to tell. His arms cramped from supporting Magee's knees; his arches complained at the weight and the unnatural load distribution; and his breathing was made difficult by the clasp of Magee's arms around his neck.

Two miles to go—maybe more. Let your weight fall forward and your foot must follow it, else you fall to the ground. It's automatic—as automatic as pulling teeth. How long is a mile? Nothing in a rocketship, thirty seconds in a pleasure car, a ten-minute crawl in a steel snail, fifteen minutes to trained troops in good condition. How far is it with a man on your back, on a rough road, when you are tired to start with?

Five thousand two hundred and eighty feet—a meaningless figure. But every step takes twenty-four inches off the total. The remainder is still incomprehensible—an infinity. Count them. Count them till you go crazy—till the figures speak themselves outside your head, and the jar!—jar!—jar! of your enormous, benumbed feet beats in your brain. Count them backward, subtracting two each time—no, that's worse; each remainder is still an unattainable, inconceivable figure.

His world closed in, lost its history and held no future. There was nothing, nothing at all but the torturing necessity of picking up his foot again and placing it forward. No feeling but the heartbreaking expenditure of will necessary to achieve that meaningless act.

MacKinnon was brought suddenly to awareness when Magee's arms relaxed from around his neck. He leaned forward and dropped to one knee to keep from spilling his burden, then eased it slowly to the ground. He thought for a moment that the Fader was dead—he could not locate his pulse, and the slack face and limp body were sufficiently corpselike, but he pressed an ear to Magee's chest and heard with relief the steady *flub-dub* of the heart.

He tied Magee's wrists together with his handkerchief and forced his own head through the encircled arms. But he was unable, in his exhausted condition, to wrestle the slack weight into position on his back.

Fader regained consciousness while MacKinnon was struggling. His first words were, "Take it easy, Dave. What's the trouble?"

Dave explained. "Better untie my wrists," advised the Fader. "I think I can walk for a while."

And walk he did, for nearly three hundred yards, before he was forced to give up again. "Look, Dave," he said after he had partially recovered, "did you bring along any more of those pepper pills?"

"Yes—but you can't take any more dosage. It would kill you."

"Yeah, I know—so they say. But that isn't the idea —yet. I was going to suggest that you might take one."

"Why, of course! Good grief, Fader, but I'm dumb."

Magee seemed no heavier than a light coat, the morning star shone brighter, and his strength seemed inexhaustible. Even when they left the highway and started up the cart trail that led to the doctor's home in the foothills, the going was tolerable and the burden not too great. MacKinnon knew that the drug burned the working tissue of his body long after his proper reserves were gone, and that it would take him days to recover from the reckless expenditure, but he did not mind. No price was too high to pay for the moment when he at last arrived at the gate of the doctor's home—on his own two feet, his charge alive and conscious.

MacKinnon was not allowed to see Magee for four days. In the meantime, he was encouraged to keep the routine of a semi-invalid himself, in order to recover the twenty-five pounds he had lost in two days and two nights, and to make up for the heavy strain on his heart during the last night. A high caloric diet, sun baths, rest, and peaceful surroundings, plus his natural good health, caused him to regain weight and strength rapidly, but he "enjoyed ill health" exceedingly be-

cause of the companionship of the doctor himself—and
Persephone.

Persephone's calendar age was fifteen. Dave never
knew whether to think of her as much older or much
younger. She had been born in Coventry, and had
lived her short life in the house of the doctor, her
mother having died in childbirth in that same house.
She was completely childlike in many respects, being
without experience in the civilized world Outside, and
having had very little contact with the inhabitants of
Coventry, except when she saw them as patients of the
doctor. But she had been allowed to read unchecked
from the library of a sophisticated and protean-minded
man of science. MacKinnon was continually being surprised at the extent of her academic and scientific
knowledge—much greater than his own. She made him
feel as if he were conversing with some aged and om-
niscient matriarch, then she would come out with some
naïve conception of the outer world, and he would be
brought up sharply with the realization that she was, in
fact, an inexperienced child.

He was mildly romantic about her. Not seriously,
of course, in view of her barely nubile age, but she was
pleasant to see, and he was hungry for feminine companionship. He was young enough himself to feel a
continual interest in the delightful differences, mental
and physical, between the male and the female of his
species. The cockbird strutted and preened his feath-
ers.

Consequently it was a blow to his pride as sharp as
had been the sentence to Coventry to discover that she
classed him with the other inhabitants of Coventry as a
poor unfortunate who needed help and sympathy because he was not quite right in his head.

He was furiously indignant, and for one whole day
he sulked alone, but the human necessity for self-justi-
fication and approval forced him to seek her out and attempt to reason with her. He explained carefully, with
complete emotional candor, the circumstances leading

up to his trial and conviction, and embellished the account with his own philosophy and evaluations, then confidently awaited her approval.

It was not forthcoming. "I don't understand your viewpoint," she said. "You did him a very real damage when you broke his nose, yet he had done you no damage of any sort. Apparently you expect me to approve that."

"But Persephone," he protested, "you ignore the fact that he called me a most insulting name."

"I don't see the connection," she said. "He made a noise with his mouth—a verbal label. If the condition designated by the verbal label does not apply to you, the noise is meaningless. If the noise is a label customarily used to designate a condition which is true in your case—if you *are* the thing that the noise refers to, you are neither more nor less that thing by reason of someone uttering the verbal label. In short, the noise has not damaged you.

"But what you did to him was another matter entirely. You broke his nose. That is damage. In sheer self-protection, the rest of society must seek you out and determine whether or not you are so unstable as to be likely to damage someone else in the future. If you are, you must be quarantined for treatment or leave society—whichever you prefer."

"You think I'm crazy, don't you?" he accused.

"Crazy? Not the way you mean it. You haven't paresis, or a brain tumor, or any other lesion that the doctor could find. But from the viewpoint of your semantic reactions you are as socially *unsane* as any fanatic witch burner."

"Come, now—that's hardly just!"

"What is justice?" She picked up the kitten she had been playing with. "I'm going in—it's getting chilly." And off she went to the house, her bare feet noiseless in the grass.

Had the science of semantics developed as rapidly as psychodynamics, and its implementing arts of propaganda and mob psychology, the United States might never have fallen into dictatorship, then been forced to undergo the Second Revolution. All of the scientific principles embodied in the Covenant which marked the end of the revolution were formulated as far back as the first quarter of the twentieth century.

But the work of the pioneer semanticists, C. K. Ogden in England and Alfred Korzybski in the United States, were known to but a handful of students, whereas psychodynamics, under the impetus of repeated wars and the frenzy of high-pressure merchandising, progressed by leaps and bounds. It is true that the mathematical aspects of semantics, as developed by Albert Einstein, Eric T. Bell, and others, were well known, even popular, but the charlatans who practiced the pseudoscience of sociology resisted every effort to apply the methods of science to their monopoly.

Semantics, "the meaning of meaning," as Ogden expressed it, or "theory of evaluations," as Korzybski preferred to call it, gave a method for the first time of applying the scientific viewpoint and procedure to every act of everyday life. Because semantics dealt with spoken and written words as a determining aspect of human behavior, it was at first mistakenly thought by many to be concerned only with words and of interest only to professional word manipulators, such as advertising copywriters and professors of etymology. A handful of unorthodox psychiatrists alone attempted to apply it to personal human problems, but their work was swept away by the epidemic mass psychoses that destroyed Europe and returned the United States to the Dark Ages.

The Covenant was the first scientific social document ever drawn up by a man, and due credit must be given to its principal author, Colonel Micah Novak, the same Novak who served as staff psychologist in the revolution. The revolutionists wished to establish in the United States the maximum personal liberty possible for everyone. Given the data—the entire social matrix

—how could they accomplish that, to a degree of high mathematical probability?

First they junked all previous concepts of justice. Examined semantically, justice has no referent—there is no observable phenomenon in the space-time-matter continuum to which one can point and say, "This is justice." Science can deal only with that which can be observed and measured. Justice is not such a matter; it can never have the same meaning to one as to another; any "noises" said about it will only add to confusion.

But damage, physical or economic, could be pointed to and measured. Citizens were forbidden by the Covenant to damage one another, and laws were passed to anticipate such damage. Any act not leading to damage, physical or economic, to some person, they declared to be legal.

As they had abandoned the concept of justice, there could be no rational standards of punishment. Penology took its place with lycanthropy and other forgotten witchcrafts. Yet, since it was not practical to permit a probable source of danger to remain in the community, social offenders were examined and potential repeaters were given their choice of psychological readjustment, or of having society withdraw itself from them—Coventry.

During the formulation of the Covenant, some assumed that the socially unsane would naturally be forced to undergo hospitalization for readjustment, particularly since current psychiatry was quite competent to cure all nonlesioned psychoses and cure or alleviate lesional psychoses, but Novak set his face against this and opposed it with all the power of his strong and subtle intellect. "Not so!" he argued. "The government must never again be permitted to tamper with the mind of any citizen without his consent, or else we set up a means of greater tyranny than we have ever experienced. Every man must be free to accept, or reject, the Covenant, even though we think him insane!"

The next time MacKinnon looked up Persephone, he found her in a state of extreme agitation. His own wounded pride was forgotten at once. "Why, my dear," he said, "whatever in the world is the matter?"

Gradually he gathered that she had been present at a conversation between Magee and the doctor, and had heard, for the first time, of the impending military operations against the United States. He patted her hand. "So that's all it is," he observed in a relieved voice. "I thought something was wrong with you yourself."

" 'That's all.' David MacKinnon, do you mean to stand there and tell me that you knew about this and don't consider it worth worrying about?"

"Me? Why should I? And for that matter, what could *I* do?"

"What could you do? You could go Outside and warn them—that's what you could do. As to why you should— Dave, you're impossible!" She burst into tears and ran from the room.

He stared after her, mouth open, then borrowed from his remotest ancestor by observing to himself that women were hard to figure out.

She did not appear at dinner. After dinner she was closeted with the doctor in his study. When she finally reappeared she went directly to her room. He finally concluded that he might as well go to bed himself.

To bed, and then to sleep, and take it up again in the morning— But it was not as simple as that. The unfriendly walls stared back at him, and the other, critical half of his mind decided to make a night of it. Fool! She doesn't want your help. Why should she? What have you got that Fader hasn't got—and better? To her you are just one of the screw-loose multitude you've seen all around you in this place.

But I'm not crazy! Just because I choose not to submit to the dictation of others doesn't make me crazy. Doesn't it though? All the rest of them in here are lame-brains; what's so fancy about you? Not all of them. How about the doctor, and— Don't kid yourself, chump, the doctor and Mother Johnston are here for their own reasons; they weren't sentenced. And Persephone was born here.

How about Magee? He was certainly rational—or seemed so. He found himself resenting, with illogical bitterness, Magee's apparent stability. Why should he be any different from the rest of us?

The rest of us? He had classed himself with the other inhabitants of Coventry. All right, all right, admit it, you fool. You're just like the rest of them; turned out because the decent people won't have you —and too damned stubborn to admit that you need treatment.

He turned on the light and tried to read. But it was no use. Why should Persephone care what happened to the people Outside? She didn't know them; she had no friends there. If he felt no obligations to them, how could she possibly care? No obligations? You had a soft, easy life for many years—all they asked was that you behave yourself. For that matter, where would you be now if the doctor had stopped to ask whether or not he owed you anything?

He was still wearily chewing the bitter cud of self-examination when the first cold and colorless light of morning filtered in. He got up, pulled a robe around him and tiptoed down the hall to Magee's room. The door was ajar. He stuck his head in and whispered, "Fader. Are you awake?"

"Come in, kid," Magee answered quietly. "What's the trouble? No can sleep?"

"No—"

"Neither can I. Sit down and we'll carry the banner together."

"Fader, I'm going to make a break for it. I'm going Outside."

"Huh? When?"

"Right away."

"Risky business, kid. Wait a few days and I'll try it with you."

"No, I can't wait for you to get well. I'm going out to warn the United States!"

Magee's eyes widened a little, but his voice was unchanged. "You haven't let that spindly kid sell you a bill of goods, Dave?"

"No. Not exactly. I'm doing this for myself. It's something I need to do. See here, Fader, what about this weapon? Have they really got something that could threaten the United States?"

"I'm afraid so," Magee admitted. "I don't know much about it, but it makes blasters look sick. More range. I don't know what they expect to do about the Barrier, but I saw 'em stringing heavy power lines before I got winged. Say, if you do get Outside, here's a chap you might look up; in fact, be sure to. He's got influence." Magee scrawled something on a scrap of paper, folded the scrap and handed it to MacKinnon, who pocketed it absent-mindedly and went on: "How closely is the gate guarded, Fader?"

"You can't get out the gate; that's out of the question. Here's what you will have to do——" He tore off another piece of paper and commenced sketching and explaining.

Dave shook hands with Magee before he left. "You'll say good-by for me, won't you? And thank the doctor? I'd rather just slide out before anyone is up."

"Of course, kid," the Fader assured him. "Well—watch out for that first step; it's a honey!"

MacKinnon crouched behind the bushes and peered cautiously at the little band of Angels filing into the bleak, ugly church. He shivered, both from fear and from the icy morning air. But his need was greater than his fear. These zealots had food—and he must have it.

The first two days after he left the house of he doctor had been fair enough. True, he had caught cold from sleeping on the ground; it had settled in his lungs and slowed him down. But he did not mind that now, if only he could refrain from sneezing or coughing until the little band of the faithful were safe inside the temple. He watched them pass—dour-looking men, women in skirts that dragged the ground, and whose work-lined faces were framed in shawls. The light had gone out of their faces. The very children were sober.

The last of them filed inside, leaving only the sexton in the churchyard, busy with some obscure duty. After an interminable time, during which MacKinnon pressed a finger against his upper lip in a frantic attempt to forestall a sneeze, the sexton, too, entered the grim building and closed the doors.

MacKinnon crept out of his hiding place and hurried to the house he had previously selected on the edge of the clearing, farthest from the church.

The dog was suspicious, but he quieted him. The house was locked, but the rear door could be forced. He was a little giddy at the sight of food when he found it—hard bread and strong, unsalted butter made from goat's milk. A misstep two days before had landed him in a mountain stream. The mishap had not seemed important until he discovered that his food tablets were a pulpy mess. He had eaten them the rest of that day, then mold had taken them and he had thrown the remainder away.

The bread lasted him through three more sleeps, but the butter melted and he was unable to carry it. He soaked as much of it as he could into the bread, then licked up the rest, after which he was very thirsty. He found one more stream, but was forced to leave it when it left the hills and entered cultivated country.

Some hours after the last of the bread was gone he reached his first objective—the main river to which all other streams in Coventry were tributary. Someplace downstream it dived under the black curtain of the Barrier, and continued seaward. With the gateway closed and guarded, its outlet constituted the only possible egress to a man unassisted.

In the meantime it was water, and the thirst was

upon him again, and his cold was worse. But he would have to wait until dark to drink; there were figures down there by the bank—some in uniform, he thought. One of them made fast a little skiff to a landing. He marked it for his own and watched it with jealous eyes. It was still there when the sun went down.

The early-morning sun struck his nose and he sneezed. He came wide awake, raised his head and looked around. The little skiff he had appropriated floated in midstream. There were no oars. He could not remember whether or not there had been any oars. The current was fairly strong; it seemed as if he should have drifted clear to the Barrier in the night. Perhaps he had passed under it—no, that was ridiculous.

Then he saw it, less than a mile away, black and ominous—but the most welcome sight he had seen in days. He was too weak and feverish to enjoy it, but it renewed the determination that kept him going.

The little boat scraped against the bottom. He saw that the current at a bend had brought him to the bank. He hopped awkwardly out, his congealed joints complaining, and drew the bow of the skiff up onto the sand. Then he thought better of it, pushed it out once more, shoved as hard as he was able and watched it disappear around the meander. No need to advertise where he had landed.

He slept most of that day, rousing himself once to move out of the sun when it grew too hot. But the sun had cooked much of the cold out of his bones, and he felt much better by nightfall.

Although the Barrier was only a mile or so away, it took most of the night to reach it by following the river bank. He knew when he had reached it by the clouds of steam that rose from the water. When the sun came up he considered the situation. The Barrier stretched across the water, but the juncture between it and the surface of the stream was hidden by billowing clouds. Someplace, down under the surface of the water—how far down he did not know—somewhere down there the Barrier ceased, and its raw edge turned the water it touched to steam.

Slowly, reluctantly and most unheroically, he commenced to strip off his clothes. The time had come and he did not relish it. He came across the scrap of paper that Magee had handed him, and attempted to examine it. But it had been pulped by his involuntary dip in the mountain stream and was quite illegible. He chucked it away.

He shivered as he stood hesitating on the bank, although the sun was warm. Then his mind was made up for him; he spied a patrol on the far bank.

Perhaps they had seen him; perhaps not. He dived.

Down, down, as far as his strength would take him. Down, and try to touch bottom, to be sure of avoiding that searing, deadly base. He felt mud with his hands. Now to swim under it. Perhaps it was death to pass under it, as well as over it; he would soon know. But which way was it? There was no direction down here.

He stayed down until his congested lungs refused. Then he rose part way and felt scalding water on his face. For a timeless interval of unutterable sorrow and loneliness he realized that he was trapped between heat and water—trapped under the Barrier.

Two private soldiers gossiped idly on a small dock which lay under the face of the Barrier. The river which poured out from beneath it held no interest for them, they had watched it for many dull tours of guard duty. An alarm clanged behind them and brought them to alertness. "What sector, Jack?"

"This bank. There he is now—see!"

They fished him out and had him spread out on the dock by the time the sergeant of the guard arrived. "Alive or dead?" he inquired.

"Dead, I think," answered the one who was not busy giving artificial resuscitation.

The sergeant clucked in a manner incongruous to his battered face and said, "Too bad. I've ordered the ambulance; send him up to the infirmary, anyhow."

The nurse tried to keep him quiet, but MacKinnon made such an uproar that she was forced to get the ward surgeon.

"Here! Here! What's all this nonsense?" the medico rebuked him, while reaching for his pulse.

Dave managed to convince him that he would not quiet down, not accept a soporific until he had told his story. They struck a working agreement that Mac-Kinnon was to be allowed to talk—"But keep it short, mind you!"—and the doctor would pass the word along to his next superior, and in return Dave would submit to a hypodermic.

The next morning two other men, unidentified, were brought to MacKinnon by the surgeon. They listened to his full story and questioned him in detail. He was transferred to corps area headquarters that afternoon by ambulance. There he was questioned again. He was regaining his strength rapidly, but he was growing quite tired of the whole rigmarole, and wanted assurance that his warning was being taken seriously. The latest of his interrogators reassured him. "Compose yourself," he told Dave, "you are to see the commanding officer this afternoon."

The corps area commander, a nice little chap with a quick, birdlike manner and a most unmilitary appearance, listened gravely while MacKinnon recited his story for what seemed to him the fiftieth time. He nodded agreement when David finished. "Rest assured, David MacKinnon, that all necessary steps are being taken."

"But how about their weapon?"

"That is taken care of—and as for the Barrier, it may not be as easy to break as our neighbors think. But your efforts are appreciated. May I do some service?"

"Well, no—not for myself, but there are two of my friends in there——" He asked that something be done to rescue Magee, and that Persephone be enabled to come out if she wished.

"I know of that girl," the general remarked. "We will get in touch with her. If at any time she wishes to become a citizen, it can be arranged. As for Magee, that is another matter——" He touched the stud of his desk visiphone. "Send Captain Randall in."

A neat, trim figure in the uniform of a captain of the United States Army entered with a light step. MacKinnon glanced at him with casual, polite interest, then his expression went to pieces. "Fader!" he yelled.

Their mutual greeting was hardly sufficiently decorous for the sanctum sanctorum of a commanding general, but the general did not seem to mind. When they had calmed down, MacKinnon had to ask the question uppermost in his mind. "But see here, Fader, all this doesn't make sense——" He paused, staring, then pointed a finger accusingly. "I know! You're in the Secret Service!"

The Fader grinned cheerfully. "Did you think," he observed, "that the United States Army would leave a plague spot like that unwatched?"

The general cleared his throat. "What do you plan to do now, David MacKinnon?"

"Eh? Me? Why, I don't have any plans——" He thought for a moment, then turned to his friend. "Do you know, Fader, I believe I'll turn in for psychological treatment, after all."

"I don't believe that will be necessary," said the general gently.

"No? Why not, sir?"

"You have cured yourself. You may not be aware of it, but four psychotechnicians have interviewed you. Their reports agree. I am authorized to tell you that your status as a free citizen has been restored, if you wish it."

The general and Captain "the Fader" Randall managed tactfully between them to terminate the interview. Randall walked back to the infirmary with his friend.

Dave wanted a thousand questions answered at once. "But, Fader," he demanded, "you must have gotten out before I did."

"A day or two."

"Then my job was unnecessary!"

"I wouldn't say that," Randall contradicted. "I might not have gotten through. As a matter of fact, they had all the details before I reported. There are others— Anyhow," he continued, to change the subject, "now that you are here, what will you do?"

"Me? It's too soon to say. It won't be classical literature, that's a cinch. If I wasn't such a dummy in math I might still try for interplanetary."

"Well, we can talk about it tonight," suggested Fader, glancing at his telechronometer. "I've got to run along, but I'll stop by later and we'll go over to the mess for dinner."

He was out of the door with an easy speed that was nostalgic of the thieves' kitchen.

Dave watched him, then said suddenly, "Hey! Fader! Why couldn't I get into the Secret Ser—"

But the Fader had gone—he must ask himself.

THE MILE-LONG SPACESHIP

by Kate Wilhelm

When this story was first reprinted in an anthology, years before I met and married the author, I described it in a book review as "dizzy and compact." I still like it, for the same reasons. It has something of the quality of the A. E. van Vogt story which follows it—the kind of roller-coaster feeling that you sometimes get in an especially good nightmare.

ALLAN NORBETT SHIVERED UNCONTROLLABLY, HUDDLING under the spotless hospital sheet seeking warmth. He stirred fretfully as consciousness slowly returned and with it the blinding stab of pain through his head. A moan escaped his lips. Immediately a nurse was at his side, gently, firmly forcing him back on the bed.

"You must remain completely still, Mr. Norbett. You're in St. Agnes' Hospital. You suffered a fractured skull in the accident, and surgery was necessary. Your wife is outside waiting to see you. She is uninjured. Do you understand me?"

The words had been spoken slowly, very clearly, but he had grasped only fragments of them.

What accident? The ship couldn't have an accident.

He'd be dead out there in space. And his wife hadn't even been there.

"What happened to the ship? How'd I get back on Earth?" The words came agonizingly, each effort cost much in pain and dizziness.

"Mr. Norbett, please calm yourself. I've rung for your doctor. He'll be here presently." The voice soothed him and a faint memory awakened. The wreck? His wife? HIS WIFE?

"Clair? Where's Clair?" Then the doctor was there and he also was soothing. Allan closed his eyes again in relief as they reassured him about Clair's safety. She would be here in a moment. The other memories receded and mingled with the anesthetic dreams he'd had. The doctor felt his pulse and listened to his heart and studied his eyes, all the while talking.

"You are a lucky man, Mr. Norbett. That was quite a wreck you were in. Your wife was even luckier. She was thrown clear when the bi-wheel first hit you."

Allan remembered it all quite clearly now and momentarily wondered how he'd come out of it at all. The doctor finally finished his examination and smiled as he said, "Everything seems perfectly normal, considering the fact that you have been traipsing all over space for the last five days."

"Days?"

"Yes. The wreck was Saturday. This is Thursday. You've been under sedation quite a bit—to help you rest. There was extensive brain injury and absolute quiet was essential. Dr. Barnsdale performed a brilliant operation Saturday night."

Allan had the feeling the doctor was purposely being so loquacious to help him over the hump of the shock of awakening after almost six days. He was in no pain now while he kept his head still, but talking brought its own punishment and he was grateful to the doctor for answering unasked questions. The doctor waited by his side for a second or two, then in a professional tone he told the nurse to bring in Clair.

And again to Allan: "She can only stay a few minutes—less if you begin talking. I'll be in again this afternoon. You rest as much as possible. If the pain becomes severe, tell your nurse. She's instructed to administer a hypo only if you request it." Again he laughed jovially. "Don't let her talk you into it, though. She is really thrilled by that space yarn you've been telling and might want to put you to sleep just to hear more."

Clair's visit was very brief and very exhausting. Afterwards he rested comfortably for nearly an hour before the pain flooded his whole being.

"Nurse."

"Yes, Mr. Norbett?" Her fingers rested lightly on his wrist for a moment.

"The pain—"

"Just try to relax, sir. It will be gone soon." He didn't feel the prick of the needle in his arm. But the pain left him in layers, gradually becoming a light enough load to permit sleep. And the coldness.

Space was so cold. No winds to blow in spurts and gusts, to relieve the cold by their absence, only the steady, numbing same black, empty cold. He turned his head to look over his shoulder and already Earth was undistinguishable among the countless stars and planets. Never had man, he told himself, seen all the stars like this. They were incredibly bright and even as he viewed them, he wondered at the movement of some of them. There was a visible pulsation, sometimes almost rhythmical, other times very erratic. A star would suddenly seem to expand enormously on one side, the protuberance around it glow even more brightly, then die down only to repeat the performance over and over. Allan wished he knew more about astronomy. He had only the most rudimentary knowledge that everyone had since the first spaceship had reached Mars. He had been out of school when space travel had become possible and had never read past the newspaper for the information necessary to understand the universe and its inhabitants.

He shivered again and thought about the advantages of eyeless seeing. There was no pupil to dilate, no retina to burn or damage, no nerves to protest with pain at the brightness of the sight. It was, he decided smugly, much better to be here without his cumbersome body to hamper him. Then he suddenly remembered the ship—the mile-long spaceship. For an instant he sent his mental gaze deep into space all around him, but the ship was nowhere to be seen. He surmised it must still be millions of light-years from Earth. As he visualized it again he slowly became aware that once more he was aboard her and the stars he was seeing were on the giant wall screen.

He watched with interest as one planet after another turned a pale violet and became nearly invisible. He had grown accustomed to the crew of the ship, so paid little heed to them. Their voices were low, monotonous to his ear, never rising or speeding up or sounding indecisive. Completely expressionless, their words defied any attempt to interpret them.

"He's back," the telepath announced.

"Good. I was afraid that he might die." The navigator in charge went calmly about his duties of sighting and marking in a complex three-dimensional chart the course of the mighty ship as it ranged among the stars.

"He's recovering from his injury. He still can't receive any impulses from me." The telepath tried again and again to create a picture in the alien mind in their midst. "Futile," he said; "the differences are too great."

"Undisciplined," said the psychologist who had been waiting ever since that first visit by the alien. "A disciplined mind can be reached by telepathy."

"Can you see his world?" This from the astro-navigator.

"Only the same intimate scenes of home-life, his

work and his immediate surroundings. He is very primitive, or perhaps merely uneducated."

"If only he knew something about astronomy." The
navigator shrugged and made a notation on his chart
as two more distant planets registered violet.

"The names he associates with stars are these." The
telepath probed deeper. "The Dipper, North Star,
Mars . . . no, that is one of the planets they have col-
onized." A wave of incredulity emanated from him,
felt by the others of the crew, but not expressed in his
voice. "He doesn't know the difference between single
stars, clusters, constellations, only that they appear as
individual stars to him, and he thinks of them as
such."

The navigator's calm voice belied the fury the others
felt well out from him. "Look at his sun, perhaps that
will give us a hint." They all knew the improbability of
this. The telepath began droning what little Allan knew
about the sun, when the captain appeared through another wall screen.

He was accompanied by the ship's ethnologist, the
expert who could reconstruct entire civilizations from
the broken remains of a tool or an object of art, or less
if necessary. The captain and his companions made
themselves comfortable near the star screen and
seemed immediately engrossed in the broken lines indi-
cating the ship's flight in the three-dimensional repro-
duced outer spaces.

"Is he still here?"

"Yes, sir."

"Is he aware yet that we have discovered his presence among us?"

"No, sir. We have made no effort to indicate our
awareness to him."

"Very good." The captain then fell silent, pondering
his particular problem as the ethnologist began adding
to the growing list of facts that were known to Allan
about Earth.

They would have a complete picture of the present and the past. As complete as the alien's mind and memory could make it. But unless they could locate his planet they might just as well go home and view space-fiction films. This exploration trip had achieved very little real success. Only fourteen planets that could be rated good with some sub-intelligent life, several hundred fair with no intelligence and only one he could conscientiously rate excellent. This mind was of an intelligent, though as yet unadvanced, humanoid race. The planet it inhabited met every requirement to be rated excellent. Of this the captain was certain.

Suddenly the telepath announced, "He's gone. He became bored watching the screen. He knows nothing about astronomy; therefore, the course loses its significance to him. He has the vague idea that we're going to a predetermined destination. The idea of an exploration, charting cruise hasn't occurred to him as yet."

"I wonder," mused the captain, "how he reconciles his conscious mind to his subconscious wandering."

The psychologist answered. "As he begins to awaken other dreams probably mingle with these memories, causing them to dim at the edges, thus becoming to his mind at any rate merely another series of especially vivid well-remembered dreams. I believe much of what lies in his subconscious is dream memory rather than fact memory." The psychologist didn't smile or indicate in any fashion the ridicule and sarcasm the others felt as he continued: "He has the memory of being always well fed. He has buried the memory of hunger so far down in his subconscious that it would take a skilled psychologist a long time to call it forth."

The telepath stirred and started to reply, then didn't. The alien's mind had been like a film, clear and easy to read. Some of the pictures had been disturbing and incomprehensible, but only through their strangeness, not because they were distorted by dream images. The psychologist never could accept anything at face value. Always probing and looking for hidden places and meanings. Just as he had when told of the world democracy existing on Earth.

"Most likely a benign dictatorship. A world couldn't be governed by a democratic government; a small area, perhaps, but not a world." Thus spoke the psychologist. But the telepath had been inside Allan's mind, and he knew it could and did work. Not only the planet Earth, but also the colonies on Mars and Venus.

The captain was still pursuing his own line of questioning.

"Has he ever shown any feeling of fear or repulsion toward us?"

"None. He accepts us as different but not to be feared because of it."

"That's because he believes we are figments of his imagination, that he can control us by awakening."

The captain ignored this explanation advanced by the psychologist. A mind intelligent enough for dreams could feel fear in the dreams—even a captain knew that. He was beginning to get the feeling that this Earth race might prove a formidable foe when and if found.

"Has he shown any interest in the drive?"

"He assumed we use an atomic drive. He has only the scantiest knowledge of atomics, however. His people use such a drive."

"The fact that the race has atomics is another reason we must find them." This would be the third planet using atomic energy. A young race, an unknown potential. They did not have interstellar travel now, but one hundred fifty years ago they hadn't had atomic energy and already they had reached their neighbor planets. It had taken three times as long for the captain's people to achieve the same success. The captain remembered the one other race located in his time that

had atomics. They were exploring space in ever-widen-
ing circles. True, they hadn't made any startling ad-
vances yet in weapons, they had found decisive bombs
and lethal rays and gases unnecessary. But they had
learned fast. They had resisted the invaders with cun-
ning and skill. Their bravery had never been questioned, but in the end the aggressors had won.

The captain felt no thrill of satisfaction in the
thought. It was a fact, accomplished long ago. The conclusion had been delayed certainly, but it had been inevitable. Only one race, one planet, one government,
could have the energy, and the right to the raw materials that made the spacelanes thoroughfares. The
slaves might ride on the masters' craft, but might not
own or operate their own. That was the law, and the
captain was determined to uphold that law to the end.

And now this. One mind freed from its body and its
Earth, roaming the universe, divulging its secrets, all
but the only one that mattered. How many millions of
stars lit the way through space? And how many of
them had their families of planets supporting life? The
captain knew there was no answer, but still he sought
ways of following the alien's mind back to his body.

Allan stirred his coffee slowly, not moving his head.
This was his first meal sitting up; now, at its conclusion, he felt too exhausted to lift his spoon from his
cup. Clair gently did it for him and held the cup to his
lips.

"Tired, darling?" Her voice was a caress.

"A little." A little! All he wanted was his bed under
him and Clair's voice whispering him to sleep. "I don't
believe I'd even need a hypo." He was startled that he
had spoken the thought, but Clair nodded, understanding.

"The doctor thinks it best to put off having anything
if you can. I'll read to you and see if you can sleep."
They had rediscovered the joy of reading books. Real

leather-bound books instead of watching the three-D set, or using the story films. Alan loved to lie quiescent, listening to the quiet voice of his wife rise and fall with the words. Often the words themselves were unimportant, but there was music in listening to Clair read them. They were beautifully articulated, falling into a pattern as rhythmic as if there were unheard drums beating the time.

He tried to remember what the sound of her voice reminded him of. Then he knew. By the very difference in tone and expression he was reminded of the crew of the mile-long spaceship in his dream. He grinned to himself at the improbability of the dream. Everyone speaking in the same metallic tone, the monotonous flight, never varying, never having any emergency to cope with.

The noises of the hospital dimmed and became obscure and then lost entirely. All was silent again as he sped toward the quiet lonesome planet he had last visited. There he had rested, gazing at the stars hanging in expanding circles over him. He had first viewed the galaxy from aboard the spaceship. Interested in the spiral shape of it, he had left the ship to seek it out at closer range. Here on this tiny planet the effect was startling. If he closed out all but the brightest and largest of the stars there was ring after ring of tiny glowing diamonds hanging directly above him. How many times had he come back? He couldn't remember, but suddenly he thought about the mile-long spaceship again.

"He's back." The telepath never moved from his position before the sky screen, nor did the astronavigator. Abruptly, however, the panorama went blank and the two moved toward the screen on the opposite wall.

"Is he coming?"

"Yes. He's curious. He thinks something is wrong."

"Good." The two stepped from the screen into a large room where a group watched a film.

The navigator and the telepath seated themselves slightly behind the rest of the assemblage. The captain had been talking; he continued as before.

"Let me know what his reactions are."

"The film interests him. The dimensional effect doesn't bother him, he appears accustomed to a form of three-dimensional films."

"Very good. Tell me the instant something strikes a responsive chord."

The film was one of their educational astronomy courses for beginners. Various stars were shown singly and in their constellations and finally in their own galaxies. Novae and supernovae, planets and satellites, appeared. The telepath dug deep into the alien's memory, but found only an increasing interest, no memories of any one scene. Suddenly the telepath said, "This one he thinks he has seen before. He has seen a similar galaxy from another position, one that shows the spiral directly overhead."

The captain asked, "Has this one been visible on the screen from such a position?"

"Not in detail. Only as part of the charted course." The navigator was making notes as he answered. "There are only three fixes for this particular effect. A minor white dwarf with six satellites and two main sequence stars, satellites unknown."

The captain thought deeply. Maybe only a similar galaxy, but again maybe he was familiar with this one.

The orders were given in the same tone he had used in carrying on the conversation. The alien had no way of knowing he was the helmsman guiding the huge ship through space.

The telepath followed the alien's mind as he gazed raptly at the ever changing film. Occasionally he reported the alien's thoughts, but nothing of importance was learned. As before, the departure of the alien was abrupt.

With the telepath's announcement, "He's gone," the film flicked off and normal activity was resumed.

Later the captain called a meeting of the psychologist, the telepath, the chief navigator and ethnologist.

"We represent the finest minds in the universe, yet when it comes to coping with one inferior intellect, we stand helpless. He flits in and out at will, telling us nothing. We are now heading light-years out of our way on what might easily prove to be a fruitless venture, merely because you"——he held the telepath in his merciless gaze——"think he recognized one of the formations." The captain's anger was a formidable thing, and the rest stirred uneasily. His voice, however, was the same monotone it always was as he asked, "And did you manage to plant the seeds in his mind as suggested at our last meeting?"

"That is hard to say. I couldn't tell." The telepath turned to the psychologist for confirmation.

"He wouldn't know himself until he began feeling the desire for more education. Even then it might be in the wrong direction. We can only wait and hope we have hit on the way to find his home planet through making him want to learn astronavigation and astronomy." Soon afterward the meeting adjourned.

Allan was back at work again, with all traces of his accident relegated to the past. His life was well-ordered and full, with no time for schooling. He told himself this over and over, to no avail. For he was still telling himself this when he filled out the registration blank at the university.

"He's here again!" The telepath had almost given up expecting the alien ever again. He kept his mind locked in the other's as he recited as though from a book. "He's completely over his injury, working again, enrolled in night classes at the school in his town. He's studying atomic engineering. He's in the engine room now getting data for something they call a thesis."

Quietly the captain rolled off a list of expletives that

would have done justice to one of the rawest space-hands. And just as quietly, calmly, and, perhaps, stoically, he pushed the red button that began the chain reaction that would completely vaporize the mile-long ship. His last breath was spent in hoping the alien would awaken with a violent headache. He did.

THE SEESAW

by A. E. van Vogt

Like Robert A. Heinlein, A. E. van Vogt has written a number of stories against a common future background. It was in "The Seesaw" that the fascinating "weapon shops" first appeared, but the author later wrote more about them in two novels, *The Weapons Shops of Isher* and *The Weapon Makers*.

You have probably noticed that most science fiction writers borrow from each other; the future worlds they describe are often pretty much alike. This is not true of van Vogt. Everything in his stories is a fresh invention—startling, nightmarish, and curiously believable.

MAGICIAN BELIEVED TO HAVE HYPNOTIZED CROWD!

June 11, 1941—Police and newspapermen believe that Middle City will shortly be advertised as the next stopping place of a master magician, and they are prepared to extend him a hearty welcome if he will condescend to explain exactly how he fooled hundreds of people into believing they saw a strange building, apparently a kind of gun shop.

The building seemed to appear on the space formerly, and still, occupied by Aunt Sally's Lunch and

115

Patterson Tailors. Only employees were inside the two aforementioned shops, and none noticed any untoward event. A large, brightly shining sign featured the front of the gun shop, which had been so miraculously conjured out of nothingness; and the sign constituted the first evidence that the entire scene was nothing but a masterly illusion. For from whichever angle one gazed at it, one seemed to be staring straight at the words, which read:

FINE WEAPONS
THE RIGHT TO BUY WEAPONS
IS THE RIGHT TO BE FREE

The window display was made up of an assortment of rather curiously shaped guns, rifles as well as small arms; and a glowing sign in the window stated:

THE FINEST ENERGY WEAPONS
IN THE KNOWN UNIVERSE

Inspector Clayton of the Investigation Branch attempted to enter the shop, but the door seemed to be locked; a few moments later, C. J. (Chris) McAllister, reporter of the *Gazette-Bulletin,* tried the door, found it opened, and entered.

Inspector Clayton attempted to follow him, but discovered that the door was again locked. McAllister emerged after some time, and was seen to be in a dazed condition. All memory of the action had apparently been hypnotized out of him, for he could make no answer to the questions of the police and spectators.

Simultaneous with his reappearance, the strange building vanished as abruptly as it had appeared.

Police state they are baffled as to how the master magician created so detailed an illusion for so long a period before so large a crowd. They are prepared to recommend his show, when it comes, without reservation.

Author's Note: The foregoing account did not mention that the police, dissatisfied with the affair, attempted to contact McAllister for a further interview, but were unable to locate him. Weeks passed, and he was still not to be found.

Herewith follows the story of what happened to McAllister from the instant that he found the door of the gun shop unlocked.

THERE WAS A CURIOUS QUALITY ABOUT THE GUN shop door. It was not so much that it opened at his first touch as that, when he pulled, it came away like a weightless thing. For a bare instant, McAllister had the impression that the knob had freed itself into his palm.

He stood quite still, startled. The thought that came finally had to do with Inspector Clayton, who a minute earlier had found the door locked.

The thought was like a signal. From behind him boomed the voice of the inspector: "Ah, McAllister, I'll handle this now."

It was dark inside the shop beyond the door, too dark to see anything, and somehow his eyes wouldn't accustom themselves to the intense gloom. . . .

Pure reporter's instinct made him step forward toward the blackness that pressed from beyond the rectangle of door. Out of the corner of one eye, he saw Inspector Clayton's hand reaching for the door handle that his own fingers had let go a moment before; and quite simply he knew that if the police officer could prevent it, no reporter would get inside that building.

His head was still turned, his gaze more on the police inspector than on the darkness in front; and it was as he began another step forward that the remarkable thing happened.

The door handle would not allow Inspector Clayton to touch it. It twisted in some queer way, in some *en-*

ergy way, for it was still there, a strange, blurred shape.
The door itself, without visible movement, so swift it
was, was suddenly touching McAllister's heel.

Light, almost weightless, was that touch; and then,
before he could think or react to what had happened,
the momentum of his forward movement had carried
him inside.

As he breasted the darkness, there was a sudden,
enormous tensing along his nerves. Then the door shut
tight, the brief, incredible agony faded. Ahead was a
brightly lit shop; behind—were unbelievable things!

For McAllister, the moment that followed was one of
blank impression. He stood, body twisted awkwardly,
only vaguely conscious of the shop's interior, but tremendously aware, in the brief moment before he was
interrupted, of what lay beyond the transparent panels
of the door through which he had just come.

There was no unyielding blackness anywhere, no Inspector Clayton, no muttering crowd of gaping spectators, no dingy row of shops across the way.

It wasn't even remotely the same street. There was
no street.

Instead, a peaceful park spread there. Beyond it,
brilliant under a noon sun, glowed a city of minarets
and stately towers—

From behind him, a husky, musical, woman's voice
said, "You will be wanting a gun?"

McAllister turned. It wasn't that he was ready to stop
feasting his eyes on the vision of the city. The movement was automatic reaction to a sound. And because
the whole affair was still like a dream, the city scene
faded almost instantly; his mind focused on the young
woman who was advancing slowly from the rear section
of the store.

Briefly, his thought wouldn't come clear. A conviction that he ought to say something was tangled with
first impressions of the girl's appearance. She had a
slender, well-shaped body; her face was creased into a
pleasant smile. She had brown eyes, neat, wavy brown

hair. Her simple frock and sandals seemed so normal at first glance that he gave them no other thought.

He was able to say: "What I can't understand is why the police officer who tried to follow me couldn't get in. And where is he now?"

To his surprise, the girl's smile became faintly apologetic. "We know that people consider it silly of us to keep harping on that ancient feud."

Her voice grew firmer: "We even know how clever the propaganda is that stresses the silliness of our stand. Meanwhile, we never allow any of *her* men in here. We continue to take our principles very seriously."

She paused as if she expected dawning comprehension from him, but McAllister saw from the slow puzzlement creeping into her eyes that his face must look as limp as were the thoughts behind it.

Her men! The girl had spoken the word as if she were referring to some personage, and in direct reply to his use of the words, police officer. That meant *her* men, whoever she was, were policemen; and they weren't allowed in this gun shop. So the door was hostile, and wouldn't admit them.

A strange emptiness struck into McAllister's mind, matching the hollowness that was beginning to afflict the pit of his stomach, a sense of unplumbed depths, the first, staggering conviction that all was not as it should be.

The girl was speaking in sharper tone: "You mean you know nothing of all this, that for generations the gunmaker's guild has existed in this age of devastating energies as the common man's only protection against enslavement. The right to buy guns——"

She stopped again, her narrowed eyes searching him; then: "Come to think of it, there's something very illogical about you. Your outlandish clothes—you're not from the northern farm plains, are you?"

He shook his head dumbly, more annoyed with his reactions every passing second. But he couldn't help it.

A tightness was growing in him, becoming more unbearable instant by instant, as if somewhere a vital mainspring were being wound to the breaking point.

The young woman went on more swiftly: "And come to think of it, it is astounding that a policeman should have tried the door and there was no alarm."

Her hand moved; metal flashed in it, metal as bright as steel in blinding sunlight. There was not the faintest hint of the apologetic in her voice as she said, "You will stay where you are, sir, till I have called my father. In our business, with our responsibility, we never take chances. Something is very wrong here."

Curiously, it was at that point that McAllister's mind began to function clearly; the thought that came paralleled hers: How had this gun shop appeared on a 1941 street? How had he come here into this fantastic world?

Something was very wrong indeed!

It was the gun that held his attention. A tiny thing it was, shaped like a pistol, but with three cubes projecting in a little half circle from the top of the slightly bulbous firing chamber.

And as he stared, his mind began to quiver on its base; for that wicked little instrument, glittering there in her browned fingers, was as real as she herself.

"Good Heaven!" he whispered. "What the devil kind of gun is it? Lower that thing and let's try to find out what all this is about."

She seemed not to be listening; and abruptly he noticed that her gaze was flicking to a point on the wall somewhat to his left. He followed her look—in time to see seven miniature white lights flash on.

Curious lights! Briefly, he was fascinated by the play of light and shade, the waxing and waning from one tiny globe to the next, a rippling movement of infinitesimal increments and decrements, an incredibly delicate effect of instantaneous reaction to some supersensitive barometer.

The lights steadied; his gaze reverted to the girl. To

his surprise, she was putting away her gun. She must have noticed his expression.

"It's all right," she said coolly. "The automatics are on you now. If we're wrong about you, we'll be glad to apologize. Meanwhile, if you're still interested in buying a gun, I'll be happy to demonstrate."

So the automatics were on him, McAllister thought ironically. He felt no relief at the information. Whatever the automatics were, they wouldn't be working in his favor; and the fact that the young woman could put away her gun in spite of her suspicions spoke volumes for the efficiency of the new watchdogs.

There was absolutely nothing he could do but play out this increasingly grim and inexplicable farce. Either he was mad, or else he was no longer on Earth, at least not the Earth of 1941—which was utter nonsense.

He'd have to get out of this place, of course. Meanwhile, the girl was assuming that a man who came into a gun shop would, under ordinary circumstances, want to buy a gun.

It struck him suddenly that, of all the things he could think of, what he wanted to see was one of those strange guns. There were implications of incredible things in the very shape of the instruments. Aloud he said, "Yes, by all means show me."

Another thought occurred to him. He added: "I have no doubt your father is somewhere in the background making some sort of study of me."

The young woman made no move to lead him anywhere. Her eyes were dark pools of puzzlement, staring at him.

"You may not realize it," she said finally, slowly, "but you have already upset our entire establishment. The lights of the automatics should have gone on the moment father pressed the buttons, as he did when I called to him. They didn't! That's unnatural, that's alien.

"And yet"—her frown deepened—"if you were one of them, how did you get through that door? Is it possible that *her* scientists have discovered human beings who do not affect the sensitive energies? And that you are one of many such, sent as an experiment to determine whether or not entrance could be gained?

"Yet that doesn't make logic either.

"If they had even a hope of success, they would not risk so lightly the chance of an overwhelming surprise. Instead you would be the entering wedge of an attack on a vast scale. She is ruthless, she's brilliant; and she craves all power during her lifetime over poor saps like you who have no more sense than to worship her amazing beauty and the splendor of the Imperial Court."

The young woman paused, with the faintest of smiles. "There I go again, off on a political speech. But you can see that there are at least a few reasons why we should be careful about you."

There was a chair over in one corner; McAllister started for it. His mind was calmer, cooler.

"Look," he began, "I don't know what you're talking about. I don't even know how I came to be in this shop. I agree with you that the whole thing requires explanation, but I mean that differently than you do. In fact . . ."

His voice trailed. He had been half lowered over the chair, but instead of sinking into it, he came erect like an old, old man. His eyes fixed on lettering that shone above a glass case of guns behind her. He said hoarsely, "Is that—a calendar?"

She followed his gaze, puzzled: "Yes, it's June third. What's wrong?"

"I don't mean that. I mean—" He caught himself with a horrible effort. "I mean those figures above that. I mean—what year is this?"

The girl looked surprised. She started to say something, then stopped and backed away. Finally: "Don't look like that! There's nothing wrong. This is eighty-four of the four thousand seven hundredth year of the Imperial House of the Isher. It's quite all right."

There was no real feeling in him. Quite deliberately

he sat down, and the conscious wonder came: exactly how *should* he feel?

Not even surprise came to his aid. Quite simply, the whole pattern of events began to make a sort of distorted logic.

The building front superimposed on those two 1941 shops; the way the door had acted; the great exterior sign with its odd linking of freedom with the right to buy weapons; the actual display of weapons in the window, *the finest energy weapons in the known universe!*

He grew aware that minutes had passed while he sat there in slow, dumb thought. And that the girl was talking earnestly with a tall, gray-haired man who was standing on the open threshold of the door through which she had originally come.

There was an odd, straining tenseness in the way they were talking. Their low-spoken words made a curious blur of sound in his ears, strangely unsettling in effect—McAllister could not quite analyze the meaning of it until the girl turned; and, in a voice dark with urgency, said, "Mr. McAllister, my father wants to know what year you're from!"

Briefly, the sense of the sentence was overshadowed by that stark urgency; then: "Huh!" said McAllister. "Do you mean that you're responsible for— And how the devil did you know my name?"

The older man shook his head. "No, we're not responsible." His voice quickened but lost none of its gravity. "There's no time to explain. What has happened is what we gunmakers have feared for generations: that sooner or later would come one who lusted for unlimited power; and who, to attain tyranny, must necessarily seek first to destroy us.

"Your presence here is a manifestation of the energy force that she has turned against us—something so new that we did not even suspect it was being used against us. But now—I have no time to waste. Get all the information you can, Lystra, and warn him of his own personal danger."

The man turned. The door closed noiselessly behind his tall figure.

McAllister asked, "What did he mean—personal danger?"

He saw that the girl's brown eyes were uneasy as they rested on him.

"It's hard to explain," she began in an uncomfortable voice. "First of all, come to the window, and I'll try to make everything clear. It's all very confusing to you, I suppose."

McAllister drew a deep breath. "Now we're getting somewhere."

His alarm was gone. The older man seemed to know what it was all about; that meant there should be no difficulty getting home again. As for all this danger to the gunmakers' guild, that was their worry, not his. Meanwhile—

He stepped forward, closer to the girl. To his amazement, she cringed away as if he had struck at her.

As he stared blankly, she turned, and laughed a humorless, uncertain laugh; finally she breathed, "don't think I'm being silly, don't be offended—but for your life's sake don't touch any human body you might come into contact with."

McAllister was conscious of a chill. It struck him with a sudden, sharp dismay that the expression of uneasiness in the girl's face was—fear!

His own fear fled before a wave of impatience. He controlled himself with an effort.

"Now, look," he began. "I want to get things clear. We can talk here without danger, providing I don't touch you or come near you. Is that straight?"

She nodded. "The floor, the walls, every piece of furniture, in fact the entire shop is made of perfect nonconducting material."

McAllister had a sudden sense of being balanced on a tightrope over a bottomless abyss. The way this girl could imply danger without making it clear what the danger was, almost petrified him.

He forced calm into his mind. "Let's start," he said, "at the beginning. How did you and your father know my name, and that I was not of"—he paused before the odd phrase, then went on—"of this time?"

"Father X-rayed you," the girl said, her voice as stiff as her body. "He X-rayed the contents of your pockets. That was how he first found out what was the matter. You see, the X-rays themselves became carriers of the energy with which you're charged. That's what was the matter; that's why the automatics wouldn't focus on you, and—"

"Just a minute!" said McAllister. His brain was a spinning world. "Energy—charged?"

The girl was staring at him. "Don't you understand?" she gasped. "You've come across five thousand years of time; and of all the energies in the universe, time is the most potent. You're charged with trillions of trillions of time-energy units. If you should step outside this shop, you'd blow up this city of the Isher and half a hundred miles of land beyond.

"You"—she finished on an unsteady, upward surge of her voice—"you could conceivably destroy the Earth!"

He hadn't noticed the mirror before; funny, too, because it was large enough, at least eight feet high, and directly in front of him on the wall where a minute before—he could have sworn—had been solid metal.

"Look at yourself," the girl was saying soothingly. "There's nothing so steadying as one's own image. Actually your body is taking the mental shock very well."

It was! He stared in dimly gathering surprise at his image. There was a paleness in the lean face that stared back at him; but the body was not actually shaking as the whirling in his mind had suggested.

He grew aware again of the girl. She was standing with one finger on one of a series of wall switches. Abruptly, he felt better.

"Thank you," he said quietly. "I certainly needed that."

She smiled encouragingly; and he was able now to be amazed at her conflicting personality. There had been on the one hand her complete inability a few minutes earlier to get to the point of his danger, a distinct incapacity for explaining things with words; yet obviously her action with the mirror showed a keen understanding of human psychology. He said, "The problem now is, from your point of view, to circumvent this—Isher—woman, and to get me back to 1941 before I blow up the Earth of . . . of whatever year this is."

The girl nodded. "Father says that you can be sent back, but—as for the rest: watch!"

He had no time for relief at the knowledge that he could be returned to his own time. She pressed another button. Instantly the mirror was gone into the metallic wall. Another button clicked—and the wall vanished.

Literally vanished. Before him stretched a park similar to the one he had already seen through the front door—obviously an extension of the same garden-like vista. Trees were there, and flowers, and green, green grass in the sun.

There was also the city again, nearer from this side, but not so pretty, immeasurably grimmer.

One vast building, as high as it was long, massively dark against the sky, dominated the entire horizon. It was a good quarter-mile away; and incredibly, it was at least that long and that high.

Neither near that monstrous building nor in the park was a living person visible. Everywhere was evidence of man's dynamic labor—but no men, not a movement; even the trees stood motionless in that strangely breathless sunlit day.

"Watch!" said the girl again, more softly.

There was no click this time. She made an adjustment on one of the buttons; and suddenly the view was no longer so clear. It wasn't that the sun had dimmed its bright intensity. It wasn't even that glass was visible where a moment before there had been nothing.

There was still no apparent substance between them and the gemlike park. But—

The park was no longer deserted!

Scores of men and machines swarmed out there. McAllister stared in frank amazement; and then as the sense of illusion faded, and the dark menace of those men penetrated, his emotion changed to dismay.

"Why," he said at last, "those men are soldiers, and the machines are—"

"Energy guns!" she said. "That's always been their problem: how to get their weapons close enough to our shops to destroy us. It isn't that the guns are not powerful over a very great distance. Even the rifles we sell can kill unprotected life over a distance of miles; but our gun shops are so heavily fortified that, to destroy us, they must use their biggest cannon at point-blank range.

"In the past, they could never do that because we own the surrounding park; and our alarm system was perfect—until now. The new energy they're using affects none of our protective instruments; and—what is infinitely worse—affords them a perfect shield against our own guns. Invisibility, of course, has long been known; but if you hadn't come, we would have been destroyed without ever knowing what happened."

"But," McAllister exclaimed sharply, "what are you going to do? They're still out there working—"

Her brown eyes burned with a fierce, yellow flame. "Where do you think Father is?" she asked. "He's warned the guild; and every member has now discovered that similar invisible guns are being set up outside his place by invisible men. Every member is working at top speed for some solution. They haven't found it yet."

She finished quietly: "I thought I'd tell you."

McAllister cleared his throat, parted his lips to speak —then closed them as he realized that no words were even near his lips. Fascinated, he watched the soldiers connecting what must have been invisible cables that led to the vast building in the background: foot-thick cables that told of the titanic power that was to be unleashed on the tiny weapon shop.

There was actually nothing to be said. The deadly reality out there overshadowed all conceivable sentences and phrases. Of all the people here, he was the most useless, his opinion the least worthwhile.

Oddly, he must have spoken aloud, but he did not realize that until the familiar voice of the girl's father came from one side of him. The older man said, "You're quite mistaken, McAllister. Of all the people here you are the *most* valuable. Through you we discovered that the Isher were actually attacking us. Furthermore, our enemies do not know of your existence, therefore have not yet realized the full effect produced by the new blanketing energy they have used.

"You, accordingly, constitute the unknown factor—our only hope, for the time left to us is incredibly short. Unless we can make immediate use of the unknown quantity you represent, all is lost!"

The man looked older, McAllister thought; there were lines of strain in his lean, sallow face as he turned toward his daughter; and his voice, when he spoke, was edged with harshness: "Lystra, number seven!"

As the girl's fingers touched the seventh button, her father explained swiftly to McAllister: "The guild supreme council is holding an immediate emergency session. We must choose the most likely method of attacking the problem, and concentrate individually and collectively on that method. Regional conversations are already in progress, but only one important idea has been put forward as yet . . . ah, gentlemen!"

He spoke past McAllister, who turned with a start, then froze.

Men were coming out of the solid wall, lightly, easily, as if it were a door and they were stepping across a threshold. One, two, three—twelve.

They were grim-faced men, all except one who glanced at McAllister, started to walk past, then stopped with a half-amused smile.

"Don't look so blank. How else do you think we could have survived these many years if we hadn't been able to transmit material objects through space? The Isher police have always been only too eager to block-ade our sources of supply. Incidentally, my name is Ca-dron—Peter Cadron!"

McAllister nodded in a perfunctory manner. He was no longer genuinely impressed by the new machines. Here were endless products of the machine age; science and invention so stupendously advanced that men made scarcely a move that did not involve a machine. He grew aware that a heavy-faced man near him was about to speak.

The man began: "We are gathered here because it is obvious that the source of the new energy is the great building just outside this shop—"

He motioned toward the wall where the mirror had been a few minutes previously, and the window through which McAllister had gazed at the monstrous structure in question.

The speaker went on: "We've known, ever since that building was completed five years ago, that it was a power building aimed against us; and now from it new energy has flown out to engulf the world, immensely potent energy, so strong that it broke the very tension of time, fortunately only at this nearest gun shop. Apparently it weakens when transmitted over distance. It—"

"Look, Dresley!" came a curt interruption from a small, thin man. "What good is all this preamble? You have been examining the various plans put forward by regional groups. Is there, or isn't there, a decent one among them?"

Dresley hesitated. To McAllister's surprise, the man's eyes fixed doubtfully on him, his heavy face worked for a moment, then hardened.

"Yes, there is a method, but it depends on compel-ling our friend from the past to take a great risk. You all know what I'm referring to. It will gain us the time we need so desperately."

"Eh!" said McAllister, and stood stunned as all eyes turned to stare at him.

The seconds fled; and it struck McAllister that what he really needed again was the mirror—to prove to him that his body was putting up a good front. Something, he thought, something to steady him.

His gaze flicked over the faces of the men. The gunmakers made a curious, confusing pattern in the way they sat, or stood, or leaned against glass cases of shining guns; and there seemed to be fewer than he had previously counted. One, two—ten, including the girl. He could have sworn there had been fourteen.

His eyes moved on, just in time to see the door of the back room closing. Four of the men had obviously gone to the laboratory or whatever lay beyond the door. Satisfied, he forgot them.

Still, he felt unsettled; and briefly his eyes were held by the purely mechanical wonder of this shop, here in this vastly future world, a shop that was an intricate machine in itself and—

He discovered that he was lighting a cigarette; and abruptly realized that that was what he needed most. The first puff tingled deliciously along his nerves. His mind grew calm; his eyes played thoughtfully over the faces before him.

He said, "I can't understand how any one of you could even think of compulsion. According to you, I'm loaded with energy. I may be wrong, but if any of you should try to thrust me back down the chute of time, or even touch me, that energy in me would do devastating things—"

"You're damned right!" chimed in a young man. He barked irritably at Dresley: "How the devil did you ever come to make such a psychological blunder? You know that McAllister will have to do as we want, to save himself; and he'll have to do it fast!"

Dresley grunted under the sharp attack. "Hell," he

said, "the truth is we have no time to waste, and I just figured there wasn't time to explain, and that he might scare easily. I see, however, that we're dealing with an intelligent man."

McAllister's eyes narrowed over the group. There was something phony here. They were talking too much, wasting the very time they needed, as if they were marking time, waiting for something to happen.

He said sharply, "And don't give me any soft soap about being intelligent. You fellows are sweating blood. You'd shoot your own grandmothers and trick me into the bargain, because the world you think right is at stake. What's this plan of yours that you were going to compel me to participate in?"

It was the young man who replied: "You are to be given insulated clothes and sent back into your own time—"

He paused. McAllister said, "That sounds okay, so far. What's the catch?"

"There is no catch!"

McAllister stared. "Now, look here," he began, "don't give me any of that. If it's as simple as that, how the devil am I going to be helping you against the Isher energy?"

The young man scowled blackly at Dresley. "You see," he said to the other, "you've made him suspicious with the talk of yours about compulsion."

He faced McAllister. "What we have in mind is an application of a sort of an energy lever and fulcrum principle. You are to be a 'weight' at the long end of a kind of energy 'crowbar,' which lifts the greater 'weight' at the short end. You will go back five thousand years in time; the machine in the great building to which your body is tuned, and which has caused all this trouble, will move ahead in time about two weeks."

"In that way," interrupted another man before McAllister could speak, "we shall have time to find a counteragent. There must be a solution, else our enemies would not have acted so secretly. Well, what do you think?"

McAllister walked slowly over to the chair that he had occupied previously. His mind was turning at furious speed, but he knew with a grim foreboding that he hadn't a fraction of the technical knowledge necessary to safeguard his interests.

He said slowly, "As I see it, this is supposed to work something like a pump handle. The lever principle, the old idea that if you had a lever long enough, and a suitable fulcrum, you could move the Earth out of its orbit."

"Exactly!" It was the heavy-faced Dresley who spoke. "Only this works in time. You go five thousand years, the building goes a few wee . . ."

His voice faded, his eagerness drained from him as he caught the expression on McAllister's face.

"Look!" said McAllister, "there's nothing more pitiful than a bunch of honest men engaged in their first act of dishonesty. You're strong men, the intellectual type, who've spent your lives enforcing an idealistic conception. You've always told yourself that if the occasion should ever require it, you would not hesitate to make drastic sacrifices. But you're not fooling anybody. *What's the catch?*"

It was quite startling to have the suit thrust at him. He hadn't observed the men emerge from the back room; and it came as a distinct shock to realize that they had actually gone for the insulated clothes before they could have known that he would use them.

McAllister stared grimly at Peter Cadron, who held the dull, grayish, limp thing toward him. A very flame of abrupt rage held him choked; before he could speak, Cadron said in a tight voice, "Get into this, and get going! It's a matter of minutes, man! When those guns out there start spraying energy, you won't be alive to argue about our honesty."

Still he hesitated; the room seemed insufferably hot;

and he was sick—sick with the deadly uncertainty. Perspiration streaked stingingly down his cheeks. His frantic gaze fell on the girl, standing silent and subdued in the background, near the front door.

He strode toward her; and either his glare or presence was incredibly frightening, for she cringed and turned white as a sheet.

"Look!" he said. "I'm in this as deep as hell. What's the risk in this thing? I've got to feel that I have some chance. Tell me, what's the catch?"

The girl was gray now, almost as gray and dead-looking as the suit Peter Cadron was holding. "It's the friction," she mumbled finally, "you may not get all the way back to 1941. You see, you'll be a sort of 'weight' and—"

McAllister whirled away from her. He climbed into the soft, almost flimsy suit, crowding the overall-like shape over his neatly pressed clothes. "It comes tight over the head, doesn't it?" he asked.

"Yes!" It was Lystra's father who answered. "As soon as you pull that zipper shut, the suit will become completely invisible. To outsiders it will seem just as if you have your ordinary clothes on. The suit is fully equipped. You could live on the Moon inside it."

"What I don't get," complained McAllister, "is why I have to wear it. I got here all right without it."

He frowned. His words had been automatic, but abruptly a thought came: "Just a minute. What becomes of the energy with which I'm charged when I'm bottled up in this insulation?"

He saw by the stiffening expressions of those around him that he had touched on a vast subject.

"So that's it!" he snapped. "The insulation is to prevent me losing any of that energy. That's how it can make a 'weight.' I have no doubt there's a connection from this suit to that other machine. Well, it's not too late. It's—"

With a desperate twist, he tried to jerk aside, to evade the clutching hands of the four men who leaped at him. Hopeless movement! They had him instantly; and their grips on him were strong beyond his power to break.

The fingers of Peter Cadron jerked the zipper tight, and Peter Cadron said, "Sorry, but when we went into that back room, we also dressed in insulated clothing. That's why you couldn't hurt us. Sorry, again!

"And remember this: There's no certainty that you are being sacrificed. The fact that there is no crater in *our* Earth proves that you did not explode in the past, and that you solved the problem in some other way. *Now, somebody open the door, quick!*"

Irresistibly he was carried forward. And then—

"Wait!"

It was the girl. The colorless gray in her face was a livid thing. Her eyes glittered like dark jewels; and in her fingers was the tiny, mirror-bright gun she had pointed in the beginning at McAllister.

The little group hustling McAllister stopped as if they had been struck. He was scarcely aware; for him there was only the girl, and the way the muscles of her lips were working, and the way her voice suddenly flamed: "This is utter outrage. Are we such cowards —is it possible that the spirit of liberty can survive only through a shoddy act of murder and gross defiance of the rights of the individual? I say no! Mr. McAllister must have the protection of the hypnotism treatment, even if we die during the wasted minutes."

"Lystra!" It was her father; and McAllister realized in the swift movement of the older man what a brilliant mind was there, and how quickly the older man grasped every aspect of the situation.

He stepped forward and took the gun from his daughter's fingers—the only man in the room, McAllister thought flashingly, who could dare approach her in that moment with the certainty she would not fire. For hysteria was in every line of her face, and the racking tears that followed showed how dangerous her stand might have been against the others.

Strangely, not for a moment had hope come. The entire action seemed divorced from his life and his thought; there was only the observation of it. He stood there for a seeming eternity and, when emotion finally came, it was surprise that he was not being hustled to his doom. With the surprise came awareness that Peter Cadron had let go his arm and stepped clear of him.

The man's eyes were calm, his head held proudly erect; he said, "Your daughter is right, sir. At this point we rise above our petty fears, and we say to this unhappy man: 'Have courage! You will not be forgotten. We can guarantee nothing, cannot even state exactly what will happen to you. But we say: if it lies in our power to help you, that help you shall have.' And now—we must protect you from the devastating psychological pressures that would otherwise destroy you, simply but effectively."

Too late, McAllister noticed that the others had turned faces away from that extraordinary wall—the wall that had already displayed so vast a versatility. He did not even see who pressed the activating button for what followed.

There was a flash of dazzling light. For an instant he felt as if his mind had been laid bare; and against that nakedness the voice of Peter Cadron pressed like some ineradicable engraving stamp: "To retain your self-control and your sanity—this is your hope: this you will do in spite of everything! And, for your sake, speak of your experience only to scientists or to those in authority who you feel will understand and help. Good luck!"

So strong remained the effect of that brief flaring light that he felt only vaguely the touch of their hands on him, propelling him. He must have fallen, but there was no pain—

He grew aware that he was lying on a sidewalk. The deep, familiar voice of Police Inspector Clayton boomed over him: "Clear the way; no crowding now!"

McAllister climbed to his feet. A pall of curious

faces gawked at him; and there was no park, no gorgeous city. Instead, a bleak row of one-story shops made a dull pattern on either side of the street.

He'd have to get away from here. These people didn't understand. Somewhere on Earth must be a scientist who could help him. After all, the record was that he hadn't exploded. Therefore, somewhere, somehow—

He mumbled answers at the questions that beat at him; and then he was clear of the disappointed crowd. There followed purposeless minutes of breakneck walking; the streets ahead grew narrower, dirtier—

He stopped, shaken. What was happening?

It was night, in a brilliant, glowing city. He was standing on an avenue that stretched jewel-like into remote distance.

A street that lived, flaming with a soft light that gleamed up from its surface—a road of light, like a river flowing under a sun that shone nowhere else, straight and smooth and—

He walked along for uncomprehending minutes, watching the cars that streamed past—and wild hope came!

Was this again the age of the Isher and the gunmakers? It could be; it looked right, and it meant they had brought him back. After all, they were not evil, and they would save him if they could. For all he knew, weeks had passed in their time and—

Abruptly, he was in the center of a blinding snowstorm. He staggered from the first, mighty, unexpected blow of that untamed wind, then, bracing himself, fought for mental and physical calm.

The shining, wondrous night city was gone; gone too the glowing road—both vanished, transformed into this deadly, wilderness world.

He peered through the driving snow. It was daylight; and he could make out the dim shadows of trees that reared up through the white mist of blizzard less than fifty feet away.

Instinctively he pressed toward their shelter, and stood finally out of that blowing, pressing wind.

He thought: One minute in the distant future; the next—where?

There was certainly no city. Only trees, an uninhabited forest and winter—

The blizzard was gone. And the trees. He stood on a sandy beach; before him stretched a blue, sunlit sea that rippled over broken white buildings. All around, scattered far into that shallow, lovely sea, far up into the weed-grown hills, were the remnants of a once tremendous city. Over all clung an aura of incredible age; and the silence of the long-dead was broken only by the gentle, timeless lapping of the waves—

Again came that instantaneous change. More prepared this time, he nevertheless sank twice under the surface of the vast, swift river that carried him on and on. It was hard swimming, but the insulated suit was buoyant with the air it manufactured each passing second; and, after a moment, he began to struggle purposefully toward the tree-lined shore a hundred feet to his right.

A thought came, and he stopped swimming. "What's the use!"

The truth was as simple as it was terrible. He was being shunted from the past to the future; he was the "weight" on the long end of an energy seesaw; and in some way he was slipping farther ahead and farther back each time. Only that could explain the catastrophic changes he had already witnessed. In a minute would come another change and—

It came! He was lying face downward on green grass, but there was no curiosity in him. He did not look up, but lay there hour after hour as the seesaw jerked on: past—future—past—future—

Beyond doubt, the gunmakers had won their respite; for at the far end of this dizzy teeter-totter was the machine that had been used by the Isher soldiers as an activating force; it too teetered up, then down, in a mad seesaw.

There remained the gunmakers' promise to help him, vain now; for they could not know what had happened. They could not find him ever in this maze of time.

There remained the mechanical law that forces must balance.

Somewhere, sometime, a balance would be struck, probably in the future—because there was still the fact that he hadn't exploded in the past. Yes, somewhere would come the balance when he would again face *that* problem. But now—

On, on, on the seesaw flashed; the world on the one hand grew bright with youth, and on the other dark with fantastic age.

Infinity yawned blackly ahead.

Quite suddenly it came to him that he knew where the seesaw would stop. It would end in the very remote past, with the release of the stupendous temporal energy he had been accumulating with each of those monstrous swings.

He would not witness, but he would cause, the formation of the planets.

NIGHTFALL

by Isaac Asimov

Isaac Asimov once ruefully remarked that although he learned to write much better after "Nightfall" was first published in 1941, he has never yet written a more popular story. The reasons are not hard to find. "Nightfall" has a powerful movement, a sense of danger and mystery, a brilliant idea, never before used in science fiction——and an easy, natural style that makes it seem that all this could be happening now, to us, even though it takes place in a distant part of the galaxy.

"If the stars should appear one night in a thousand years, how would men believe and adore, and preserve for many generations the remembrance of the city of God?"
—EMERSON

ATON 77, DIRECTOR OF SARO UNIVERSITY, THRUST OUT a belligerent lower lip and glared at the young newspaperman in a hot fury.

Theremon 762 took that fury in his stride. In his earlier days, when his now widely syndicated column was only a mad idea in a cub reporter's mind, he had specialized in "impossible" interviews. It had cost him bruises, black eyes, and broken bones; but it had given him an ample supply of coolness and self-confidence.

So he lowered the outthrust hand that had been so pointedly ignored and calmly waited for the aged director to get over the worst. Astronomers were queer ducks, anyway, and if Aton's actions of the last two months meant anything, this same Aton was the queerduckiest of the lot.

Aton 77 found his voice, and though it trembled with restrained emotion, the careful, somewhat pedantic phraseology, for which the famous astronomer was noted, did not abandon him.

"Sir," he said, "you display an infernal gall in coming to me with that impudent proposition of yours."

The husky telephotographer of the Observatory, Beenay 25, thrust a tongue's tip across dry lips and interposed nervously, "Now, sir, after all——"

The director turned to him and lifted a white eyebrow. "Do not interfere, Beenay. I will credit you with good intentions in bringing this man here; but I will tolerate no insubordination now."

Theremon decided it was time to take a part. "Director Aton, if you'll let me finish what I started saying, I think——"

"I don't believe, young man," retorted Aton, "that anything you could say now would count much as compared with your daily columns of these last two months. You have led a vast newspaper campaign against the efforts of myself and my colleagues to organize the world against the menace which it is now too late to avert. You have done your best with your highly personal attacks to make the staff of this Observatory objects of ridicule."

The director lifted a copy of the Saro City *Chronicle* from the table and shook it at Theremon furiously. "Even a person of your well-known impudence should have hesitated before coming to me with a request that he be allowed to cover today's events for his paper. Of all newsmen, you!"

Aton dashed the newspaper to the floor, strode to the window, and clasped his arms behind his back.

"You may leave," he snapped over his shoulder. He stared moodily out at the skyline where Gamma, the brightest of the planet's six suns, was setting. It had already faded and yellowed into the horizon mists, and Aton knew he would never see it again as a sane man.

He whirled. "No, wait, come here!" He gestured peremptorily. "I'll give you your story."

The newsman had made no motion to leave, and now he approached the old man slowly. Aton gestured outward. "Of the six suns, only Beta is left in the sky. Do you see it?"

The question was rather unnecessary. Beta was almost at zenith, its ruddy light flooding the landscape to an unusual orange as the brilliant rays of setting Gamma died. Beta was at aphelion. It was small; smaller than Theremon had ever seen it before, and for the moment it was undisputed ruler of Lagash's sky.

Lagash's own sun, Alpha, the one about which it revolved, was at the antipodes, as were the two distant companion pairs. The red dwarf Beta—Alpha's immediate companion—was alone, grimly alone.

Aton's upturned face flushed redly in the sunlight. "In just under four hours," he said, "civilization, as we know it, comes to an end. It will do so because, as you see, Beta is the only sun in the sky." He smiled grimly. "Print that! There'll be no one to read it."

"But if it turns out that four hours pass—and another four—and nothing happens?" asked Theremon softly.

"Don't let that worry you. Enough will happen."

"Granted! And *still*—if nothing happens?"

For a second time, Beenay 25 spoke. "Sir, I think you ought to listen to him."

Theremon said, "Put it to a vote, Director Aton."

There was a stir among the remaining five members of the Observatory staff, who till now had maintained an attitude of wary neutrality.

"That," stated Aton flatly, "is not necessary." He drew out his pocket watch. "Since your good friend,

Beenay, insists so urgently, I will give you five minutes. Talk away."

"Good! Now, just what difference would it make if you allowed me to take down an eyewitness account of what's to come? If your prediction comes true, my presence won't hurt; for in that case my column would never be written. On the other hand, if nothing comes of it, you will just have to expect ridicule or worse. It would be wise to leave that ridicule to friendly hands."

Aton snorted. "Do you mean yours when you speak of friendly hands?"

"Certainly!" Theremon sat down and crossed his legs. "My columns may have been a little rough, but I gave you people the benefit of the doubt every time. After all, this is not the century to preach 'The end of the world is at hand' to Lagash. You have to understand that people don't believe the *Book of Revelations* anymore, and it annoys them to have scientists turn about-face and tell us the Cultists are right after all—"

"No such thing, young man," interrupted Aton. "While a great deal of our data has been supplied us by the Cult, our results contain none of the Cult's mysticism. Facts are facts, and the Cult's so-called mythology *has* certain facts behind it. We've exposed them and ripped away their mystery. I assure you that the Cult hates us now worse than you do."

"I don't hate you. I'm just trying to tell you that the public is in an ugly humor. They're angry."

Aton twisted his mouth in derision. "Let them be angry."

"Yes, but what about tomorrow?"

"There'll be no tomorrow!"

"But if there is. Say that there is—just to see what happens. That anger might take shape into something serious. After all, you know, business has taken a nose-dive these last two months. Investors don't really believe the world is coming to an end, but just the same they're being cagey with their money until it's all over. Johnny Public doesn't believe you, either, but the new spring furniture might just as well wait a few months—just to make sure.

"You see the point. Just as soon as this is all over, the business interests will be after your hide. They'll say that if crackpots—begging your pardon—can upset the country's prosperity any time they want, simply by making some cockeyed prediction—it's up to the planet to prevent them. The sparks will fly, sir."

The director regarded the columnist sternly. "And just what were you proposing to do to help the situation?"

"Well"—Theremon grinned—"I was proposing to take charge of the publicity. I can handle things so that only the ridiculous side will show. It would be hard to stand, I admit, because I'd have to make you all out to be a bunch of gibbering idiots, but if I can get people laughing at you, they might forget to be angry. In return for that, all my publisher asks is an exclusive story."

Beenay nodded and burst out, "Sir, the rest of us think he's right. These last two months we've considered everything but the million-to-one chance that there is an error somewhere in our theory or in our calculations. We ought to take care of that, too."

There was a murmur of agreement from the men grouped about the table, and Aton's expression became that of one who found his mouth full of something bitter and couldn't get rid of it.

"You may stay if you wish, then. You will kindly refrain, however, from hampering us in our duties in any way. You will also remember that I am in charge of all activities here, and in spite of your opinions as expressed in your columns, I will expect full cooperation and full respect—"

His hands were behind his back, and his wrinkled face thrust forward determinedly as he spoke. He might have continued indefinitely but for the intrusion of a new voice.

"Hello, hello, hello!" It came in a high tenor, and the

plump cheeks of the newcomer expanded in a pleased smile. "What's this morgue-like atmosphere about here? No one's losing his nerve, I hope."

Aton started in consternation and said peevishly, "Now what the devil are you doing here, Sheerin? I thought you were going to stay behind in the Hideout."

Sheerin laughed and dropped his tubby figure into a chair. "Hideout be blowed! The place bored me. I wanted to be here, where things are getting hot. Don't you suppose I have my share of curiosity? I want to see these Stars the Cultists are forever speaking about." He rubbed his hands and added in a soberer tone, "It's freezing outside. The wind's enough to hang icicles on your nose. Beta doesn't seem to give any heat at all, at the distance it is."

The white-haired director ground his teeth in sudden exasperation. "Why do you go out of your way to do crazy things, Sheerin? What kind of good are you around here?"

"What kind of good am I around there?" Sheerin spread his palms in comical resignation. "A psychologist isn't worth his salt in the Hideout. They need men of action and strong, healthy women that can breed children. Me? I'm a hundred pounds too heavy for a man of action, and I wouldn't be a success at breeding children. So why bother them with an extra mouth to feed? I feel better over here."

Theremon spoke briskly. "Just what is the Hideout, sir?"

Sheerin seemed to see the columnist for the first time. He frowned and blew his ample cheeks out. "And just who in Lagash are you, redhead?"

Aton compressed his lips and then muttered sullenly, "That's Theremon 762, the newspaper fellow. I suppose you've heard of him."

The columnist offered his hand. "And, of course, you're Sheerin 501 of Saro University. I've heard of you." Then he repeated, "What is this Hideout, sir?"

"Well," said Sheerin, "we had managed to convince

a few people of the validity of our prophecy of—er—doom, to be spectacular about it, and those few have taken proper measures. They consist mainly of the immediate members of the families of the Observatory staff, certain of the faculty of Saro University, and a few outsiders. Altogether, they number about three hundred, but three quarters are women and children."

"I see! They're supposed to hide where the Darkness and the—er—Stars can't get at them, and then hold out when the rest of the world goes poof."

"If they can. It won't be easy. With all of mankind insane, with the great cities going up in flames—environment will not be conducive to survival. But they have food, water, shelter, and weapons—"

"They've got more," said Aton. "They've got all our records, except for what we will collect today. Those records will mean everything to the next cycle, and *that's* what must survive. The rest can go hang."

Theremon uttered a long, low whistle and sat brooding for several minutes. The men about the table had brought out a multichess board and started a six-member game. Moves were made rapidly and in silence. All eyes bent in furious concentration on the board. Theremon watched them intently and then rose and approached Aton, who sat apart in whispered conversation with Sheerin.

"Listen," he said, "let's go somewhere where we won't bother the rest of the fellows. I want to ask some questions."

The aged astronomer frowned sourly at him, but Sheerin chirped up, "Certainly. It will do me good to talk. It always does. Aton was telling me about your ideas concerning world reaction to a failure of the prediction—and I agree with you. I read your column pretty regularly, by the way, and as a general thing I like your views."

"Please, Sheerin," growled Aton.

"Eh? Oh, all right. We'll go into the next room. It has softer chairs, anyway."

There were softer chairs in the next room. There were also thick red curtains on the windows and a maroon carpet on the floor. With the bricky light of Beta pouring in, the general effect was one of dried blood.

Theremon shuddered. "Say, I'd give ten credits for a decent dose of white light for just a second. I wish Gamma or Delta were in the sky."

"What are your questions?" asked Aton. "Please remember that our time is limited. In a little over an hour and a quarter we're going upstairs, and after that there will be no time for talk."

"Well, here it is." Theremon leaned back and folded his hands on his chest. "You people seem so all-fired serious about this that I'm beginning to believe you. Would you mind explaining what it's all about?"

Aton exploded, "Do you mean to sit there and tell me that you've been bombarding us with ridicule without even finding out what we've been trying to say?"

The columnist grinned sheepishly. "It's not that bad, sir. I've got the general idea. You say there is going to be a world-wide Darkness in a few hours and that all mankind will go violently insane. What I want now is the science behind it."

"No, you don't. No, you don't," broke in Sheerin. "If you ask Aton for that—supposing him to be in the mood to answer at all—he'll trot out pages of figures and volumes of graphs. You won't make head or tail of it. Now if you were to ask me, I could give you the layman's standpoint."

"All right; I ask you."

"Then first I'd like a drink." He rubbed his hands and looked at Aton.

"Water?" grunted Aton.

"Don't be silly!"

"Don't you be silly. No alcohol today. It would be too easy to get my men drunk. I can't afford to tempt them."

The psychologist grumbled wordlessly. He turned to

Theremon, impaled him with his sharp eyes, and began.

"You realize, of course, that the history of civilization on Lagash displays a cyclic character—but I mean, *cyclic!*"

"I know," replied Theremon cautiously, "that that is the current archaeological theory. Has it been accepted as a fact?"

"Just about. In this last century it's been generally agreed upon. This cyclic character is—or rather, was —one of the great mysteries. We've located series of civilizations, nine of them definitely, and indications of others as well, all of which have reached heights comparable to our own, and all of which, without exception, were destroyed by fire at the very height of their culture.

"And no one could tell why. All centers of culture were thoroughly gutted by fire, with nothing left behind to give a hint as to the cause."

Theremon was following closely. "Wasn't there a Stone Age, too?"

"Probably, but as yet practically nothing is known of it, except that men of that age were little more than rather intelligent apes. We can forget about that."

"I see. Go on!"

"There have been explanations of these recurrent catastrophes, all of a more or less fantastic nature. Some say that there are periodic rains of fire; some that Lagash passes through a sun every so often; some even wilder things. But there is one theory, quite different from all of these that has been handed down over a period of centuries."

"I know. You mean this myth of the 'Stars' that the Cultists have in their *Book of Revelations.*"

"Exactly," rejoined Sheerin with satisfaction. "The Cultists said that every two thousand and fifty years Lagash entered a huge cave, so that all the suns disappeared, and there came *total darkness all over the world!* And then, they say, things called Stars appeared, which robbed men of their souls and left them unreasoning brutes, so that they destroyed the civilization they themselves had built up. Of course they mix all this up with a lot of religio-mystic notions, but that's the central idea."

There was a short pause in which Sheerin drew a long breath. "And now we come to the Theory of Universal Gravitation." He pronounced the phrase so that the capital letters sounded—and at that point Aton turned from the window, snorted loudly, and stalked out of the room.

The two stared after him, and Theremon said, "What's wrong?"

"Nothing in particular," replied Sheerin. "Two of the men were due several hours ago and haven't shown up yet. He's terrifically short-handed, of course, because all but the really essential men have gone to the Hideout."

"You don't think the two deserted, do you?"

"Who? Faro and Yimot? Of course not. Still, if they're not back within the hour, things would be a little sticky." He got to his feet suddenly, and his eyes twinkled. "Anyway, as long as Aton is gone—"

Tiptoeing to the nearest window, he squatted, and from the low window box beneath withdrew a bottle of red liquid that gurgled suggestively when he shook it.

"I *thought* Aton didn't know about this," he remarked as he trotted back to the table. "Here! We've only got one glass so, as the guest, you can have it. I'll keep the bottle." And he filled the tiny cup with judicious care.

Theremon rose to protest, but Sheerin eyes him sternly. "Respect your elders, young man."

The newsman seated himself with a look of anguish on his face. "Go ahead, then, you old villain."

The psychologist's Adam's apple wobbled as the bottle upended, and then, with a satisfied grunt and a smack of the lips, he began again. "But what do you know about gravitation?"

"Nothing, except that it is a very recent development, not too well established, and that the math is so hard that only twelve men in Lagash are supposed to understand it."

"*Tcha!* Nonsense! Baloney! I can give you all the essential math in a sentence. The Law of Universal Gravitation states that there exists a cohesive force among all bodies of the universe, such that the amount of this force between any two given bodies is proportional to the product of their masses divided by the square of the distance between them."

"Is that all?"

"That's enough! It took four hundred years to develop it."

"Why that long? It sounded simple enough, the way you said it."

"Because great laws are not divined by flashes of inspiration, whatever you may think. It usually takes the combined work of a world full of scientists over a period of centuries. After Genovi 41 discovered that Lagash rotated about the sun Alpha rather than vice versa—and that was four hundred years ago—astronomers have been working. The complex motions of the six suns were recorded and analyzed and unwoven. Theory after theory was advanced and checked and counterchecked and modified and abandoned and revived and converted to something else. It was a devil of a job."

Theremon nodded thoughtfully and held out his glass for more liquor. Sheerin grudgingly allowed a few ruby drops to leave the bottle.

"It was twenty years ago," he continued after remoistening his own throat, "that it was finally demonstrated that the Law of Universal Gravitation accounted exactly for the orbital motions of the six suns. It was a great triumph."

Sheerin stood up and walked to the window, still clutching his bottle. "And now we're getting to the point. In the last decade, the motions of Lagash about

Alpha were computed according to gravity, and *it did not account for the orbit observed;* not even when all perturbations due to the other suns were included. Either the law was invalid, or there was another, as yet unknown factor involved."

Theremon joined Sheerin at the window and gazed out past the wooded slopes to where the spires of Saro City gleamed bloodily in the horizon. The newsman felt the tension of uncertainty grow within him as he cast a short glance at Beta. It glowered redly at zenith, dwarfed and evil.

"Go ahead, sir," he said softly.

Sheerin replied, "Astronomers stumbled about for years, each proposed theory more untenable than the one before—until Aton had the inspiration of calling in the Cult. The head of the Cult, Sor 5, had access to certain data that simplified the problem considerably. Aton set to work on a new track.

"What if there were another nonluminous planetary body such as Lagash? If there were, you know, it would shine only by reflected light, and if it were composed of bluish rock, as Lagash itself largely is, then, in the redness of the sky, the eternal blaze of the suns would make it invisible—drown it out completely."

Theremon whistled. "What a screwy idea!"

"You think *that's* screwy? Listen to this: Suppose this body rotated about Lagash at such a distance and in such an orbit and had such a mass that its attraction would exactly account for the deviations of Lagash's orbit from theory— do you know what would happen?"

The columnist shook his head.

"Well, sometimes this body would get in the way of a sun." And Sheerin emptied what remained in the bottle at a draft.

"And it does, I suppose," said Theremon flatly.

"Yes! But only one sun lies in its place of revolution." He jerked a thumb at the shrunken sun above. "Beta! And it has been shown that the eclipse will occur only when the arrangement of the suns is such that Beta is alone in its hemisphere and at maximum distance, at which time the moon is invariably at minimum distance. The eclipse that results, with the moon seven times the apparent diameter of Beta, covers all of Lagash and lasts well over half a day, so that no spot on the planet escapes the effects. *That eclipse comes once every two thousand and forty-nine years."*

Theremon's face was drawn into an expressionless mask. "And that's my story?"

The psychologist nodded. "That's all of it. First the eclipse—which will start in three quarters of an hour —then universal Darkness and, maybe, these mysterious Stars—then madness, and end of the cycle."

He brooded. "We had two months' leeway—we at the Observatory—and that wasn't enough time to persuade Lagash of the danger. Two centuries might not have been enough. But our records are at the Hideout, and today we photograph the eclipse. The next cycle will *start off* with the truth, and when the *next* eclipse comes, mankind will at last be ready for it. Come to think of it, that's part of your story too."

A thin wind ruffled the curtains at the window as Theremon opened it and leaned out. It played coldly with his hair as he stared at the crimson sunlight on his hand. Then he turned in sudden rebellion.

"What is there in Darkness to drive *me* mad?"

Sheerin smiled to himself as he spun the empty liquor bottle with abstracted motions of his hand. "Have you ever experienced Darkness, young man?"

The newsman leaned against the wall and considered. "No. Can't say I have. But I know what it is. Just—uh—" He made vague motions with his fingers and then brightened. "Just no light. Like in caves."

"Have you ever been in a cave?"

"In a *cave!* Of course not!"

"I thought not. *I* tried last week—just to see—but I got out in a hurry. I went in until the mouth of the cave was just visible as a blur of light, with black everywhere else. I never thought a person my weight could run that fast."

Theremon's lip curled. "Well, if it comes to that, I guess I wouldn't have run if I had been there."

The psychologist studied the young man with an annoyed frown.

"My, don't you talk big! I dare you to draw the curtain."

Theremon looked his surprise and said, "What for? If we had four or five suns out there, we might want to cut the light down a bit for comfort, but now we haven't enough light as it is."

"That's the point. Just draw the curtain; then come here and sit down."

"All right." Theremon reached for the tasseled string and jerked. The red curtain slid across the wide window, the brass rings hissing their way along the crossbar, and a dusk-red shadow clamped down on the room.

Theremon's footsteps sounded hollowly in the silence as he made his way to the table, and then they stopped halfway. "I can't see you, sir," he whispered.

"Feel your way," ordered Sheerin in a strained voice.

"But I can't see you, sir." The newsman was breathing harshly. "I can't see anything."

"What did you expect?" came the grim reply. "Come here and sit down!"

The footsteps sounded again, waveringly, approaching slowly. There was the sound of someone fumbling with a chair. Theremon's voice came thinly, "Here I am. I feel . . . ulp . . . all right."

"You like it, do you?"

"N—no. It's pretty awful. The walls seem to be—" He paused. "They seem to be closing in on me. I keep wanting to push them away. But I'm not going *mad*! In fact, the feeling isn't as bad as it was."

"All right. Draw the curtain back again."

There were cautious footsteps through the dark, the

rustle of Theremon's body against the curtain as he felt for the tassel, and then the triumphant *ro-o-sh* of the curtain slithering back. Red light flooded the room, and with a cry of joy Theremon looked up at the sun.

Sheerin wiped the moistness off his forehead with the back of a hand and said shakily, "And that was just a dark room."

"It can be stood," said Theremon lightly.

"Yes, a dark room can. But were you at the Jonglor Centennial Exposition two years ago?"

"No, it so happens I never got around to it. Six thousand miles was just a bit too much to travel, even for the exposition."

"Well, I was there. You remember hearing about the 'Tunnel of Mystery' that broke all records in the amusement area—for the first month or so, anyway?"

"Yes. Wasn't there some fuss about it?"

"Very little. It was hushed up. You see, that Tunnel of Mystery was just a mile-long tunnel—with no lights. You got into a little open car and jolted along through Darkness for fifteen minutes. It was very popular—while it lasted."

"Popular?"

"Certainly. There's a fascination in being frightened *when it's part of a game*. A baby is born with three instinctive fears: of loud noises, of falling, and of the absence of light. That's why it's considered funny to jump at someone and shout 'Boo!' That's why it's such fun to ride a roller coaster. And that's why that Tunnel of Mystery started cleaning up. People came out of that Darkness shaking, breathless, half dead with fear, but they kept on paying to get in."

"Wait a while, I remember now. Some people came out dead, didn't they? There were rumors of that after it shut down."

The psychologist snorted. "Bah! Two or three dead. That was nothing! They paid off the families of the dead ones and argued the Jonglor City Council into forgetting it. After all, they said, if people with weak hearts want to go through the tunnel, it was at their own risk—and besides, it wouldn't happen again. So they put a doctor in the front office and had every customer go through a physical examination before getting into the car. That actually *boosted* ticket sales."

"Well, then?"

"But you see, there was something else. People sometimes came out in perfect order, except that they refused to go into buildings—any buildings; including palaces, mansions, apartment houses, tenements, cottages, huts, shacks, lean-tos, and tents."

Theremon looked shocked. "You mean they refused to come in out of the open? Where'd they sleep?"

"In the open."

"They should have *forced* them inside."

"Oh, they did, they did. Whereupon these people went into violent hysterics and did their best to bat their brains out against the nearest wall. Once you got them inside, you couldn't keep them there without a strait jacket and a shot of morphine."

"They must have been crazy."

"Which is exactly what they were. One person out of every ten who went into that tunnel came out that way. They called in the psychologists, and we did the only thing possible. We closed down the exhibit." He spread his hands.

"What was the matter with these people?" asked Theremon finally.

"Essentially the same thing that was the matter with you when you thought the walls of the room were crushing in on you in the dark. There is a psychological term for mankind's instinctive fear of the absence of light. We call it 'claustrophobia,' because the lack of light is always tied up with enclosed places, so that fear of one is fear of the other. You see?"

"And those people of the tunnel?"

"Those people of the tunnel consisted of those unfortunates whose mentality did not quite possess the resiliency to overcome the claustrophobia that overtook them in the Darkness. Fifteen minutes without light is a long time; you only had two or three minutes, and I believe you were fairly upset.

"The people of the tunnel had what is called a 'claustrophobic fixation.' Their latent fear of Darkness and enclosed places had crystalized and become active, and, as far as we can tell, permanent. That's what fifteen minutes in the dark will do."

There was a long silence, and Theremon's forehead wrinkled slowly into a frown. "I don't believe it's that bad."

"You mean you don't want to believe," snapped Sheerin. "You're afraid to believe. Look out the window!"

Theremon did so, and the psychologist continued without pausing. "Imagine Darkness—everywhere. No light, as far as you can see. The houses, the trees, the fields, the earth, the sky—black! And Stars thrown in, for all I know—whatever *they* are. Can you conceive it?"

"Yes, I can," declared Theremon truculently.

And Sheerin slammed his fist down upon the table in sudden passion. "You lie! You can't conceive that. Your brain wasn't built for the conception any more than it was built for the conception of infinity or of eternity. You can only talk about it. A fraction of the reality upsets you, and when the real thing comes, your brain is going to be presented with the phenomenon outside its limits of comprehension. You will go mad, completely and permanently! There is no question of it!"

He added sadly, "And another couple of millennia of painful struggle comes to nothing. Tomorrow there won't be a city standing unharmed in all Lagash."

Theremon recovered part of his mental equilibrium. "That doesn't follow. I still don't see that I can go loony just because there isn't a sun in the sky—but even if I did, and everyone else did, how does that harm the cities? Are we going to blow them down?"

But Sheerin was angry, too. "If you were in Darkness, what would you want more than anything else: what would it be that every instinct would call for? Light, damn you, *light!*"

"Well?"

"And how would you get light?"

"I don't know," said Theremon flatly.

"What's the *only* way to get light, short of a sun?"

"How should I know?"

They were standing face to face and nose to nose.

Sheerin said, "You burn something, mister. Ever see a forest fire? Ever go camping and cook a stew over a wood fire? Heat isn't the only thing burning wood gives off, you know. It gives off light, and people know that. And when it's dark they want light, and they're going to *get* it."

"So they burn wood?"

"So they burn whatever they can get. They've got to have light. They've got to burn something, and wood isn't handy—so they'll burn whatever is nearest. They'll have their light—and every center of habitation goes up in flames!"

Eyes held each other as though the whole matter were a personal affair of respective will powers, and then Theremon broke away wordlessly. His breathing was harsh and ragged, and he scarcely noted the sudden hubbub that came from the adjoining room behind the closed door.

Sheerin spoke, and it was with an effort that he made it sound matter-of-fact. "I think I heard Yimot's voice. He and Faro are probably back. Let's go in and see what kept them."

"Might as well!" muttered Theremon. He drew a long breath and seemed to shake himself. The tension was broken.

The room was in an uproar, with members of the staff clustering about two young men who were removing outer garments even as they parried the miscellany of questions being thrown at them.

Aton bustled through the crowd and faced the new-comers angrily. "Do you realize that it's less than half an hour before deadline? Where have you two been?"

Faro 24 seated himself and rubbed his hands. His cheeks were red with the outdoor chill. "Yimot and I have just finished carrying through a little crazy experiment of our own. We've been trying to see if we couldn't construct an arrangement by which we could simulate the appearance of Darkness and Stars so as to get an advance notion as to how it looked."

There was a confused murmur from the listeners, and a sudden look of interest entered Aton's eyes. "There wasn't anything said of this before. How did you go about it?"

"Well," said Faro, "the idea came to Yimot and myself long ago, and we've been working it out in our spare time. Yimot knew of a low one-story house down in the city with a domed roof—it had once been used as a museum, I think. Anyway, we bought it—"

"Where did you get the money?" interrupted Aton peremptorily.

"Our bank accounts," grunted Yimot 70. "It cost two thousand credits." Then, defensively, "Well, what of it? Tomorrow, two thousand credits will be two thousand pieces of paper. That's all."

"Sure," agreed Faro. "We bought the place and rigged it up with black velvet from top to bottom so as to get as perfect a Darkness as possible. Then we punched tiny holes in the ceiling and through the roof and covered them with little metal caps, all of which could be shoved aside simultaneously at the close of a switch. At least we didn't do that part ourselves; we got a carpenter and an electrician and some others—money didn't count. The point was that we could get the light to shine through those holes in the roof, so that we could get a starlike effect."

Not a breath was drawn during the pause that followed. Aton said stiffly, "You had no right to make a private—"

Faro seemed abashed. "I know, sir—but, frankly, Yimot and I thought the experiment was a little dangerous. If the effect really worked, we half expected to go mad—from what Sheerin says about all this, we thought that would be rather likely. We wanted to take the risk ourselves. Of course if we found we could retain sanity, it occurred to us that we might develop immunity to the real thing, and then expose the rest of you the same way. But things didn't work out at all—"

"Why, what happened?"

It was Yimot who answered. "We shut ourselves in and allowed our eyes to get accustomed to the dark. It's an extremely creepy feeling because the total Darkness makes you feel as if the walls and ceiling are crushing in on you. But we got over that and pulled the switch. The caps fell away and the roof glittered all over with little dots of light—"

"Well?"

"Well—nothing. That was the whacky part of it. Nothing happened. It was just a roof with holes in it, and that's just what it looked like. We tried it over and over again—that's what kept us so late—but there just isn't any effect at all."

There followed a shocked silence, and all eyes turned to Sheerin, who sat motionless, mouth open.

Theremon was the first to speak. "You know what this does to this whole theory you've built up, Sheerin, don't you?" He was grinning with relief.

But Sheerin raised his hand. "Now wait a while. Just let me think this through." And then he snapped his fingers, and when he lifted his head there was neither surprise nor uncertainty in his eyes. "Of course—"

He never finished. From somewhere up above there sounded a sharp clang, and Beenay, starting to his feet, dashed up the stairs with a "What the devil!"

The rest followed after.

Things happened quickly. Once up in the dome,

Beenay cast one horrified glance at the shattered photographic plates and at the man bending over them; and then hurled himself fiercely at the intruder, getting a death grip on his throat. There was a wild threshing, and as others of the staff joined in, the stranger was swallowed up and smothered under the weight of half a dozen angry men.

Aton came up last, breathing heavily. "Let him up!"

There was a reluctant unscrambling and the stranger, panting harshly, with his clothes torn and his forehead bruised, was hauled to his feet. He had a short yellow beard curled elaborately in the style affected by the Cultists.

Beenay shifted his hold to a collar grip and shook the man savagely. "All right, rat, what's the idea? These plates—"

"I wasn't after *them*," retorted the Cultist coldly. "That was an accident."

Beenay followed his glowering stare and snarled, "I see. You were after the cameras themselves. The accident with the plates was a stroke of luck for you, then. If you had touched Snapping Bertha or any of the others, you would have died by slow torture. As it is—" He drew his fist back.

Aton grabbed his sleeve. "Stop that! Let him go!"

The young technician wavered, and his arm dropped reluctantly. Aton pushed him aside and confronted the Cultist. "You're Latimer, aren't you?"

The Cultist bowed stiffly and indicated the symbol upon his hip. "I am Latimer 25, adjutant of the third class to his serenity, Sor 5."

"And"—Aton's white eyebrows lifted—"you were with his serenity when he visited me last week, weren't you?"

Latimer bowed a second time.

"Now, then, what do you want?"

"Nothing that you would give me of your own free will."

"Sor 5 sent you, I suppose—or is this your own idea?"

"I won't answer that question."

"Will there be any further visitors?"

"I won't answer that, either."

Aton glanced at his timepiece and scowled. "Now, man, what is it your master wants of me? I have fulfilled my end of the bargain."

Latimer smiled faintly, but said nothing.

"I asked him," continued Aton angrily, "for data only the Cult could supply, and it was given to me. For that, thank you. In return I promised to prove the essential truth of the creed of the Cult."

"There was no need to prove that," came the proud retort. "It stands proven by the *Book of Revelations*."

"For the handful that constitute the Cult, yes. Don't pretend to mistake my meaning. I offered to present scientific backing for your beliefs. And I did!"

The Cultist's eyes narrowed bitterly. "Yes, you did —with a fox's subtlety, for your pretended explanation backed our beliefs, and at the same time removed all necessity for them. You made of the Darkness and of the Stars a natural phenomenon and removed all its real significance. That was blasphemy."

"If so, the fault isn't mine. The facts exist. What can I do but state them?"

"Your 'facts' are a fraud and a delusion."

Aton stamped angrily. "How do you know?"

And the answer came with the certainty of absolute faith. "I know!"

The director purpled and Beenay whispered urgently. Aton waved him silent. "And what does Sor 5 want us to do? He still thinks, I suppose, that in trying to warn the world to take measures against the menace of madness, we are placing innumerable souls in jeopardy. We aren't succeeding, if that means anything to him."

"The attempt itself has done harm enough, and your

vicious effort to gain information by means of your devilish instruments must be stopped. We obey the will of the Stars, and I only regret that my clumsiness prevented me from wrecking your infernal devices."

"It wouldn't have done you too much good," returned Aton. "All our data, except for the direct evidence we intend collecting right now, is already safely cached and well beyond possibility of harm." He smiled grimly. "But that does not affect your present status as an attempted burglar and criminal."

He turned to the men behind him. "Someone call the police at Saro City."

There was a cry of distaste from Sheerin. "Damn it, Aton, what's wrong with you? There's no time for that. Here"—he bustled his way forward—"let me handle this."

Aton stared down his nose at the psychologist. "This is not the time for your monkeyshines, Sheerin. Will you please let me handle this my own way? Right now you are a complete outsider here, and don't forget it."

Sheerin's mouth twisted eloquently. "Now why should we go to the impossible trouble of calling the police—with Beta's eclipse a matter of minutes from now—when this young man here is perfectly willing to pledge his word of honor to remain and cause no trouble whatsoever?"

The Cultist answered promptly, "I will do no such thing. You're free to do what you want, but it's only fair to warn you that just as soon as I can get my chance I'm going to finish what I came out here to do. If it's my word of honor you're relying on, you'd better call the police."

Sheerin smiled in a friendly fashion. "You're a determined cuss, aren't you? Well, I'll explain something. Do you see that young man at the window? He's a strong, husky fellow, quite handy with his fists, and he's an outsider besides. Once the eclipse starts there will be nothing for him to do except keep an eye on

you. Besides him, there will be myself—a little too
stout for active fisticuffs, but still able to help."

"Well, what of it?" demanded Latimer frozenly.

"Listen and I'll tell you," was the reply. "Just as
soon as the eclipse starts, we're going to take you,
Theremon and I, and deposit you in a little closet with
one door, to which is attached one giant lock and no
windows. You will remain there for the duration."

"And afterward," breathed Latimer fiercely,
"there'll be no one to let me out. I know as well as you
do what the coming of the Stars means—I know it far
better than you. With all your minds gone, you are not
likely to free me. Suffocation or slow starvation, is it?
About what I might have expected from a group of
scientists. But I don't give my word. It's a matter of
principle, and I won't discuss it further."

Aton seemed perturbed. His faded eyes were troubled. "Really, Sheerin, locking him—"

"Please!" Sheerin motioned him impatiently to silence. "I don't think for a moment things will go that
far. Latimer has just tried a clever little bluff, but I'm
not a psychologist just because I like the sound of the
word." He grinned at the Cultist. "Come now, you
don't really think I'm trying anything as crude as slow
starvation. My dear Latimer, if I lock you in the
closet, you are not going to see the Darkness, and you
are not going to see the Stars. It does not take much
knowledge of the fundamental creed of the Cult to
realize that for you to be hidden from the Stars when
they appear means the loss of your immortal soul.
Now, I believe you to be an honorable man. I'll accept
your word of honor to make no further effort to dis-
rupt proceedings, if you'll offer it."

A vein throbbed in Latimer's temple, and he seemed
to shrink within himself as he said thickly, "You have
it!" And then he added with swift fury, "But it is my
consolation that you will all be damned for your deeds
of today." He turned on his heel and stalked to the
high three-legged stool by the door.

Sheerin nodded to the columnist. "Take a seat next to him, Theremon—just as a formality. Hey, Theremon!"

But the newspaperman didn't move. He had gone pale to the lips. "Look at that!" The finger he pointed toward the sky shook, and his voice was dry and cracked.

There was one simultaneous gasp as every eye followed the pointing finger and, for one breathless moment, stared frozenly.

Beta was chipped on one side!

The tiny bit of encroaching blackness was perhaps the width of a fingernail, but to the staring watchers it magnified itself into the crack of doom.

Only for a moment they watched, and after that there was a shrieking confusion that was even shorter of duration and which gave way to an orderly scurry of activity—each man at his prescribed job. At the crucial moment there was no time for emotion. The men were merely scientists with work to do. Even Aton had melted away.

Sheerin said prosaically, "First contact must have been made fifteen minutes ago. A little early, but pretty good considering the uncertainties involved in the calculation." He looked about him and then tiptoed to Theremon, who still remained staring out the window, and dragged him away gently.

"Aton is furious," he whispered, "so stay away. He missed first contact on account of this fuss with Latimer, and if you get in his way he'll have you thrown out the window."

Theremon nodded shortly and sat down. Sheerin stared in surprise at him.

"The devil, man," he exclaimed, "you're shaking."

"Eh?" Theremon licked dry lips and then tried to smile. "I don't feel very well, and that's a fact."

The psychologist's eyes hardened. "You're not losing your nerve?"

"No!" cried Theremon in a flash of indignation.

"Give me a chance, will you? I haven't really believed this rigmarole—not way down beneath, anyway—till just this minute. Give me a chance to get used to the idea. You've been preparing yourself for two months or more."

"You're right, at that," replied Sheerin thoughtfully. "Listen! Have you got a family—parents, wife, children?"

Theremon shook his head. "You mean the Hideout, I suppose. No, you don't have to worry about that. I have a sister, but she's two thousand miles away. I don't even know her exact address."

"Well, then, what about yourself? You've got time to get there, and they're one short anyway, since I left. After all, you're not needed here, and you'd make a darned fine addition—"

Theremon looked at the other wearily. "You think I'm scared stiff, don't you? Well, get this, mister, I'm a newspaperman and I've been assigned to cover a story. I intend covering it."

There was a faint smile on the psychologist's face. "I see. Professional honor, is that it?"

"You might call it that. But, man, I'd give my right arm for another bottle of that sockeroo juice even half the size of the one you hogged. If ever a fellow needed a drink, I do."

He broke off. Sheerin was nudging him violently. "Do you hear that? Listen!"

Theremon followed the motion of the other's chin and stared at the Cultist, who, oblivious to all about him, faced the window, a look of wild elation on his face, droning to himself the while in singsong fashion.

"What's he saying?" whispered the columnist.

"He's quoting *Book of Revelations,* fifth chapter," replied Sheerin. Then, urgently, "Keep quiet and listen, I tell you."

The Cultist's voice had risen in a sudden increase of fervor: " 'And it came to pass that in those days the Sun, Beta, held lone vigil in the sky for ever longer periods as the revolutions passed; until such time as for full half a revolution, it alone, shrunken and cold, shone down upon Lagash.

" 'And men did assemble in the public squares and in the highways, there to debate and to marvel at the sight, for a strange depression had seized them. Their minds were troubled and their speech confused, for the souls of men awaited the coming of the Stars.

" 'And in the city of Trigon, at high noon, Vendret 2 came forth and said unto the men of Trigon, "Lo, ye sinners! Though ye scorn the ways of righteousness, yet will the time of reckoning come. Even now the Cave approaches to swallow Lagash; yea, and all it contains."

" 'And even as he spoke the lip of the Cave of Darkness passed the edge of Beta so that to all Lagash it was hidden from sight. Loud were the cries of men as it vanished, and great the fear of soul that fell upon them.

" 'It came to pass that the Darkness of the Cave fell upon Lagash, and there was no light on all the surface of Lagash. Men were even as blinded, nor could one man see his neighbor, though he felt his breath upon his face.

" 'And in this blackness there appeared the Stars, in countless numbers, and to the strains of music of such beauty that the very leaves of the trees cried out in wonder.

" 'And in that moment the souls of men departed from them, and their abandoned bodies became even as beasts; yea, even as brutes of the wild; so that through the blackened streets of the cities of Lagash they prowled with wild cries.

" 'From the Stars there then reached down the Heavenly Flame, and where it touched, the cities of Lagash flamed to utter destruction, so that of man and of the works of man nought remained.

" 'Even then—' "

There was a subtle change in Latimer's tone. His

eyes had not shifted, but somehow he had become aware of the absorbed attention of the other two. Easily, without pausing for breath, the timbre of his voice shifted and the syllables became more liquid.

Theremon, caught by surprise, stared. The words seemed on the border of familiarity. There was un elusive shift in the accent, a tiny change in the vowel stress; nothing more—yet Latimer had become thoroughly unintelligible.

Sheerin smiled slyly. "He shifted to some old-cycle tongue, probably their traditional second cycle. That was the language in which the *Book of Revelations* was originally written, you know."

"It doesn't matter; I've heard enough." Theremon shoved his chair back and brushed his hair back with hands that no longer shook. "I feel much better now."

"You do?" Sheerin seemed mildly surprised.

"I'll say I do. I had a bad case of jitters just a while back. Listening to you and your gravitation and seeing that eclipse start almost finished me. But this"—he jerked a contemptuous thumb at the yellow-bearded Cultist—"*this* is the sort of thing my nurse used to tell me. I've been laughing at that sort of thing all my life. I'm not going to let it scare me *now*."

He drew a deep breath and said with a hectic gaiety. "But if I expect to keep on the good side of myself, I'm going to turn my chair away from the window."

Sheerin said, "Yes, but you'd better talk lower. Aton just lifted his head out of that box he's got it stuck into and gave you a look that should have killed you."

Theremon made a mouth. "I forgot about the old fellow." With elaborate care he turned the chair from the window, cast one distasteful look over his shoulder, and said, "It has occurred to me that there must be considerable immunity against this Star madness."

The psychologist did not answer immediately. Beta was past its zenith now, and the square of bloody sunlight that outlined the window upon the floor had lifted into Sheerin's lap. He stared at its dusky color thoughtfully and then bent and squinted into the sun itself.

The chip in its side had grown to a black encroachment that covered a third of Beta. He shuddered, and when he straightened once more his florid cheeks did not contain quite as much color as they had had previously.

With a smile that was almost apologetic, he reversed his chair also. "There are probably two million people in Saro City that are all trying to join the Cult at once in one gigantic revival." Then, ironically, "The Cult is in for an hour of unexampled prosperity. I trust they'll make the most of it. Now, what was it you said?"

"Just this. How do the Cultists manage to keep the *Book of Revelations* going from cycle to cycle, and how on Lagash did it get written in the first place? There must have been some sort of immunity, for if everyone had gone mad, who would be left to write the book?"

Sheerin stared at his questioner ruefully. "Well, now, young man, there isn't any eyewitness answer to that, but we've got a few damned good notions as to what happened. You see, there are three kinds of people who might remain relatively unaffected. First, the very few who don't see the Stars at all: the blind, those who drink themselves into a stupor at the beginning of the eclipse and remain so to the end. We leave them out—because they aren't really witnesses.

"Then there are children below six, to whom the world as a whole is too new and strange for them to be too frightened at Stars and Darkness. They would be just another item in an already surprising world. You see that, don't you?"

The other nodded doubtfully. "I suppose so."

"Lastly, there are those whose minds are too coarsely grained to be entirely toppled. The very insensitive would be scarcely affected—oh, such people as some of our older, work-broken peasants. Well, the children would have fugitive memories, and that, combined with the confused, incoherent babblings of the half-mad morons, formed the basis for the *Book of Revelations.*

"Naturally, the book was based, in the first place, on the testimony of those least qualified to serve as historians; that is, children and morons; and was probably edited and re-edited through the cycles."

"Do you suppose," broke in Theremon, "that they carried the book through the cycles the way we're planning on handing on the secret of gravitation?"

Sheerin shrugged. "Perhaps, but their exact method is unimportant. They do it, somehow. The point I was getting at was that the book can't help but be a mass of distortion, even if it is based on fact. For instance, do you remember the experiment with the holes in the roof that Faro and Yimot tried—the one that didn't work?"

"Yes."

"You know why it didn't w—" He stopped and rose in alarm, for Aton was approaching, his face a twisted mask of consternation. *"What's happened?"*

Aton drew him aside and Sheerin could feel the fingers on his elbow twitching.

"Not so loud!" Aton's voice was low and tortured. "I've just gotten word from the Hideout on the private line."

Sheerin broke in anxiously. "They are in trouble?"

"Not *they*," Aton stressed the pronoun significantly. "They sealed themselves off just a while ago, and they're going to stay buried till day after tomorrow. They're safe. But the *city*, Sheerin—it's a shambles. You have no idea—" He was having difficulty in speaking.

"Well?" snapped Sheerin impatiently. "What of it? It will get worse. What are you shaking about?" Then, suspiciously, "How do you feel?"

Aton's eyes sparked angrily at the insinuation, and then faded to anxiety once more. "You don't understand. The Cultists are active. They're rousing the peo-

ple to storm the Observatory—promising them immediate entrance into grace, promising them salvation, promising them anything. What are we to do,
Sheerin?"

Sheerin's head bent, and he stared in long abstraction at his toes. He tapped his chin with one knuckle,
then looked up and said crisply, "Do? What is there to
do? Nothing at all. Do the men know of this?"

"No, of course not!"

"Good! Keep it that way. How long till totality?"

"Not quite an hour."

"There's nothing to do but gamble. It will take time
to organize any really formidable mob, and it will take
more time to get them out here. We're a good five
miles from the city—"

He glared out the window, down the slopes to where
the farmed patches gave way to clumps of white
houses in the suburbs; down to where the metropolis
itself was a blur on the horizon—a mist in the waning
blaze of Beta.

He repeated without turning, "It will take time.
Keep on working and pray that totality comes first."

Beta was cut in half, the line of division pushing a
slight concavity into the still-bright portion of the Sun.
It was like a gigantic eyelid shutting slantwise over the
light of a world.

The faint clatter of the room in which he stood
faded into oblivion, and he sensed only the thick silence of the fields outside. The very insects seemed
frightened mute. And things were dim.

He jumped at the voice in his ear. Theremon said,
"Is something wrong?"

"Er? Er—no. Get back to the chair. We're in the
way." They slipped back to their corner, but the psychologist did not speak for a time. He lifted a finger
and loosened his collar. He twisted his neck back and
forth but found no relief. He looked up suddenly.

"Are you having any difficulty in breathing?"

The newspaperman opened his eyes wide and drew two or three long breaths. "No. Why?"

"I looked out the window too long, I suppose. The dimness got me. Difficulty in breathing is one of the first symptoms of a claustrophobic attack."

Theremon drew another long breath. "Well, it hasn't got me yet. Say, here's another of the fellows."

Beenay had interposed his bulk between the light and the pair in the corner, and Sheerin squinted up at him anxiously. "Hello, Beenay."

The astronomer shifted his weight to the other foot and smiled feebly. "You won't mind if I sit down awhile and join in the talk? My cameras are set, and there's nothing to do till totality." He paused and eyed the Cultist, who fifteen minutes earlier had drawn a small, skin-bound book from his sleeve and had been poring intently over it ever since. "That rat hasn't been making trouble, has he?"

Sheerin shook his head. His shoulders were thrown back and he frowned his concentration as he forced himself to breathe regularly. He said, "Have you had any trouble breathing, Beenay?"

Beenay sniffed the air in his turn. "It doesn't seem stuffy to me."

"A touch of claustrophobia," explained Sheerin apologetically.

"Ohhh! It worked itself differently with me. I get the impression that my eyes are going back on me. Things seem to blur and—well, nothing is clear. And it's cold, too."

"Oh, it's cold, all right. That's no illusion." Theremon grimaced. "My toes feel as if I've been shipping them cross-country in a refrigerating car."

"What we need," put in Sheerin, "is to keep our minds busy with extraneous affairs. I was telling you a while ago, Theremon, why Faro's experiments with the holes in the roof came to nothing."

"You were just beginning," replied Theremon. He

encircled a knee with both arms and nuzzled his chin against it.

"Well, as I started to say, they were misled by taking the *Book of Revelations* literally. There probably wasn't any sense in attaching any physical significance to the Stars. It might be, you know, that in the presence of total Darkness, the mind finds it absolutely necessary to create light. This illusion of light might be all the Stars there really are."

"In other words," interposed Theremon, "you mean the Stars are the results of the madness and not one of the causes. Then, what good will Beenay's photographs be?"

"To prove that it is an illusion, maybe; or to prove the opposite; for all I know. Then again——"

But Beenay had drawn his chair closer, and there was an expression of sudden enthusiasm on his face. "Say, I'm glad you two got onto this subject." His eyes narrowed and he lifted one finger. "I've been thinking about these Stars and I've got a really cute notion. Of course it's strictly ocean foam, and I'm not trying to advance it seriously, but I think it's interesting. Do you want to hear it?"

He seemed half reluctant, but Sheerin leaned back and said, "Go ahead! I'm listening."

"Well, then, supposing there were other suns in the universe." He broke off a little bashfully. "I mean suns that are so far away that they're too dim to see. It sounds as if I've been reading some of that fantastic fiction, I suppose."

"Not necessarily. Still, isn't that possibility eliminated by the fact that, according to the Law of Gravitation, they would make themselves evident by their attractive forces?"

"Not if they were far enough off," rejoined Beenay, "really far off—maybe as much as four light years, or even more. We'd never be able to detect perturbations then, because they'd be too small. Say that there were a lot of suns that far off; a dozen or two, maybe."

Theremon whistled melodiously. "What an idea for a good Sunday supplement article. Two dozen suns in a universe eight lights years across. Wow! That would shrink our world into insignificance. The readers would eat it up."

"Only an idea," said Beenay with a grin, "but you see the point. During an eclipse, these dozen suns would become visible because there'd be no *real* sunlight to drown them out. Since they're so far off, they'd appear small, like so many little marbles. Of course the Cultists talk of millions of Stars, but that's probably exaggeration. There just isn't any place in the universe you could put a million suns—unless they touch one another."

Sheerin had listened with gradually increasing interest. "You've hit something there, Beenay. And exaggeration is just exactly what would happen. Our minds, as you probably know, can't grasp directly any number higher than five; above that there is only the concept of 'many.' A dozen would become a million just like that. A damn good idea!"

"And I've got another cute little notion," Beenay said. "Have you ever thought what a simple problem gravitation would be if only you had a sufficiently simple system? Supposing you had a universe in which there was a planet with only one sun. The planet would travel in a perfect ellipse and the exact nature of the gravitational force would be so evident it could be accepted as an axiom. Astronomers on such a world would start off with gravity probably before they even invented the telescope. Naked-eye observation would be enough."

"But would such a system be dynamically stable?" questioned Sheerin doubtfully.

"Sure! They call it the 'one-and-one' case. It's been worked out mathematically, but it's the philosophical implications that interest me."

"It's nice to think about," admitted Sheerin, "as a

pretty abstraction—like a perfect gas, or absolute zero."

"Of course," continued Beenay, "there's the catch that life would be impossible on such a planet. It wouldn't get enough heat and light, and if it rotated there would be total Darkness half of each day. You couldn't expect life—which is fundamentally dependent upon light—to develop under those conditions. Besides—"

Sheerin's chair went over backward as he sprang to his feet in a rude interruption. "Aton's brought out the lights."

Beenay said, "Huh," turned to stare, and then grinned halfway around his head in open relief.

There were half a dozen foot-long, inch-thick rods cradled in Aton's arms. He glared over them at the assembled staff members.

"Get back to work, all of you. Sheerin, come here and help me!"

Sheerin trotted to the older man's side and, one by one, in utter silence, the two adjusted the rods in makeshift metal holders suspended from the walls.

With the air of one carrying through the most sacred item of a religious ritual, Sheerin scraped a large, clumsy match into spluttering life and passed it to Aton, who carried the flame to the upper end of one of the rods.

It hesitated there awhile, playing futilely about the tip, until a sudden, crackling flare cast Aton's lined face into yellow highlights. He withdrew the match and a spontaneous cheer rattled the window.

The rod was topped by six inches of wavering flame! Methodically, the other rods were lighted, until six independent fires turned the rear of the room yellow.

The light was dim, dimmer even than the tenuous sunlight. The flames reeled crazily, giving birth to drunken, swaying shadows. The torches smoked devilishly and smelled like a bad day in the kitchen. But they emitted yellow light.

There was something about yellow light, after four hours of somber, dimming Beta. Even Latimer had lifted his eyes from his book and stared in wonder.

Sheerin warmed his hands at the nearest, regardless of the soot that gathered upon them in a fine, gray powder, and muttered ecstatically to himself. "Beautiful! Beautiful! I never realized before what a wonderful color yellow is."

But Theremon regarded the torches suspiciously. He wrinkled his nose at the rancid odor and said, "What are those things?"

"Wood," said Sheerin shortly.

"Oh, no, they're not. They aren't burning. The top inch is charred and the flame just keeps shooting up out of nothing."

"That's the beauty of it. This is a really efficient artificial-light mechanism. We made a few hundred of them, but most went to the Hideout, of course. You see"—he turned and wiped his blackened hands upon his handkerchief—"you take the pithy core of coarse water reeds, dry them thoroughly, and soak them in animal grease. Then you set fire to it and the grease burns, little by little. These torches will burn for almost half an hour without stopping. Ingenious, isn't it? It was developed by one of our own young men at Saro University."

After the momentary sensation, the dome had quieted. Latimer had carried his chair directly beneath a torch and continued reading, lips moving in the monotonous recital of invocations to the Stars. Beenay had drifted away to his cameras once more, and Theremon seized the opportunity to add to his notes on the article he was going to write for the Saro City *Chronicle* the next day—a procedure he had been following for the last two hours in a perfectly methodical, perfectly conscientious and, as he was well aware, perfectly meaningless fashion.

But, as the gleam of amusement in Sheerin's eyes indicated, careful note-taking occupied his mind with

something other than the fact that the sky was gradually turning a horrible deep purple-red, as if it were
one gigantic, freshly peeled beet; and so it fulfilled its
purpose.

The air grew, somehow, denser. Dusk, like a palpa-
ble entity, entered the room, and the dancing circle of
yellow light about the torches etched itself into ever-
sharper distinction against the gathering grayness beyond. There was the odor of smoke and the presence
of little chuckling sounds that the torches made as they
burned; the soft pad of one of the men circling the
table at which he worked, on hesitant tiptoes; the occa-
sional indrawn breath of someone trying to retain com-
posure in a world that was retreating into the shadow.

It was Theremon who first heard the extraneous
noise. It was a vague, unorganized *impression* of sound
that would have gone unnoticed but for the dead silence that prevailed within the dome.

The newsman sat upright and replaced his notebook. He held his breath and listened; then, with considerable reluctance, threaded his way between the solarscope and one of Beenay's cameras and stood before the window.

The silence ripped to fragments at his startled
shout: *"Sheerin!"*

Work stopped! The psychologist was at his side in a
moment. Aton joined him. Even Yimot 70, high in his
little lean-back seat at the eyepiece of the gigantic solarscope, paused and looked downward.

Outside, Beta was a mere smoldering splinter, taking
one last desperate look at Lagash. The eastern horizon, in the direction of the city, was lost in Darkness,
and the road from Saro to the Observatory was a
dull-red line bordered on both sides by wooded tracts,
the trees of which had somehow lost individuality and
merged into a continuous shadowy mass.

But it was the highway itself that held attention, for
along it there surged another, and infinitely menacing,
shadowy mass.

Aton cried in a cracked voice, "The madmen from the city! They've come!"

"How long to totality?" demanded Sheerin.

"Fifteen minutes, but . . . but they'll be here in five."

"Never mind, keep the men working. We'll hold them off. This place is built like a fortress. Aton, keep an eye on our young Cultist just for luck. Theremon, come with me."

Sheerin was out the door, and Theremon was at his heels. The stairs stretched below them in tight, circular sweeps about the central shaft, fading into a dank and dreary grayness.

The first momentum of their rush had carried them fifty feet down, so that the dim, flickering yellow from the open door of the dome had disappeared and both above and below the same dusky shadow crushed in upon them.

Sheerin paused, and his pudgy hand clutched at his chest. His eyes bulged and his voice was a dry cough. "I can't . . . breathe. . . . Go down . . . yourself. Close all doors——"

Theremon took a few downward steps, then turned. "Wait! Can you hold out a minute?" He was panting himself. The air passed in and out his lungs like so much molasses, and there was a little germ of screeching panic in his mind at the thought of making his way into the mysterious Darkness below by himself.

Theremon, after all, was afraid of the dark!

"Stay here," he said. "I'll be back in a second." He dashed upward two steps at a time, heart pounding—not altogether from the exertion—tumbled into the dome and snatched a torch from its holder. It was foul-smelling, and the smoke smarted his eyes almost blind, but he clutched that torch as if he wanted to kiss it for joy, and its flame streamed backward as he hurtled down the stairs again.

Sheerin opened his eyes and moaned as Theremon

bent over him. Theremon shook him roughly. "All right, get a hold on yourself. We've got light."

He held the torch at tiptoe height and, propping the tottering psychologist by an elbow, made his way downward in the middle of the protecting circle of illumination.

The offices on the ground floor still possessed what light there was, and Theremon felt the horror about him relax.

"Here," he said brusquely, and passed the torch to Sheerin. "You can hear *them* outside."

And they could. Little scraps of hoarse, wordless shouts.

But Sheerin was right; the Observatory was built like a fortress. Erected in the last century, when the neo-Gavottian style of architecture was at its ugly height, it had been designed for stability and durability rather than for beauty.

The windows were protected by the grillwork of inch-thick iron bars sunk deep into the concrete sills. The walls were solid masonry that an earthquake couldn't have touched, and the main door was a huge oaken slab reinforced with iron. Theremon shot the bolts and they slid shut with a dull clang.

At the other end of the corridor, Sheerin cursed weakly. He pointed to the lock of the back door which had been neatly jimmied into uselessness.

"That must be how Latimer got in," he said.

"Well, don't stand there," cried Theremon impatiently. "Help drag up the furniture—and keep that torch out of my eyes. The smoke's killing me."

He slammed the heavy table up against the door as he spoke, and in two minutes had built a barricade which made up for what it lacked in beauty and symmetry by the sheer inertia of its massiveness.

Somewhere, dimly, far off, they could hear the battering of naked fists upon the door; and the screams and yells from outside had a sort of half reality.

That mob had set off from Saro City with only two

things in mind: the attainment of Cultist salvation by
the destruction of the Observatory, and a maddening
fear that all but paralyzed them. There was no time to
think of ground cars, or of weapons, or of leadership,
or even of organization. They made for the Observatory on foot and assaulted it with bare hands.

And now that they were there, the last flash of Beta,
the last ruby-red drop of flame, flickered feebly over a
humanity that had left only stark, universal fear!

Theremon groaned, "Let's get back to the dome!"

In the dome, only Yimot, at the solarscope, had
kept his place. The rest were clustered about the cameras, and Beenay was giving his instructions in a
hoarse, strained voice.

"Get it straight, all of you. I'm snapping Beta just
before totality and changing the plate. That will leave
one of you to each camera. You all know about . . .
about times of exposure—"

There was a breathless murmur of agreement.

Beenay passed a hand over his eyes. "Are the
torches still burning? Never mind, I see them!" He was
leaning hard against the back of a chair. "Now remember, don't . . . don't try to look for good shots. Don't
waste time trying to get t-two stars at a time in the
scope field. One is enough. And . . . and if you feel
yourself going *get away from the camera.*"

At the door, Sheerin whispered to Theremon, "Take
me to Aton. I don't see him."

The newsman did not answer immediately. The
vague forms of the astronomers wavered and blurred,
and the torches overhead had become only yellow
splotches.

"It's dark," he whimpered.

Sheerin held out his hand. "Aton." He stumbled forward. "Aton!"

Theremon stepped after and seized his arm. "Wait,
I'll take you." Somehow he made his way across the

room. He closed his eyes against the Darkness and his mind against the chaos within it.

No one heard them or paid attention to them. Sheerin stumbled against the wall. "Aton!"

The psychologist felt shaking hands touching him, then withdrawing, and a voice muttering, "Is that you, Sheerin?"

"Aton!" He strove to breathe normally. "Don't worry about the mob. The place will hold them off."

Latimer, the Cultist, rose to his feet, and his face twisted in desperation. His word was pledged, and to break it would mean placing his soul in mortal peril. Yet that word had been forced from him and had not been given freely. The Stars would come soon! He could not stand by and allow— And yet his word was pledged.

Beenay's face was dimly flushed as it looked upward at Beta's last ray, and Latimer, seeing him bend over his camera, made his decision. His nails cut the flesh of his palms as he tensed himself.

He staggered crazily as he started his rush. There was nothing before him but shadows; the very floor beneath his feet lacked substance. And then someone was upon him and he went down with clutching fingers at his throat.

He doubled his knee and drove it hard into his assailant. "Let me up or I'll kill you."

Theremon cried out sharply and muttered through a blinding haze of pain. "You double-crossing rat!"

The newsman seemed conscious of everything at once. He heard Beenay croak, "I've got it. At your cameras, men!" and then there was the strange awareness that the last thread of sunlight had thinned out and snapped.

Simultaneously he heard one last choking gasp from Beenay, and a queer little cry from Sheerin, a hysterical giggle that cut off in a rasp—and a sudden silence, a strange, deadly silence from outside.

And Latimer had gone limp in his loosening grasp.

Theremon peered into the Cultist's eyes and saw the blankness of them, staring upward, mirroring the feeble yellow of the torches. He saw the bubble of froth upon Latimer's lips and heard the low animal whimper in Latimer's throat.

With the slow fascination of fear, he lifted himself on one arm and turned his eyes toward the blood-curdling blackness of the window.

Through it shone the Stars!

Not Earth's feeble thirty-six hundred Stars visible to the eye; Lagash was in the center of a giant cluster. Thirty thousand mighty suns shone down in a soul-searing splendor that was more frighteningly cold in its awful indifference than the bitter wind that shivered across the cold, horribly bleak world.

Theremon staggered to his feet, his throat constricting him to breathlessness, all the muscles of his body writhing in an intensity of terror and sheer fear beyond bearing. He was going mad and knew it, and somewhere deep inside a bit of sanity was screaming, struggling to fight off the hopeless flood of black terror. It was very horrible to go mad and know that you were going mad—to know that in a little minute you would be here physically and yet all the real essence would be dead and drowned in the black madness. For this was the Dark—the Dark and the Cold and the Doom. The bright walls of the universe were shattered and their awful black fragments were falling down to crush and squeeze and obliterate him.

He jostled someone crawling on hands and knees, but stumbled somehow over him. Hands groping at his tortured throat, he limped toward the flame of the torches that filled all his mad vision.

"Light!" he screamed.

Aton, somewhere, was crying, whimpering horribly like a terribly frightened child. "Stars—all the Stars— we didn't know at all. We didn't know anything. We thought six stars in a universe is something the Stars didn't notice is Darkness forever and ever and ever and the walls are breaking in and we didn't know we couldn't know and anything—"

Someone clawed at the torch, and it fell and snuffed out. In the instant, the awful splendor of the indifferent Stars leaped nearer to them.

On the horizon outside the window, in the direction of Saro City, a crimson glow began growing, strengthening in brightness, that was not the glow of a sun.

The long night had come again.

THE MILLION-YEAR PICNIC

by Ray Bradbury

Ray Bradbury's Mars is not meant to be taken
as seriously as Alan Nourse's Mercury, or even
Clifford D. Simak's Jupiter, in the story that
follows this one. It is an imaginary planet, which
does not even try to fit itself into the picture
that astronomers have of the real Mars. But
once again, this is in a great tradition——the
tradition of Edgar Rice Burroughs, Leigh Brack-
ett, and many others who have written about
a Mars where human beings could live and
breathe and have memorable adventures.

SOMEHOW THE IDEA WAS BROUGHT UP BY MOM THAT
perhaps the whole family would enjoy a fishing trip.
But they weren't Mom's words; Timothy knew that.
They were Dad's words, and Mom used them for him
somehow.

Dad shuffled his feet in a clutter of Martian pebbles
and agreed. So immediately there was a tumult and a
shouting, and very quickly the camp was tucked into
capsules and containers, Mom slipped into traveling
jumpers and blouse, Dad stuffed his pipe full with
trembling hands, his eyes on the Martian sky, and the
three boys piled yelling into the motorboat, none of
them really keeping an eye on Mom and Dad, except
Timothy.

Dad pushed a stud. The water boat sent a humming sound up into the sky. The water shook back and the boat nosed ahead, and the family cried "Hurrah!"

Timothy sat in the back of the boat with Dad, his small fingers atop Dad's hairy ones, watching the canal twist, leaving the crumbled place behind where they had landed in their small family rocket all the way from Earth. He remembered the night before they left Earth, the hustling and hurrying, the rocket that Dad had found somewhere, somehow, and the talk of a vacation on Mars. A long way to go for a vacation, but Timothy said nothing because of his younger brothers. They came to Mars and now, first thing, or so they said, they were going fishing.

Dad had a funny look in his eyes as the boat went up-canal. A look that Timothy couldn't figure. It was made of strong light and maybe a sort of relief. It made the deep wrinkles laugh instead of worry or cry.

So there went the cooling rocket, around a bend, gone.

"How far are we going?" Robert splashed his hand. It looked like a small crab jumping in the violet water.

Dad exhaled. "A million years."

"Gee," said Robert.

"Look, kids." Mother pointed one soft long arm. "There's a dead city."

They looked with fervent anticipation, and the dead city lay dead for them alone, drowsing in a hot silence of summer made on Mars by a Martian weatherman.

And Dad looked as if he was pleased that it was dead.

It was a futile spread of pink rocks sleeping on a rise of sand, a few tumbled pillars, one lonely shrine, and then the sweep of sand again. Nothing else for miles. A white desert around the canal and a blue desert over it.

Just then a bird flew up. Like a stone thrown across a blue pond, hitting, falling deep, and vanishing.

Dad got a frightened look when he saw it. "I thought it was a rocket."

Timothy looked at the deep ocean sky, trying to see Earth and the war and the ruined cities and the men killing each other since the day he was born. But he saw nothing. The war was as removed and far off as two flies battling to the death in the arch of a great high and silent cathedral. And just as senseless.

William Thomas wiped his forehead and felt the touch of his son's hand on his arm, like a young tarantula, thrilled. He beamed at his son. "How goes it, Timmy?"

"Fine, Dad."

Timothy hadn't quite figured out what was ticking inside the vast adult mechanism beside him. The man with the immense hawk nose, sunburnt, peeling—and the hot blue eyes like agate marbles you play with after school in summer back on Earth, and the long thick columnar legs in the loose riding breeches.

"What are you looking at so hard, Dad?"

"I was looking for Earthian logic, common sense, good government, peace, and responsibility."

"All that up there?"

"No. I didn't find it. It's not there anymore. Maybe it'll never be there again. Maybe we fooled ourselves that it was ever there."

"Huh?"

"See the fish," said Dad, pointing.

There rose a soprano clamor from all three boys as they rocked the boat arching their tender necks to see. They *oohed* and *ahed*. A silver ring fish floated by them, undulating, and closing like an iris, instantly, around food particles, to assimilate them.

Dad looked at it. His voice was deep and quiet.

"Just like war. War swims along, sees food, contracts. A moment later—Earth is gone."

"William," said Mom.

"Sorry," said Dad.

They sat still and felt the canal water rush cool,

swift, and glassy. The only sound was the motor hum, the glide of water, the sun expanding the air.

"When do we see the Martians?" cried Michael.

"Quite soon, perhaps," said Father. "Maybe tonight."

"Oh, but the Martians are a dead race now," said Mom.

"No, they're not. I'll show you some Martians, all right," Dad said presently.

Timothy scowled at that but said nothing. Everything was odd now. Vacations and fishing and looks between people.

The other boys were already engaged making shelves of their small hands and peering under them toward the seven-foot stone banks of the canal, watching for Martians.

"What do they look like?" demanded Michael.

"You'll know them when you see them." Dad sort of laughed, and Timothy saw a pulse beating time in his cheek.

Mother was slender and soft, with a woven plait of spun-gold hair over her head in a tiara, and eyes the color of the deep cool canal water where it ran in shadow, almost purple, with flecks of amber caught in it. You could see her thoughts swimming around in her eyes, like fish—some bright, some dark, some fast, quick, some slow and easy, and sometimes, like when she looked up where Earth was, being color and nothing else. She sat up in the boat's prow, one hand resting on the side, the other on the lap of her dark blue breeches, and a line of sunburnt soft neck showing where her blouse opened like a white flower.

She kept looking ahead to see what was there, and not being able to see it clearly enough, she looked backward toward her husband, and through his eyes, reflected then, she saw what was ahead; and since he added part of himself to this reflection, a determined firmness, her face relaxed and she accepted it and she turned back, knowing suddenly what to look for.

Timothy looked too. But all he saw was a straight pencil line of canal going violet through a wide shallow valley penned by low, eroded hills, and on until it fell over the sky's edge. And this canal went on and on, through cities that would have rattled like beetles in a dry skull if you shook them. A hundred or two hundred cities dreaming hot summer-day dreams and cool summer-night dreams. . . .

They had come millions of miles for this outing—to fish. But there had been a gun on the rocket. This was a vacation. But why all the food, more than enough to last them years and years, left hidden back there near the rocket? Vacation. Just behind the veil of the vacation was not a soft face of laughter, but something hard and bony and perhaps terrifying. Timothy could not lift the veil, and the two other boys were busy being ten and eight years old, respectively.

"No Martians yet. Nuts." Robert put his V-shaped chin on his hands and glared at the canal.

Dad had brought an atomic radio along, strapped to his wrist. It functioned on an old-fashioned principle: you held it against the bones near your ear and it vibrated singing or talking to you. Dad listened to it now. His face looked like one of those fallen Martian cities, caved in, sucked dry, almost dead.

Then he gave it to Mom to listen. Her lips dropped open.

"What—" Timothy started to question, but never finished what he wished to say.

For at that moment there were two titanic, marrow-jolting explosions that grew upon themselves, followed by a half dozen minor concussions.

Jerking his head up, Dad notched the boat speed higher immediately. The boat leaped and jounced and spanked. This shook Robert out of his funk and elicited yelps of frightened but ecstatic joy from Michael, who clung to Mom's legs and watched the water pour by his nose in a wet torrent.

Dad swerved the boat, cut speed, and ducked the

craft into a little branch canal and under an ancient, crumbling stone wharf that smelled of crab flesh. The boat rammed the wharf hard enough to throw them all forward, but no one was hurt, and Dad was already twisted to see if the ripples on the canal were enough to map their route into hiding. Water lines went across, lapped the stones, and rippled back to meet each other, settling, to be dappled by the sun. It all went away.

Dad listened. So did everybody.

Dad's breathing echoed like fists beating against the cold wet wharf stones. In the shadow, Mom's cat eyes just watched Father for some clue to what next.

Dad relaxed and blew out a breath, laughing at himself.

"The rocket, of course. I'm getting jumpy. The rocket."

Michael said, "What happened, Dad, what happened?"

"Oh, we just blew up our rocket, is all," said Timothy, trying to sound matter-of-fact. "I've heard rockets blown up before. Ours just blew."

"Why did we blow up our rocket?" asked Michael. "Huh, Dad?"

"It's part of the game, silly!" said Timothy.

"A game!" Michael and Robert loved the word.

"Dad fixed it so it would blow up and no one'd know where we landed or went! In case they ever came looking, see?"

"Oh boy, a secret!"

"Scared by my own rocket," admitted Dad to Mom. "I *am* nervous. It's silly to think there'll ever *be* any more rockets. Except *one,* perhaps, if Edwards and his wife get through with *their* ship."

He put his tiny radio to his ear again. After two minutes he dropped his hand as you would drop a rag.

"It's over at last," he said to Mom. "The radio just went off the atomic beam. Every other world station's gone. They dwindled down to a couple in the last few years. Now the air's completely silent. It'll probably remain silent."

"For how long?" asked Robert.

"Maybe—your great-grandchildren will hear it again," said Dad. He just sat there, and the children were caught in the center of his awe and defeat and resignation and acceptance.

Finally he put the boat out into the canal again, and they continued in the direction in which they had originally started.

It was getting late. Already the sun was down the sky, and a series of dead cities lay ahead of them.

Dad talked very quietly and gently to his sons. Many times in the past he had been brisk, distant, removed from them, but now he patted them on the head with just a word and they felt it.

"Mike, pick a city."

"What, Dad?"

"Pick a city, son. Any one of these cities we pass."

"All right," said Michael. "How do I pick?"

"Pick the one you like the most. You, too, Robert and Tim. Pick the city you like best."

"I want a city with Martians in it," said Michael.

"You'll have that," said Dad. "I promise." His lips were for the children, but his eyes were for Mom.

They passed six cities in twenty minutes. Dad didn't say anything more about the explosions; he seemed much more interested in having fun with his sons, keeping them happy, than anything else.

Michael liked the first city they passed, but this was vetoed because everyone doubted quick first judgments. The second city nobody liked. It was an Earthman's settlement, built of wood and already rotting into sawdust. Timothy liked the third city because it was large. The fourth and fifth were too small and the sixth brought acclaim from everyone, including Mother, who joined in the Gees, Goshes, and Look-at-thats!

There were fifty or sixty huge structures still standing, streets were dusty but paved, and you could see one or two old centrifugal fountains still pulsing wetly in the plazas. That was the only life—water leaping in the late sunlight.

"This is the city," said everybody.

Steering the boat to a wharf, Dad jumped out.

"Here we are. This is ours. This is where we live from now on!"

"From now on?" Michael was incredulous. He stood up, looking, and then turned to blink back at where the rocket used to be. "What about the rocket? What about Minnesota?"

"Here," said Dad.

He touched the small radio to Michael's blond head. "Listen."

Michael listened.

"Nothing," he said.

"That's right. Nothing. Nothing at all anymore. No more Minneapolis, no more rockets, no more Earth."

Michael considered the lethal revelation and began to sob little dry sobs.

"Wait a moment," said Dad the next instant. "I'm giving you a lot more in exchange, Mike!"

"What?" Michael held off the tears, curious, but quite ready to continue in case Dad's further revelation was as disconcerting as the original.

"I'm giving you this city, Mike. It's yours."

"Mine?"

"For you and Robert and Timothy, all three of you, to own for yourselves."

Timothy bounded from the boat. "Look, guys, all for *us!* All of *that!*" He was playing the game with Dad, playing it large and playing it well. Later, after it was all over and things had settled, he could go off by himself and cry for ten minutes. But now it was still a game, still a family outing, and the other kids must be kept playing.

Mike jumped out with Robert. They helped Mom.

"Be careful of your sister," said Dad, and nobody knew what he meant until later.

They hurried into the great pink-stoned city, whispering among themselves, because dead cities have a way of making you want to whisper, to watch the sun go down.

"In about five days," said Dad quietly, "I'll go back down to where our rocket was and collect the food hidden in the ruins there and bring it here; and I'll hunt for Bert Edwards and his wife and daughters there."

"Daughters?" asked Timothy. "How many?"

"I can see that'll cause trouble later." Mom nodded slowly.

"Girls." Michael made a face like an ancient Martian stone image. "Girls."

"Are they coming in a rocket too?"

"Yes. If they make it. Family rockets are made for travel to the Moon, not Mars. We were lucky we got through."

"Where did you get the rocket?" whispered Timothy, for the other boys were running ahead.

"I saved it. I saved it for twenty years, Tim. I had it hidden away, hoping I'd never have to use it. I suppose I should have given it to the government for the war, but I kept thinking about Mars. . . ."

"And a picnic?"

"Right. This is between you and me. When I saw everything was finishing on Earth, after I'd waited until the last moment, I packed us up. Bert Edwards had a ship hidden, too, but we decided it would be safer to take off separately, in case anyone tried to shoot us down."

"Why'd you blow up the rocket, Dad?"

"So we can't go back, ever. And so if any of those evil men ever come to Mars they won't know we're here."

"Is that why you looked up all the time?"

"Yes, it's silly. They won't follow us, ever. They

haven't anything to follow with. I'm being too careful, is all."

Michael came running back. "Is this really *our* city, Dad?"

"The whole darn planet belongs to us, kids. The whole darn planet."

They stood there, King of the Hill, Top of the Heap, Ruler of All They Surveyed, Unimpeachable Monarchs and Presidents, trying to understand what it meant to own a world and how big a world really was.

Night came quickly in the thin atmosphere, and Dad left them in the square by the pulsing fountain, went down to the boat, and came walking back carrying a stack of paper in his big hands.

He laid the papers in a clutter in an old courtyard and set them afire. To keep warm, they crouched around the blaze and laughed, and Timothy saw the little letters leap like frightened animals when the flames touched and engulfed them. The papers crinkled like an old man's skin, and the cremation surrounded innumerable words:

"GOVERNMENT BONDS; Business Graph, 1999; Religious Prejudice: An Essay; The Science of Logistics; Problems of the Pan-American Unity; Stock Report for July 3, 1998; The War Digest . . ."

Dad had insisted on bringing these papers for this purpose. He sat there and fed them into the fire, one by one, with satisfaction, and told his children what it all meant.

"It's time I told you a few things. I don't suppose it was fair, keeping so much from you. I don't know if you'll understand, but I have to talk, even if only part of it gets over to you."

He dropped a leaf in the fire.

"I'm burning a way of life, just like that way of life is being burned clean off Earth right now. Forgive me if I talk like a politician. I am, after all, a former state governor, and I was honest and they hated me for it. Life on Earth never settled down to doing anything very good. Science ran too far ahead of us too quickly, and the people got lost in a mechanical wilderness, like children making over pretty things, gadgets, helicopters, rockets; emphasizing the wrong items, emphasizing machines instead of how to run the machines. Wars got bigger and bigger and finally killed Earth. That's what the silent radio means. That's what we ran away from.

"We were lucky. There aren't any more rockets left. It's time you knew this isn't a fishing trip at all. I put off telling you. · Earth is gone. Interplanetary travel won't be back for centuries, maybe never. But that way of life proved itself wrong, and strangled itself with its own hands. You're young. I'll tell you this again every day until it sinks in."

He paused to feed more papers to the fire.

"Now we're alone. We and a handful of others who'll land in a few days. Enough to start over. Enough to turn away from all that back on Earth and strike out on a new line—"

The fire leaped up to emphasize his talking. And then all the papers were gone except one. All the laws and beliefs of Earth were burnt into small hot ashes which soon would be carried off in a wind.

Timothy looked at the last thing that Dad tossed in the fire. It was a map of the World, and it wrinkled and distorted itself hotly and went—flimpf—and was gone like a warm, black butterfly. Timothy turned away.

"Now I'm going to show you the Martians," said Dad. "Come on, all of you. Here, Alice." He took her hand.

Michael was crying loudly, and Dad picked him up and carried him, and they walked down through the ruins toward the canal.

The canal. Where tomorrow or the next day their future wives would come up in a boat, small laughing girls now, with their father and mother.

The night came down around them, and there were

stars. But Timothy couldn't find Earth. It had already set. That was something to think about.

A night bird called among the ruins as they walked. Dad said, "Your mother and I will try to teach you. Perhaps we'll fail. I hope not. We've had a good lot to see and learn from. We planned this trip years ago, before you were born. Even if there hadn't been a war we would have come to Mars, I think, to live and form our own standard of living. It would have been another century before Mars would have been really poisoned by the Earth civilization. Now, of course——"

They reached the canal. It was long and straight and cool and wet and reflective in the night.

"I've always wanted to see a Martian," said Michael. "Where are they, Dad? You promised."

"There they are," said Dad, and he shifted Michael on his shoulder and pointed straight down.

The Martians were there. Timothy began to shiver.

The Martians were there—in the canal—reflected in the water. Timothy and Michael and Robert and Mom and Dad.

The Martians stared back up at them for a long, long silent time from the rippling water. . . .

DESERTION

by Clifford D. Simak

If we are ever to live and breathe without
artificial aid on the surfaces of other planets,
like the methane giant Jupiter, it will be necessary to "terraform" them—change them so
that we can live there . . . or else (and what a
curious and disturbing thought this is!) change
ourselves to suit them. Clifford Simak's "Desertion" is a longtime favorite of mine for its
mystery and its surprise ending, and the genuine touch of wonder in it.

FOUR MEN, TWO BY TWO, HAD GONE INTO THE HOWL-
ing maelstrom that was Jupiter and had not returned.
They had walked into the keening gale—or rather,
they had loped, bellies low against the ground, wet
sides gleaming in the rain.

For they did not go in the shape of men.

Now the fifth man stood before the desk of Kent
Fowler, head of Dome No. 3, Jovian Survey Commission.

Under Fowler's desk, old Towser scratched a flea,
then settled down to sleep again.

Harold Allen, Fowler saw with a sudden pang, was
young—too young. He had the easy confidence of
youth, the face of one who never had known fear. And

194

that was strange. For men in the domes of Jupiter did know fear—fear and humility. It was hard for Man to reconcile his puny self with the mighty forces of the monstrous planet.

"You understand," said Fowler, "that you need not do this. You understand that you need not go."

It was formula, of course. The other four had been told the same thing, but they had gone. This fifth one, Fowler knew, would go as well. But suddenly he felt a dull hope stir within him that Allen wouldn't go.

"When do I start?" asked Allen.

There had been a time when Fowler might have taken quiet pride in that answer, but not now. He frowned briefly.

"Within the hour," he said.

Allen stood waiting, quietly.

"Four other men have gone out and have not returned," said Fowler. "You know that, of course. We want you to return. We don't want you going off on any heroic rescue expedition. The main thing, the only thing, is that you come back, that you prove man can live in a Jovian form. Go to the first survey stake, no farther, then come back. Don't take any chances. Don't investigate anything. Just come back."

Allen nodded. "I understand all that."

"Miss Stanley will operate the converter," Fowler went on. "You need have no fear on that particular score. The other men were converted without mishap. They left the converter in apparently perfect condition. You will be in thoroughly competent hands. Miss Stanley is the best qualified conversion operator in the solar system. She has had experience on most of the other planets. That is why she's here."

Allen grinned at the woman and Fowler saw something flicker across Miss Stanley's face—something that might have been pity, or rage—or just plain fear. But it was gone again and she was smiling back at the youth who stood before the desk. Smiling in that prim, schoolteacherish way she had of smiling, almost as if she hated herself for doing it.

"I shall be looking forward," said Allen, "to my conversion."

And the way he said it, he made it all a joke, a vast, ironic joke.

But it was no joke.

It was serious business, deadly serious. Upon these tests, Fowler knew, depended the fate of men on Jupiter. If the tests succeeded, the resources of the giant planet would be thrown open. Man would take over Jupiter as he already had taken over the other smaller planets. And if they failed—

If they failed, Man would continue to be chained and hampered by the terrific pressure, the greater force of gravity, the weird chemistry of the planet. He would continue to be shut within the domes, unable to set actual foot upon the planet, unable to see it with direct, unaided vision, forced to rely upon the awkward tractors and televisor, forced to work with clumsy tools and mechanisms or through the medium of robots that themselves were clumsy.

For Man, unprotected and in his natural form, would be blotted out by Jupiter's terrific pressure of fifteen thousand pounds per square inch, pressure that made terrestrial sea bottoms seem a vacuum by comparison.

Even the strongest metal Earthmen could devise couldn't exist under pressure such as that, under the pressure and the alkaline rains that forever swept the planet. It grew brittle and flaky, crumbling like clay, or it ran away in little streams and puddles of ammonia salts. Only by stepping up the toughness and strength of that metal, by increasing its electronic tension, could it be made to withstand the weight of thousands of miles of swirling, choking gases that made up the atmosphere. And even when that was done, everything had to be coated with tough quartz to keep away the rain—the liquid ammonia that fell as bitter rain.

Fowler sat listening to the engines in the sub-floor of the dome—engines that ran on endlessly, the dome never quiet of them. They had to run and keep on running, for if they stopped the power flowing into the metal walls of the dome would stop, the electronic tension would ease up and that would be the end of everything.

Towser roused himself under Fowler's desk and scratched another flea, his leg thumping hard against the floor.

"Is there anything else?" asked Allen.

Fowler shook his head. "Perhaps there's something you want to do," he said. "Perhaps you—"

He had meant to say write a letter and he was glad he caught himself quick enough so he didn't say it.

Allen looked at his watch. "I'll be there on time," he said. He swung around and headed for the door.

Fowler knew Miss Stanley was watching him and he didn't want to turn and meet her eyes. He fumbled with a sheaf of papers on the desk before him.

"How long are you going to keep this up?" asked Miss Stanley, and she bit off each word with a vicious snap.

He swung around in his chair and faced her then. Her lips were drawn into a straight, thin line, her hair seemed skinned back from her forehead tighter than ever, giving her face that queer, almost startling death-mask quality.

He tried to make his voice cool and level. "As long as there's any need of it," he said. "As long as there's any hope."

"You're going to keep on sentencing them to death," she said. "You're going to keep marching them out face to face with Jupiter. You're going to sit in here safe and comfortable and send them out to die."

"There is no room for sentimentality, Miss Stanley," Fowler said, trying to keep the note of anger from his voice. "You know as well as I do why we're doing this.

You realize that Man in his own form simply cannot cope with Jupiter. The only answer is to turn men into the sort of things that can cope with it. We've done it on the other planets.

"If a few men die, but we finally succeed, the price is small. Through the ages men have thrown away their lives on foolish things, for foolish reasons. Why should we hesitate, then, at a little death in a thing as great as this?"

Miss Stanley sat stiff and straight, hands folded in her lap, the lights shining on her graying hair and Fowler, watching her, tried to imagine what she might feel, what she might be thinking. He wasn't exactly afraid of her, but he didn't feel quite comfortable when she was around. Those sharp blue eyes saw too much, her hands looked far too competent. She should be somebody's aunt sitting in a rocking chair with her knitting needles. But she wasn't. She was the top-notch conversion unit operator in the solar system and she didn't like the way he was doing things.

"There is something wrong, Mr. Fowler," she declared.

"Precisely," agreed Fowler. "That's why I'm sending young Allen out alone. He may find out what it is."

"And if he doesn't?"

"I'll send someone else."

She rose slowly from her chair, started toward the door, then stopped before his desk.

"Some day," she said, "you will be a great man. You never let a chance go by. This is your chance. You knew it was when this dome was picked for the tests. If you put it through, you'll go up a notch or two. No matter how many men may die, you'll go up a notch or two."

"Miss Stanley," he said and his voice was curt, "young Allen is going out soon. Please be sure that your machine—"

"My machine," she told him icily, "is not to blame. It operates along the coordinates the biologists set up."

He sat hunched at his desk, listening to her footsteps go down the corridor.

What she said was true, of course. The biologists had set up the coordinates. But the biologists could be wrong. Just a hairbreadth of difference, one iota of digression, and the converter would be sending out something that wasn't the thing they meant to send. A mutant that might crack up, go haywire, come unstuck under some condition or stress of circumstance wholly unsuspected.

For Man didn't know much about what was going on outside. Only what his instruments told him was going on. And the samplings of those happenings furnished by those instruments and mechanisms had been no more than samplings, for Jupiter was unbelievably large and the domes were very few.

Even the work of the biologists in getting the data on the Lopers, apparently the highest form of Jovian life, had involved more than three years of intensive study and after that two years of checking to make sure. Work that could have been done on Earth in a week or two. But work that, in this case, couldn't be done on Earth at all, for one couldn't take a Jovian life form to Earth. The pressure here on Jupiter couldn't be duplicated outside of Jupiter and at Earth pressure and temperature the Lopers would simply have disappeared in a puff of gas.

Yet it was work that had to be done if Man ever hoped to go about Jupiter in the life form of the Lopers. For before the converter could change a man to another life form, every detailed physical characteristic of that life form must be known—surely and positively, with no chance of mistake.

Allen did not come back.

The tractors, combing the nearby terrain, found no trace of him, unless the skulking thing reported by one of the drivers had been the missing Earthman in Loper form.

The biologists sneered their most accomplished academic sneers when Fowler suggested the coordinates might be wrong. Carefully they pointed out the coordinates worked. When a man was put into the converter and the switch was thrown, the man became a Loper. He left the machine and moved away, out of sight, into the soupy atmosphere.

Some quirk, Fowler had suggested; some tiny deviation from the thing a Loper should be, some minor defect. If there were, the biologists said, it would take years to find it.

And Fowler knew that they were right.

So there were five men now instead of four and Harold Allen had walked out into Jupiter for nothing at all. It was as if he'd never gone, so far as knowledge was concerned.

Fowler reached across his desk and picked up the personnel file, a thin sheaf of paper neatly clipped together. It was a thing he dreaded but a thing he had to do. Somehow the reason for these strange disappearances must be found. And there was no other way than to send out more men.

He sat for a moment listening to the howling of the wind above the dome, the everlasting thundering gale that swept across the planet in boiling, twisting wrath.

Was there some threat out there, he asked himself? Some danger they did not know about? Something that lay in wait and gobbled up the Lopers, making no distinction between Lopers that were bona fide and Lopers that were men? To the gobblers, of course, it would make no difference.

Or had there been a basic fault in selecting the Lopers as the type of life best fitted for existence on the surface of the planet? The evident intelligence of the Lopers, he knew, had been one factor in that determination. For if the thing Man became did not have capacity for intelligence, Man could not for long retain his own intelligence in such a guise.

Had the biologists let that one factor weigh too heavily, using it to offset some other factor that might be unsatisfactory, even disastrous? It didn't seem likely. Stiffnecked as they might be, the biologists knew their business.

Or was the whole thing impossible, doomed from the very start? Conversion to other life forms had worked on other planets, but that did not necessarily mean it would work on Jupiter. Perhaps Man's intelligence could not function correctly through the sensory apparatus provided Jovian life. Perhaps the Lopers were so alien there was no common ground for human knowledge and the Jovian conception of existence to meet and work together.

Or the fault might lie with Man, be inherent with the race. Some mental aberration which, coupled with what they found outside, wouldn't let them come back. Although it might not be an aberration, not in the human sense. Perhaps just one ordinary human trait, accepted as commonplace on Earth, would be so violently at odds with Jovian existence that it would blast human sanity.

Claws rattled and clicked down the corridor. Listening to them, Fowler smiled wanly. It was Towser coming back from the kitchen, where he had gone to see his friend, the cook.

Towser came into the room, carrying a bone. He wagged his tail at Fowler and flopped down beside the desk, bone between his paws. For a long moment his rheumy old eyes regarded his master, and Fowler reached down a hand to ruffle a ragged ear.

"You still like me, Towser?" Fowler asked, and Towser thumped his tail.

"You're the only one," said Fowler.

He straightened and swung back to the desk. His hand reached out and picked up the file.

Bennett? Bennett had a girl waiting for him back on Earth.

Andrews? Andrews was planning on going back to Mars Tech just as soon as he earned enough to see him through a year.

Olson? Olson was nearing pension age. All the time telling the boys how he was going to settle down and grow roses.

Carefully, Fowler laid the file back on the desk.

Sentencing men to death. Miss Stanley had said that, her pale lips scarcely moving in her parchment face. Marching men out to die while he, Fowler, sat here safe and comfortable.

They were saying it all through the dome, no doubt, especially since Allen had failed to return. They wouldn't say it to his face, of course. Even the man or men he called before this desk and told they were the next to go wouldn't say it to him.

But he would see it in their eyes.

He picked up the file again. Bennett, Andrews, Olson. There were others, but there was no use in going on.

Kent Fowler knew that he couldn't do it, couldn't face them, couldn't send more men out to die.

He leaned forward and flipped up the toggle on the intercommunicator.

"Yes, Mr. Fowler."

"Miss Stanley, please."

He waited for Miss Stanley, listening to Towser chewing half-heartedly on the bone. Towser's teeth were getting bad.

"Miss Stanley," said Miss Stanley's voice.

"Just wanted to tell you, Miss Stanley, to get ready for two more."

"Aren't you afraid," asked Miss Stanley, "that you'll run out of them? Sending out one at a time, they'd last longer, give you twice the satisfaction."

"One of them," said Fowler, "will be a dog."

"A dog!"

"Yes, Towser."

He heard the quick, cold rage that iced her voice. "Your own dog! He's been with you all these years——"

"That's the point," said Fowler. "Towser would be unhappy if I left him behind."

It was not the Jupiter he had known through the televisor. He had expected it to be different, but not like this. He had expected a hell of ammonia rain and stinking fumes and the deafening, thundering tumult of the storm. He had expected swirling clouds and fog and the snarling flicker of monstrous thunderbolts.

He had not expected that the lashing downpour would be reduced to drifting purple mist that moved like fleeing shadows over a red and purple sward. He had not even guessed the snaking bolts of lightning would be flares of pure ecstasy across a painted sky.

Waiting for Towser, Fowler flexed the muscles of his body, amazed at the smooth, sleek strength he found. Not a bad body, he decided, and grimaced at remembering how he had pitied the Lopers when he glimpsed them through a television screen.

For it had been hard to imagine a living organism based upon ammonia and hydrogen rather than upon water and oxygen, hard to believe that such a form of life could know the same quick thrill of life that humankind could know. Hard to conceive of life out in the soupy maelstrom that was Jupiter, not knowing, of course, that through Jovian eyes it was no soupy maelstrom at all.

The wind brushed against him with what seemed gentle fingers and he remembered with a start that by Earth standards the wind was a roaring gale, a two-hundred-mile-an-hour howler laden with deadly gases.

Pleasant scents seeped into his body. And yet scarcely scents, for it was not the sense of smell as he remembered it. It was as if his whole being was soaking up the sensation of lavender—and yet not lavender. It was something, he knew, for which he had no word, undoubtedly the first of many enigmas in terminology. For the words he knew, the thought symbols that served him as an Earthman would not serve him as a Jovian.

The lock in the side of the dome opened and

Towser came tumbling out—at least he thought it must be Towser.

He started to call to the dog, his mind shaping the words he meant to say. But he couldn't say them. There was no way to say them. He had nothing to say them with.

For a moment his mind swirled in muddy terror, a blind fear that eddied in little puffs of panic through his brain.

How did Jovians talk? How—

Suddenly he was aware of Towser, intensely aware of the bumbling, eager friendliness of the shaggy animal that had followed him from Earth to many planets. As if the thing that was Towser had reached out and for a moment sat within his brain.

And out of the bubbling welcome that he sensed, came words.

"Hiya, pal."

Not words really, better than words. Thought symbols in his brain, communicated thought symbols that had shades of meaning words could never have.

"Hiya, Towser," he said.

"I feel good," said Towser. "Like I was a pup. Lately I've been feeling pretty punk. Legs stiffening up on me and teeth wearing down to almost nothing. Hard to mumble a bone with teeth like that. Besides, the fleas give me hell. Used to be I never paid much attention to them. A couple of fleas more or less never meant much in my early days."

"But . . . but—" Fowler's thoughts tumbled awkwardly. "You're talking to me!"

"Sure thing," said Towser. "I always talked to you, but you couldn't hear me. I tried to say things to you, but I couldn't make the grade."

"I understood you sometimes," Fowler said.

"Not very well," said Towser. "You knew when I wanted food and when I wanted a drink, and when I wanted out, but that's about all you ever managed."

"I'm sorry," Fowler said.

"Forget it," Towser told him. "I'll race you to the cliff."

For the first time, Fowler saw the cliff, apparently many miles away, but with a strange crystalline beauty that sparkled in the shadow of the many-colored clouds.

Fowler hesitated. "It's a long way—"

"Ah, come on," said Towser, and even as he said it he started for the cliff.

Fowler followed, testing his legs, testing the strength in that new body of his, a bit doubtful at first, amazed a moment later, then running with a sheer joyousness that was one with the red and purple sward, with the drifting smoke of the rain across the land.

As he ran the consciousness of music came to him, a music that beat into his body, that surged throughout his being, that lifted him on wings of silver speed. Music like bells might make from some steeple on a sunny springtime hill.

As the cliff drew nearer the music deepened and filled the universe with a spray of magic sound. And he knew the music came from the tumbling waterfall that feathered down the face of the shining cliff.

Only, he knew, it was no waterfall, but an ammonia-fall, and the cliff was white because it was oxygen, solidified.

He skidded to a stop beside Towser where the waterfall broke into a glittering rainbow of many hundred colors. Literally many hundred, for here, he saw, was no shading of one primary to another such as human beings saw, but a clear-cut selectivity that broke the prism down to its last ultimate classification.

"The music," said Towser.

"Yes, what about it?"

"The music," said Towser, "is vibrations. Vibrations of water falling."

"But, Towser, you don't know about vibrations."

"Yes, I do," contended Towser. "It just popped into my head."

Fowler gulped mentally. "Just popped!"

And suddenly, within his own head, he held a formula—the formula for a process that would make metal to withstand the pressure of Jupiter.

He stared, astounded, at the waterfall and swiftly his mind took the many colors and placed them in their exact sequence in the spectrum. Just like that. Just out of blue sky. Out of nothing, for he knew nothing either of metals or of colors.

"Towser," he cried. "Towser, something's happening to us!"

"Yeah, I know," said Towser.

"It's our brains," said Fowler. "We're using them, all of them, down to the last hidden corner. Using them to figure out things we should have known all the time. Maybe the brains of Earth-things naturally are slow and foggy. Maybe we are the morons of the universe. Maybe we are fixed so we have to do things the hard way."

And, in the new sharp clarity of thought that seemed to grip him, he knew that it would not only be the matter of colors in a waterfall or metals that would resist the pressure of Jupiter. He sensed other things, things not yet quite clear. A vague whispering that hinted of greater things, of mysteries beyond the pale of human thought, beyond even the pale of human imagination. Mysteries, fact, logic built on reasoning. Things that any brain should know if it used all its reasoning power.

"We're still mostly Earth," he said. "We're just beginning to learn a few of the things we are to know—a few of the things that were kept from us as human beings, perhaps because we were human beings. Because our human bodies were poor bodies. Poorly equipped for thinking, poorly equipped in certain senses that one has to have to know. Perhaps even lacking in certain senses that are necessary to true knowledge."

He stared back at the dome, a tiny black thing dwarfed by the distance.

Back there were men who couldn't see the beauty that was Jupiter. Men who thought that swirling clouds and lashing rain obscured the planet's face. Unseeing human eyes. Poor eyes. Eyes that could not see the beauty in the clouds, that could not see through the storm. Bodies that could not feel the thrill of trilling music stemming from the rush of broken water.

Men who walked alone, in terrible loneliness, talking with their tongues like Boy Scouts wigwagging out their messages, unable to reach out and touch one another's mind as he could reach out and touch Towser's mind. Shut off forever from that personal, intimate contact with other living things.

He, Fowler, had expected terror inspired by alien things out here on the surface, had expected to cower before the threat of unknown things, had steeled himself against disgust of a situation that was not of Earth.

But instead he had found something greater than Man had ever known. A swifter, surer body. A sense of exhilaration, a deeper sense of life. A sharper mind. A world of beauty that even the dreamers of the Earth had not yet imagined.

"Let's get going," Towser urged.

"Where do you want to go?"

"Anywhere," said Towser. "Just start going and see where we end up. I have a feeling . . . well, a feeling—"

"Yes, I know," said Fowler.

For he had the feeling, too. The feeling of high destiny. A certain sense of greatness. A knowledge that somewhere off beyond the horizons lay adventure and things greater than adventure.

Those other five had felt it, too. Had felt the urge to go and see, the compelling sense that here lay a life of fullness and of knowledge.

That, he knew, was why they had not returned.

"I won't go back," said Towser.

"We can't let them down," said Fowler.

Fowler took a step or two, back toward the dome, then stopped.

Back to the dome. Back to that aching, poison-laden body he had left. It hadn't seemed aching before, but now he knew it was.

Back to the fuzzy brain. Back to muddled thinking. Back to the flapping mouths that formed signals others understood. Back to eyes that now would be worse than no sight at all. Back to squalor, back to crawling, back to ignorance.

"Perhaps some day," he said, muttering to himself.

"We got a lot to do and a lot to see," said Towser. "We got a lot to learn. We'll find things—"

Yes, they could find things. Civilizations, perhaps. Civilizations that would make the civilization of Man seem puny by comparison. Beauty and, more important, an understanding of that beauty. And a comradeship no one had ever known before—that no man, no dog had ever known before.

And life. The quickness of life after what seemed a drugged existence.

"I can't go back," said Towser.

"Nor I," said Fowler.

"They would turn me back into a dog," said Towser.

"And me," said Fowler, "back into a man."

TWILIGHT

by Don A. Stuart

Don A. Stuart is the name under which John W. Campbell, now the famous editor of the magazine *Analog*, began in the Thirties to write a new and different kind of science fiction story. Unlike the gadgety stories he wrote under his own name, this story hints at more than it says; you should listen to it as if it were a piece of music.

"SPEAKING OF HITCHHIKERS," SAID JIM BENDELL in a rather bewildered way, "I picked up a man the other day that certainly was a queer cuss." He laughed, but it wasn't a real laugh. "He told me the queerest yarn I ever heard. Most of them tell you how they lost their good jobs and tried to find work out here in the wide spaces of the West. They don't seem to realize how many people we have out here. They think all this great beautiful country is uninhabited."

Jim Bendell's a real-estate man, and I knew how he could go on. That's his favorite line, you know. He's real worried because there's a lot of homesteading plots still open out in our state. He talks about the beautiful country, but he never went farther into the desert than the edge of town. 'Fraid of it actually. So I sort of steered him back on the track.

"What did he claim, Jim? Prospector who couldn't find land to prospect?"

"That's not very funny, Bart. No; it wasn't only what he claimed. He didn't even claim it, just said it. You know, he didn't say it was true, he just said it. That's what gets me. Darn it, I know it ain't true, but the way he said it— Oh, I don't know."

By which I knew he didn't. Jim Bendell's usually pretty careful about his English—real proud of it. When he slips, that means he's disturbed. Like the time he thought the rattlesnake was a stick of wood and wanted to put it on the fire.

Jim went on: And he had funny clothes, too. They looked like silver, but they were soft as silk. And at night they glowed just a little.

I picked him up about dusk. Really picked him up. He was lying off about ten feet from the South Road. I thought, at first, somebody had hit him, and then hadn't stopped. Didn't see him very clearly, you know. I picked him up, put him in the car, and started on. I had about three hundred miles to go, but I thought I could drop him at Warren Spring with Doc Vance. But he came to in about five minutes, and opened his eyes. He looked up straight off, and he looked first at the car, then at the moon. "Thank God!" he says, and then looks at me. It gave me a shock. He was beautiful. No; he was handsome.

He wasn't either one. He was magnificent. He was about six feet two, I think, and his hair was brown, with a touch of red-gold. It seemed like fine copper wire that's turned brown. It was crisp and curly. His forehead was wide, twice as wide as mine. His features were delicate, but tremendously impressive; his eyes were gray, like etched iron, and bigger than mine—a lot.

That suit he wore—it was more like a bathing suit with pajama trousers. His arms were long and muscled smoothly as an Indian's. He was white, though, tanned lightly with a golden, rather than a brown, tan.

But he was magnificent. Most wonderful man I ever saw. I don't know, darn it!

"Hello!" I said. "Have an accident?"

"No; not this time, at least."

And his voice was magnificent, too. It wasn't an ordinary voice. It sounded like an organ talking, only it was human.

"But maybe my mind isn't quite steady yet. I tried an experiment. Tell me what the date is—year and all, and let me see," he went on.

"Why—December 9, 1932," I said.

And it didn't please him. He didn't like it a bit. But the wry grin that came over his face gave way to a chuckle.

"Over a thousand—" he says reminiscently. "Not as bad as seven million. I shouldn't complain."

"Seven million what?"

"Years," he said, steadily enough. Like he meant it. "I tried an experiment once. Or I will try it. Now I'll have to try it again. The experiment was—in 3059. I'd just finished the release experiment. Testing space then. Time—it wasn't that, I still believe. It was space. I felt myself caught in that field, but I couldn't pull away. Field gamma-H 481, intensity 935 in the Pellman range. It sucked men in—and I went out.

"I think it took a short cut through space to the position the solar system will occupy. Through a higher dimension, effecting a speed exceeding light, and throwing me into the future plane."

He wasn't telling me, you know. He was just thinking out loud. Then he began to realize I was there.

"I couldn't read their instruments, seven million years of evolution changed everything. So I overshot my mark a little coming back. I belong in 3059. But tell me, what's the latest scientific invention of this year?"

He startled me so, I answered almost before I thought.

"Why—television, I guess. And radio and airplanes."

"Radio—good. They will have instruments."

"But see here—who are you?"

"Ah—I'm sorry. I forgot," he replied in that organ voice of his. "I am Ares Sen Kenlin. And you?"

"James Waters Bendell."

"Waters—what does that mean—I do not recognize it?"

"Why—it's a name, of course. Why should you recognize it?"

"I see—you have not the classification, then. 'Sen' stands for science."

"Where did you come from, Mr. Kenlin?"

"Come from?" He smiled, and his voice was slow and soft. "I came out of space across seven million years or more. They had lost count—the men had. The machines had eliminated the unneeded service. They didn't know what year it was. But before that—my home is in the Neva'th City in the year 3059."

That's when I began to think he was a nut.

"I was an experimenter," he went on. "Science, as I have said. My father was a scientist, too, but in human genetics. I myself am an experiment. He proved his point, and all the world followed suit. I was the first of the new race. The new race—oh, holy destiny—what has—what will— What is its end? I have seen it—almost. I saw them—the little men—bewildered—lost. And the machines. Must it be—can't anything sway it? Listen—I heard this song."

He sang the song. Then he didn't have to tell me about the people. I knew them. I could hear their voices, in the queer, crackling, un-English words. I could read their bewildered longings. It was a minor key, I think. It called, it called and asked, and hunted hopelessly. And over it all the steady rumble and whine of the unknown, forgotten machines.

The machines that couldn't stop, because they had been started, and the little men who had forgotten how to stop them, or even what they were for, looking at them and listening—and wondering. They couldn't read or write anymore, and the language had changed, you see, so the phonic records of their ancestors meant nothing to them.

But that song went on, and they wondered. And they looked out across space and they saw the warm, friendly stars—too far away. Nine planets they knew and inhabited. And locked by infinite distance, they couldn't see another race, a new life.

And through it all—two things. The machines. Bewildered forgetfulness. And maybe one more. Why?

That was the song, and it made me cold. It shouldn't be sung around people of today. It almost killed something. It seemed to kill hope. After that song—I—well, I believed him.

When he finished the song, he didn't talk for a while. Then he sort of shook himself.

You won't understand (he continued). Not yet—but I have seen them. They stand about, little misshapen men with huge heads. But their heads contain only brains. They had machines that could think—but somebody turned them off a long time ago, and no one knew how to start them again. That was the trouble with them. They had wonderful brains. Far better than yours or mine. But it must have been millions of years ago when they were turned off, too, and they just hadn't thought since then. Kindly little people. That was all they knew.

When I slipped into that field it grabbed me like a gravitational field whirling a space transport down to a planet. It sucked me in—and through. Only the other side must have been seven million years in the future. That's where I was. It must have been in exactly the same spot on Earth's surface, but I never knew why.

It was night then, and I saw the city a little way off. The moon was shining on it, and the whole scene looked wrong. You see, in seven million years, men had done a lot with the positions of the planetary bodies, what with moving space liners, clearing lanes through the asteroids, and such. And seven million years is long enough for natural things to change positions a little. The moon must have been fifty thousand miles farther out. And it was rotating on its axis. I lay there awhile and watched it. Even the stars were different.

There were ships going out of the city. Back and forth, like things sliding along a wire, but there was only a wire of force, of course. Part of the city, the lower part, was brightly lighted with what must have been mercury-vapor glow, I decided. Blue-green. I felt sure men didn't live there—the light was wrong for eyes. But the top of the city was so sparsely lighted.

Then I saw something coming down out of the sky. It was brightly lighted. A huge globe, and it sank straight to the center of the great black-and-silver mass of the city.

I don't know what it was, but even then I knew the city was deserted. Strange that I could even imagine that, I who had never seen a deserted city before. But I walked the fifteen miles over to it and entered it. There were machines going about the streets, repair machines, you know. They couldn't understand that the city didn't need to go on functioning, so they were still working. I found a taxi machine that seemed fairly familiar. It had a manual control that I could work.

I don't know how long that city had been deserted. Some of the men from other cities said it was a hundred and fifty thousand years. Some went as high as three hundred thousand years. Three hundred thousand years since human foot had been in that city. The taxi machine was in perfect condition, functioned at once. It was clean, and the city was clean and orderly. I saw a restaurant and I was hungry. Hungrier still for humans to speak to. There were none, of course, but I didn't know.

The restaurant had the food displayed directly, and I made a choice. The food was three hundred thousand years old, I suppose. I didn't know, and the machines that served it to me didn't care, for they made things synthetically, you see, and perfectly. When they made those cities, they forgot one thing. They didn't realize that things shouldn't go on forever.

It took me six months to make my apparatus. And near the end I was ready to go mad from seeing those machines go blindly, perfectly, on in the orbits of their duties with the tireless, ceaseless perfection their designers had incorporated in them, long after those designers and their sons, and their sons' sons had no use for them. . . .

When Earth is cold, and the sun has died out, those machines will go on. When Earth begins to crack and break, those perfect, ceaseless machines will try to repair her—

I left the restaurant and cruised about the city in the taxi. The machine had a little, electric-power motor, I believe, but it gained its power from the great, central power radiator. I knew before long that I was far in the future. The city was divided into two sections, a section of many strata where machines functioned smoothly, save for a deep, humming heat that echoed through the whole city like a vast, unending song of power. The entire metal framework of the place echoed with it, transmitted it, hummed with it. But it was soft and restful, a reassuring beat.

There must have been thirty levels above ground and twenty more below, a solid block of metal walls and metal floors and metal and glass and force machines. The only light was the blue-green glow of the mercury vapor arcs. The light of mercury vapor is rich in high-energy quanta which stimulate the alkali metal atoms readily to photo-electric activity. Or perhaps that is beyond the science of your day? I have forgotten.

But they had used that light because many of their worker machines needed sight. They were marvelous. For five hours I wandered through the vast power plant on the very lowest level, watching them, and because there was motion, and that pseudo, mechanical life, I felt less alone.

The generators I saw were a development of the release I had discovered—when? The release of the energy of matter, I mean, and I knew when I saw that for what countless ages they could continue.

The entire lower block of the city was given over to the machines. Thousands. But most of them seemed idle, or, at most, running under light load. I recognized a telephone apparatus, and not a single signal came through. There was no life in the city. Yet when I pressed a little stud beside the screen on one side of the room, the machine began working instantly. It was ready. Only no one needed it any more. The men knew how to die, and be dead, but the machines didn't.

Finally I went up to the top of the city, the upper level. It was a paradise. There were shrubs and trees and parks, glowing in the soft light that they had learned to make in the very air. They had learned it five million years or more before. Two million years ago they forgot. But the machines didn't, and they were still making it. It hung in the air, soft, silvery light, slightly rosy, and the gardens were shadowy with it. There were no machines here now, but I knew that in daylight they must come out and work on these gardens, keeping them a paradise for masters who had died, and stopped moving, as they could not.

In the desert outside the city it had been cool, and very dry. Here the air was soft, warm, and sweet with the scent of blooms that men had spent several hundreds of thousands of years perfecting.

Then somewhere music began. It began in the air and spread softly through it. The moon was just setting now, and as it set, the rosy-silver glow waned and the music grew stronger.

It came from everywhere and from nowhere. It was within me. I do not know how they did it. And I do not know how such music could be written.

Savages make music too simple to be beautiful, but it is stirring. Semisavages write music beautifully simple, and simply beautiful. Your Negro music was your best. They knew music when they heard it and sang it as they felt it. Semicivilized peoples write great music. They are proud of their music, and make sure it is known for great music. They make it so great it is top-heavy.

I had always thought our music good. But that which came through the air was the song of triumph, sung by a mature race, the race of man in its full triumph! It was man singing his triumph in majestic sound that swept me up; it showed me what lay before me; it carried me on.

And it died in the air as I looked at the deserted city. The machines should have forgotten that song. Their masters had, long before.

I came to what must have been one of their homes; it was a dimly seen doorway in the dusky light, but as I stepped up to it, the lights which had not functioned in three hundred thousand years illuminated it for me with a green-white glow, like a firefly, and I stepped into the room beyond. Instantly something happened to the air in the doorway behind me; it was as opaque as milk. The room in which I stood was a room of metal and stone. The stone was some jet black substance with the finish of velvet, and the metals were silver and gold. There was a rug on the floor, a rug of just such material as I am wearing now, but thicker and softer. There were divans about the room, low and covered with these soft metallic materials. They were black and gold and silver too.

I had never seen anything like that. I never shall again, I suppose, and my language and yours were not made to describe it.

The builders of that city had right and reason to sing that song of sweeping triumph, triumph that swept them over the nine planets and the fifteen habitable moons.

But they weren't there anymore, and I wanted to leave. I thought of a plan and went to a subtelephone office to examine a map I had seen. The old world looked much the same. Seven or even seventy million years doesn't mean much to old Mother Earth. She may even succeed in wearing down those marvelous machine cities. She can wait a hundred million or a thousand million years, or even a hundred thousand million years before she is beaten.

I tried calling different city centers shown on the map. I had quickly learned the system when I examined the central apparatus.

I tried once—twice—thrice—a round dozen times. Yawk City, Lunnon City, Paree, Shkago, Singpor, others. I was beginning to feel that there were no more men on all Earth. And I felt crushed, as at each city the machines replied and did my bidding. The machines were there in each of those far vaster cities, for I was in the Neva City of their time. A small city. Yawk City was more than fifty kilometers in diameter.

In each city I had tried several numbers. Then I tried San Frisco. There was someone there, and a voice answered and the picture of a human appeared on the little glowing screen. I could see him start and stare in surprise at me. Then he started speaking to me. I couldn't understand, of course. I can understand your speech, and you mine, because your speech of this day is largely recorded on records of various types and has influenced our pronunciation.

Some things are changed, names of cities particularly, because names of cities are apt to be polysyllabic and used a great deal. People tend to elide them, shorten them. I am in—Nee-vah-dah—as you would say? We say only Neva. And Yawk State. But it is Ohio and Iowa still. Over a thousand years, effects were small on words because they were recorded.

But seven million years had passed, and the men had forgotten the old records, used them less as time went on, and their speech varied till the time came when they could no longer understand the records. They were not written any more, of course.

Some men must have arisen occasionally among that

last race and sought for knowledge, but it was denied them. An ancient writing can be translated if some basic rule is found. An ancient voice though—and when the race has forgotten the laws of science and the labor of mind—

So his speech was strange to me as he answered over the circuit. His voice was high in pitch, his words liquid, the tones sweet. It was almost a song as he spoke. He was excited and called others. I could not understand them, but I knew where they were. I could go to them.

So I went down from the paradise of gardens, and as I prepared to leave, I saw the dawn in the sky. The strange, bright stars winked and twinkled and faded. Only one, bright, rising star was familiar—Venus. She shone golden now. Finally, as I stood watching for the first time that strange heaven, I began to understand what had first impressed me with the wrongness of the view. The stars, you see, were all different.

In my time—and yours—the solar system is a lone wanderer that, by chance, is passing across an intersection point of galactic traffic. The stars we see at night are the stars of moving clusters, you know. In fact our system is passing through the heart of the Ursa Major group. Half a dozen other groups center within five hundred light-years of us.

But during those seven millions of years, the sun had moved out of the group. The heavens were almost empty to the eye. Only here and there shone a single faint star. And across the vast sweep of black sky swung the band of the Milky Way. The sky was empty.

That must have been another thing those men meant in their songs—felt in their hearts. Loneliness—not even the close, friendly stars. We have stars within half a dozen light-years. They told me that their instruments, which gave directly the distance to any star, showed that the nearest was one hundred and fifty light-years away. It was enormously bright. Brighter even than Sirius of our heavens. And that made it even

less friendly, because it was a blue-white supergiant.
Our sun would have served as a satellite for that star.

I stood there and watched the lingering rose-silver
glow die as the powerful blood-red light of the sun
swept over the horizon. I knew by the stars now that it
must have been several millions of years since my day,
since I had last seen the sun sweep up. And that blood-
red light made me wonder if the sun itself was dying.

An edge of it appeared, blood-red and huge. It
swung up, and the color faded, till in half an hour it was
the familiar yellow-gold disk.

It hadn't changed in all that time.

I had been foolish to think that it would. Seven million years—that is nothing to Earth, how much less to
the sun? Some two thousand thousand thousand times it
had risen since I last saw it rise. Two thousand thousand thousand days. If it had been that many years—I
might have noticed a change.

The universe moves slowly. Only life is not enduring;
only life changes swiftly. Seven short millions of years.
Seven days in the life of Earth—and the race was
dying. It had left something, machines. But they would
die, too, even though they could not understand. So I
felt. I—may have changed that. I will tell you. Later.

For when the sun was up, I looked again at the sky
and the ground, some fifty floors below. I had come to
the edge of the city.

Machines were moving on that ground, leveling it
perhaps. A great, wide line of gray stretched off across
the level desert straight to the east. I had seen it glowing
faintly before the sun rose—a roadway for ground machines. There was no traffic on it.

I saw an airship slip in from the east. It came with
soft, muttering whine of air, like a child complaining in
sleep; it grew to my eyes like an expanding balloon. It
was huge when it settled in a great port-slip in the city
below. I could hear now the clang and mutter of ma-

chines, working on the materials brought in, no doubt. The machines had ordered raw materials. The machines in other cities had supplied them. The freight machines had carried them here.

San Frisco and Jacksville were the only two cities on North America still used. But the machines went on in all the others because they couldn't stop. They hadn't been ordered to.

Then, high above, something appeared, and from the city beneath me, from a center section, three small spheres rose. They, like the freight ship, had no visible driving mechanisms. The point in the sky above, like a black star in a blue space, had grown to a moon. The three spheres met it high above. Then, together, they descended and lowered into the center of the city, where I could not see them.

It was a freight transport from Venus. The one I had seen land the night before had come from Mars, I learned.

I moved after that and looked for some sort of a taxi-plane. They had none that I recognized in scouting about the city. I searched the higher levels, and here and there saw deserted ships, but far too large for me, and without controls.

It was nearly noon—and I ate again. The food was good.

I knew then that this was a city of the dead ashes of human hopes. The hopes of not a race, not the whites, nor the yellows, nor the blacks, but the human race. I was made to leave it. I was afraid to try the ground road to the west, for the taxi I drove was powered from some source in the city and I knew it would fail before many miles.

It was afternoon when I found a small hangar near the outer wall of the vast city. It contained three ships. I had been searching through the lower strata of the human section—the upper part. There were restaurants and shops and theaters there. I entered one place where, at my entrance, soft music began, and colors and forms began to rise on a screen before me.

They were the triumph songs, in form and sound and color, of a mature race, a race that had marched steadily upward through five millions of years—and didn't see the path that faded out ahead, when they were dead and had stopped and the city itself was dead; but it hadn't stopped. I hastened out of there—and the song that had not been sung in three hundred thousand years died behind me.

But I found the hangar. It was a private one, likely. Three ships. One must have been fifty feet long and fifteen in diameter. It was a yacht, a space yacht probably. One was some fifteen feet long and five feet in diameter. That must have been the family air machine. The third was a tiny thing, little more than ten feet long and two in diameter. I had to lie down within it, evidently.

There was a periscopic device that gave me a view ahead and almost directly above. A window that permitted me to see what lay below—and a device that moved a map under a frosted-glass screen and projected it onto the screen in such a way that the cross-hairs of the screen always marked my position.

I spent half an hour attempting to understand what the makers of that ship had made. But the men who made that were men who held behind them the science and knowledge of five millions of years and the perfect machines of those ages. I saw the release mechanism that powered it. I understood the principles of that and, vaguely, the mechanics. But there were no conductors, only pale beams that pulsed so swiftly you could hardly catch the pulsations from the corner of the eye. They had been glowing and pulsating steadily, some half dozen of them, for three hundred thousand years at least; probably more.

I entered the machine, and instantly half a dozen more beams sprang into being, there was a slight suggestion of a quiver, and a queer strain ran through my body. I understood in an instant, for the machine was resting on gravity nullifiers. That had been my hope when I worked on the space fields I discovered after the release.

But they had had it for millions of years before they built that perfect, deathless machine. My weight, entering it, had forced it to readjust itself and simultaneously to prepare for operation. Within, an artificial gravity equal to Earth's had gripped me, and the neutral zone between the outside and the interior had caused the strain.

The machine was ready. It was fully fueled, too. You see they were equipped to tell automatically their wants and needs. They were almost living things, every one. A caretaker machine kept them supplied, adjusted, even repaired them when need be, and when possible. If it was not possible, I learned later, they were carried away in a service truck that came automatically, replaced by an exactly similar machine, and carried to the shops where they were made, and automatic machines made them over.

The machine waited patiently for me to start. The controls were simple, obvious. There was a lever at the left that you pushed forward to move forward, pulled back to go back. On the right a horizontal, pivoted bar. If you swung it left, the ship spun left; if right, the ship spun right. If tipped up, the ship followed it, and likewise for all motions other than backward and forward. Raising it bodily raised the ship as depressing it depressed the ship.

I lifted it slightly, a needle moved a bit on a gauge comfortably before my eyes as I lay there, and the floor dropped beneath me. I pulled the other control back, and the ship gathered speed as it moved gently out into the open. Releasing both controls into neutral, the machine continued till it stopped at the same elevation, the motion absorbed by air friction. I turned it about, and another dial before my eyes moved, showing my position. I could not read it, though. The map did not move, as I had hoped it would. So I started toward what I felt was west.

I could feel no acceleration in that marvelous machine. The ground simply began leaping backward, and in a moment the city was gone. The map unrolled rapidly beneath me now, and I saw that I was moving south of west. I turned northward slightly and watched the compass. Soon I understood that, too, and the ship sped on.

I had become too interested in the map and the compass, for suddenly there was a sharp buzz and, without my volition, the machine rose and swung to the north. There was a mountain ahead of me; I had not seen, but the ship had.

I noticed then what I should have seen before—two little knobs that would move the map. I started to move them and heard a sharp clicking, and the pace of the ship began decreasing. A moment and it had steadied at a considerably lower speed, the machine swinging to a new course. I tried to right it, but to my amazement the controls did not affect it.

It was the map, you see. It would either follow the course or the course would follow it. I had moved it and the machine had taken over control of its own accord. There was a little button I could have pushed—but I didn't know. I couldn't control the ship until it finally came to rest and lowered itself to a stop six inches from the ground in the center of what must have been the ruins of a great city, Sacramento, probably.

I understood now, so I adjusted the map for San Frisco, and the ship went on at once. It steered itself around a mass of broken stone, turned back to its course, and headed on, a bullet-shaped, self-controlled dart.

It didn't descend when it reached San Frisco. It simply hung in the air and sounded a soft musical hum. Twice. Then it waited. I waited too, and looked down.

There were people here. I saw the humans of that

age for the first time. They were graceful, slim people with heads disproportionately large. But not extremely so.

Their eyes impressed me most. They were huge, and when they looked at me there was a power in them that seemed sleeping, but too deeply to be roused.

I took the manual controls then and landed. And no sooner had I got out than the ship rose automatically and started off by itself. They had automatic parking devices. The ship had gone to a public hangar, the nearest, where it would be automatically serviced and cared for. There was a little call set I should have taken with me when I got out. Then I could have pressed a button and called it to me—wherever I was in that city.

The people about me began talking—singing almost —among themselves. Others were coming up leisurely. Men and women—but there seemed no old and few young. What few young there were, were treated almost with respect, lest a careless step knock them down.

There was reason, you see. They lived a tremendous time. Some lived as long as three thousand years. Then —they simply died. They didn't grow old, and it never had been learned why people died as they did. The heart stopped, the brain ceased thought—and they died. But the young children, children not yet mature, were treated with the utmost care. Only one child was born in the course of a month in that city of one hundred thousand people. The human race was growing sterile.

And have I told you that they were lonely? Their loneliness was beyond hope. For, you see, as man strode toward maturity, he destroyed all forms of life that menaced him. Disease. Insects. Then the last of the insects, and finally the last of the man-eating animals.

The balance of nature was destroyed then, so they

had to go on. It was like the machines. They started them—and now they couldn't stop. So they had to destroy weeds of all sorts, then many formerly harmless plants. Then the herbivora, too, the deer and the antelope and the rabbit and the horse. They were a menace, they attacked man's machine-tended crops. Man was still eating natural foods.

You can understand. The thing was beyond their control. In the end they killed off the denizens of the sea, also, in self-defense. Without the many creatures that had kept them in check, they were swarming beyond bounds. And the time had come when synthetic foods replaced natural. The air was purified of all life about two and half million years after our day, all microscopic life.

That meant that the water must be purified. It was —and then came the end of life in the ocean. There were minute organisms that lived on bacterial forms, and tiny fish that lived on the minute organisms, and small fish that lived on the tiny fish, and big fish that lived on the small fish—and the beginning of the chain was gone. The sea was devoid of life in a generation. That meant about one thousand and five hundred years to them. Even the sea plants had gone.

And on all Earth there was only man and the organisms he had protected—the plants he wanted for decoration, and certain ultrahygienic pets, as long-lived as their masters. Dogs. They must have been remarkable animals. Man was reaching his maturity then, and his animal friend, the friend that had followed him through a thousand millennia to your day and mine, and another four thousand millennia to the day of man's early maturity, had grown in intelligence. In an ancient museum—a wonderful place, for they had, perfectly preserved, the body of a great leader of mankind who had died five and a half million years before I saw him—in that museum, deserted then, I saw one of those canines. His skull was nearly as large as mine. They had simple ground machines that dogs could be trained to drive, and they held races in which the dogs drove those machines.

Then man reached his full maturity. It extended over a period of a full million years. So tremendously did he stride ahead, the dog ceased to be a companion. Less and less were they wanted. When the million years had passed, and man's decline began, the dog was gone. It had died out.

And now this last dwindling group of men still in the system had no other life form to make their successor. Always before when one civilization toppled, on its ashes rose a new one. Now there was but one civilization, and all other races, even other species, were gone, save in the plants. And man was too far along in his old age to bring intelligence and mobility to the plants. Perhaps he could have, in his prime.

Other worlds were flooded with man during that million years—*the* million years. Every planet and every moon of the system had its quota of men. Now only the planets had their populations, the moons had been deserted. Pluto had been left before I landed, and men were coming from Neptune, moving in toward the sun and the home planet, while I was there. Strangely quiet men, viewing, most of them, for the first time, the planet that had given their race life.

But as I stepped from that ship and watched it rise away from me, I saw why the race of man was dying. I looked back at the faces of those men, and on them I read the answer. There was one single quality gone from the still-great minds—minds far greater than yours or mine. I had to have the help of one of them in solving some of my problems. In space, you know, there are twenty coordinates, ten of which are zero, six have fixed values, and the four others represent our changing, familiar dimensions in spacetime. That means that integrations must proceed not in double, or triple, or quadruple—but ten integrations.

It would have taken me too long. I would never
have solved all the problems I must work out. I could
not use their mathematics machines, and mine, of
course, were seven million years in the past. But one
of those men was interested and helped me. He did
quadruple and quintuple integration, even quadruple
integration between varying exponential limits—in his
head.

When I asked him to. For the one thing that had
made man great had left him. As I looked in their
faces and eyes on landing I knew it. They looked at
me, interested at this rather unusual-looking stranger
—and went on. They had come to see the arrival of a
ship. A rare event, you see. But they were merely wel-
coming me in a friendly fashion. They were not curious! Man had lost the instinct of curiosity.

Oh, not entirely! They wondered at the machines,
they wondered at the stars. But they did nothing about
it. It was not wholly lost to them yet, but nearly. It
was dying. In the six short months I stayed with them,
I learned more than they had learned in the two or
even three thousand years they had lived among the
machines.

Can you appreciate the crushing hopelessness it
brought to me? I, who love science, who see in it, or
have seen in it, the salvation, the raising of mankind
—to see those wondrous machines of man's triumphant maturity forgotten and misunderstood. The
wondrous, perfect machines that tended, protected,
and cared for those gentle, kindly people who had—
forgotten.

They were lost in it. The city was a magnificent ruin
to them, a thing that rose stupendous about them.
Something not understood, a thing that was of the nature of the world. It was. It had not been made; it simply was. Just like the mountains and the deserts and
the waters of the seas.

Do you understand—can you see that the time since
those machines were new was longer than the time

from our day to the birth of the race? Do we know the legends of our first ancestors? Do we remember their lore of forest and cave? The secret of chipping a flint till it had a sharp-cutting edge? The secret of trailing and killing a sabertooth tiger without being killed oneself?

They were not in similar straits, though the time had been longer, because the language had taken a long step toward perfection, and because the machines maintained everything for them through generation after generation.

Why, the entire planet of Pluto had been deserted —yet on Pluto, where the largest mines of one of their metals were located, the machines still functioned. A perfect unity existed throughout the system. A unified system of perfect machines.

And all those people knew was that doing a certain thing to a certain lever produced certain results. Just as men in the Middle Ages knew that taking a certain material, wood, and placing it in contact with other pieces of wood heated red, would cause the wood to disappear and become heat. They did not understand that the wood was being oxidized with the release of the heat of formation of carbon dioxide and water. So those people did not understand the things that fed and clothed and carried them.

I stayed with them there for three days. And then I went to Jacksville. Yawk City, too. That was enormous. It stretched over—well, from north of where Boston is today to south of Washington—that was what they called Yawk City.

"I never believed that, when he said it," said Jim, interrupting himself.

I knew he didn't. If he had, I think he'd have bought land somewhere along there and held for a rise in value. I know Jim. He'd have the idea that seven million years was something like seven hundred, and maybe his great-grandchildren would be able to sell it.

Anyway, went on Jim, he said it was all because the cities had spread so. Boston spread south. Washington north. And Yawk City spread all over. And the cities between grew into them.

And it was all one vast machine. It was perfectly ordered and perfectly neat. They had a transportation system that took me from the North End to the South End in three minutes. I timed it. They had learned to neutralize acceleration.

Then I took one of the great spaceliners to Neptune. There were still some running. Some people, you see, were coming the other way.

The ship was huge. Mostly it was a freight liner. It floated up from Earth, a great metal cylinder three quarters of a mile long, and a quarter of a mile in diameter. Outside the atmosphere it began to accelerate. I could see Earth dwindle. I have ridden one of our own liners to Mars, and it took me, in 3048, five days. In half an hour on this liner Earth was just a star, with a smaller, dimmer star near it. In an hour we passed Mars. Eight hours later we landed on Neptune. M'reen was the city. Large as the Yawk City of my day—and no one living there.

The planet was cold and dark—horribly cold. The sun was a tiny, pale disk, heatless and almost lightless. But the city was perfectly comfortable. The air was fresh and cool, moist with the scent of growing blossoms, perfumed with them. And the whole, giant metal framework trembled just slightly with the humming, powerful beat of the mighty machines that cared for it.

I learned from records I deciphered, because of my knowledge of the ancient tongue that their tongue was based on, and the tongue of that day when man was dying, that that city was built three million, seven hundred and thirty thousand, one hundred and fifty years after my birth. Not a machine had been touched by the hand of man since that day.

Yet the air was perfect for man. And the warm,

rose-silver glow hung in the air here and supplied the only illumination.

I visited some of their other cities, where there were men. And there, on the retreating outskirts of man's domain, I first heard the Song of Longings, as I called it.

And another, the Song of Forgotten Memories. Listen—

"He sang another of those songs. There's one thing I know," declared Jim. That bewildered note was stronger in his voice, and by that time I guess I pretty well understood his feelings. Because, you have to remember, I heard it only secondhand from an ordinary man, and Jim had heard it from an eye-and-ear witness that was not ordinary, and heard it in that organ voice.

Anyway, I guess Jim was right when he said: "He wasn't any ordinary man. No ordinary man could think of those songs. They weren't right. When he sang that song, it was full of more of those plaintive minors. I could feel him searching his mind for something he had forgotten. Something he desperately wanted to remember—something he knew he should have known —and I felt it eternally elude him. I felt it get further away from him as he sang. I heard that lonely, frantic searcher attempting to recall that thing—that thing that would save him.

"And I heard him give a little sob of defeat—and the song ended." Jim tried a few notes. He hasn't a good ear for music—but that was too powerful to forget. Just a few hummed notes. Jim hasn't much imagination, I guess, or when that man of the future sang to him he would have gone mad. It shouldn't be sung to modern men; it isn't meant for them. You've heard those heartrending cries some animals give, like human cries, almost? A loon, now—he sounds like a lunatic being murdered horribly.

That's just unpleasant. That song made you feel just exactly what the singer meant—because it didn't just sound human—it was human. It was the essence of

humanity's last defeat, I guess. You always feel sorry
for the chap who loses after trying hard. Well, you
could feel the whole of humanity trying hard—and losing. And you knew they couldn't afford to lose, because they couldn't try again.

He said he'd been interested before, Jim went on.
And still not wholly upset by those machines that
couldn't stop. But that was too much for him.

I knew after that, he said, that these weren't men I
could live among. They were dying men, and I was
alive with the youth of the race. They looked at me
with the same longing, hopeless wonder with which
they looked at the stars and the machines. They knew
what I was, but couldn't understand.

I began to work on leaving.

It took six months. It was hard because my instruments were gone, of course, and theirs didn't read in
the same units. And there were few instruments, anyway. The machines didn't read instruments; they acted
on them. They were sensory organs to them.

But Reo Lantal helped where he could. And I came
back.

I did just one thing before I left that may help. I
may even try to get back there sometime. To see, you
know.

I said they had machines that could really think? But
that someone had stopped them a long time ago, and
no one knew how to start them?

I found some records and deciphered them. I started
one of the latest and best of them and started it on a
great problem. It is only fitting it should be done. The
machine can work on it, not for a thousand years but
for a million, if it must.

I started five of them actually and connected them
together as the records directed.

They are trying to make a machine with something
man had lost. It sounds rather comical. But stop to
think before you laugh. And remember that Earth as

I saw it from the ground level of Neva City just before Reo Lantal threw the switch.

Twilight—the sun has set. The desert out beyond, in its mystic, changing colors. The great, metal city rising straight-walled to the human city above, broken by spires and towers and great trees with scented blossoms. The silvery-rose glow in the paradise of gardens above.

And all the great city-structure throbbing and humming to the steady, gentle beat of perfect, deathless machines built more than three million years before—and never touched since that time by human hands. And they go on. The dead city. The men that have lived, and hoped, and built—and died to leave behind them those little men who can only wonder and look and long for a forgotten kind of companionship. They wander through the vast cities their ancestors built, knowing less of it than the machines themselves.

And the songs. Those tell the story best, I think. Little, hopeless, wondering men amid vast, unknowing, blind machines that started three million years before —and just never knew how to stop. They are dead— and can't die and be still.

So I brought another machine to life and set it to a task which, in time to come, it will perform.

I ordered it to make a machine which would have what man had lost. A curious machine.

And then I wanted to leave quickly and go back. I had been born in the first full light of man's day. I did not belong in the lingering, dying glow of man's twilight.

So I came back. A little too far back. But it will not take me long to return—accurately this time.

"Well, that was his story," Jim said. "He didn't tell me it was true—didn't say anything about it. And he had me thinking so hard, I didn't even see him get off in Reno when we stopped for gas.

"But—he wasn't an ordinary man," repeated Jim, in a rather belligerent tone.

Jim claims he doesn't believe the yarn, you know. But he does; that's why he always acts so determined about it when he says he wasn't an ordinary man.

No, he wasn't, I guess. I think he lived and died, too, probably, sometime in the thirty-first century. And I think he saw the twilight of the race, too.

HAPPY ENDING

by Henry Kuttner

Henry Kuttner was an inventive and ingenious writer, whose special pleasure was to take the ordinary pulp science fiction story apart and put it back together in previously undreamed-of ways. Here is one of his most spectacular successes.

THIS IS THE WAY THE STORY ENDED: JAMES KELVIN concentrated very hard on the thought of the chemist with the red moustache who had promised him a million dollars. It was simply a matter of tuning in on the man's brain, establishing a rapport. He had done it before. Now it was more important than ever that he do it this one last time. He pressed the button on the gadget the robot had given him, and thought hard.

Far off, across limitless distances, he found the rapport.

He clamped on the mental tight beam.

He rode it. . . .

The red-moustached man looked up, gaped, and grinned delightedly.

"So there you are!" he said. "I didn't hear you come in. Good grief, I've been trying to find you for two weeks."

"Tell me one thing quick," Kelvin said. "What's your name?"

"George Bailey. Incidentally, what's yours?"

But Kelvin didn't answer. He had suddenly remembered the other thing the robot had told him about that gadget which established rapport when he pressed the button. He pressed it now—and nothing happened. The gadget had gone dead. Its task was finished, which obviously meant he had at last achieved health, fame and fortune. The robot had warned him, of course. The thing was set to do one specialized job. Once he got what he wanted, it would work no more.

So Kelvin got the million dollars.

And he lived happily ever after. . . .

This is the middle of the story:

As he pushed aside the canvas curtain something—a carelessly hung rope—swung down at his face, knocking the horn-rimmed glasses askew. Simultaneously a vivid bluish light blazed into his unprotected eyes. He felt a curious, sharp sense of disorientation, a shifting motion that was almost instantly gone.

Things steadied before him. He let the curtain fall back into place, making legible again the painted inscription: HOROSCOPES—LEARN YOUR FUTURE—and he stood staring at the remarkable horomancer.

It was a—oh, impossible!

The robot said in a flat, precise voice, "You are James Kelvin. You are a reporter. You are thirty years old, unmarried, and you came to Los Angeles from Chicago today on the advice of your physician. Is that correct?"

In his astonishment Kelvin called on the Deity. Then he settled his glasses more firmly and tried to remember an exposé of charlatans he had once written. There was some obvious way they worked things like this, miraculous as it sounded.

The robot looked at him impassively out of its faceted eye.

"On reading your mind," it continued in the pedantic voice, "I find this is the year nineteen forty-nine. My plans will have to be revised. I had meant to arrive in the year nineteen seventy. I will ask you to assist me."

Kelvin put his hands in his pockets and grinned.

"With money, naturally," he said. "You had me going for a minute. How do you do it, anyhow? Mirrors? Or like Maelzel's chess player?"

"I am not a machine operated by a dwarf, nor am I an optical illusion," the robot assured him. "I am an artificially created living organism, originating at a period far in your future."

"And I'm not the sucker you take me for," Kelvin remarked pleasantly. "I came in here to—"

"You lost your baggage checks," the robot said. "While wondering what to do about it, you had a few drinks and took the Wilshire bus at exactly—exactly eight thirty-five post meridian."

"Lay off the mind-reading," Kelvin said. "And don't tell me you've been running this joint very long with a line like that. The cops would be after you. *If* you're a real robot, ha, ha."

"I have been running this joint," the robot said, "for approximately five minutes. My predecessor is unconscious behind that chest in the corner. Your arrival here was sheer coincidence." It paused very briefly, and Kelvin had the curious impression that it was watching to see if the story so far had gone over well.

The impression was curious because Kelvin had no feeling at all that there was a man in the large, jointed figure before him. If such as a thing as a robot were possible, he would have believed implicitly that he confronted a genuine specimen. Such things being impossible, he waited to see what the gimmick would be.

"My arrival here was also accidental," the robot informed him. "This being the case, my equipment will have to be altered slightly. I will require certain substitute mechanisms. For that, I gather as I read your mind, I will have to engage in your peculiar barter system of economics. In a word, coinage or gold or silver certificates will be necessary. Thus I am—temporarily—a horomancer."

"Sure, sure," Kelvin said. "Why not a simple mugging? If you're a robot, you could do a super-mugging job with a quick twist of the gears."

"It would attract attention. Above all, I require secrecy. As a matter of fact, I am—" the robot paused, searched Kelvin's brain for the right phrase, and said, "—on the lam. In my era, time-traveling is strictly forbidden, even by accident, unless government-sponsored."

There was a fallacy there somewhere, Kelvin thought, but he couldn't quite spot it. He blinked at the robot intently. It looked pretty unconvincing.

"What proof do you need?" the creature asked. "I read your brain the minute you came in, didn't I? You must have felt the temporary amnesia as I drew out the knowledge and then replaced it."

"So that's what happened," Kelvin said. He took a cautious step backward. "Well, I think I'll be getting along."

"Wait," the robot commanded. "I see you have begun to distrust me. Apparently you now regret having suggested a mugging job. You fear I may act on the suggestion. Allow me to reassure you. It is true that I could take your money and assure secrecy by killing you, but I am not permitted to kill humans. The alternative is to engage in the barter system. I can offer you something valuable in return for a small amount of gold. Let me see." The faceted gaze swept around the tent, dwelt piercingly for a moment on Kelvin. "A horoscope," the robot said. "It is supposed to help you achieve health, fame and fortune. Astrology, however, is out of my line. I can merely offer a logical scientific method of attaining the same results."

"Uh-huh," Kelvin said skeptically. "How much? And why haven't *you* used that method?"

"I have other ambitions," the robot said in a cryptic manner. "Take this." There was a brief clicking. A panel opened in the metallic chest. The robot extracted a small, flat case and handed it to Kelvin, who automatically closed his fingers on the cold metal.

"Be careful. Don't push that button until—"

But Kelvin had pushed it. . . .

He was driving a figurative car that had got out of control. There was somebody else inside his head. There was a schizophrenic, double-tracked locomotive that was running wild and his hand on the throttle couldn't slow it down an instant. His mental steering-wheel had snapped.

Somebody else was thinking for him!

Not quite a human being. Not quite sane, probably, from Kelvin's standards. But awfully sane from his own. Sane enough to have mastered the most intricate principles of non-Euclidean geometry in the nursery.

The senses got synthesized in the brain into a sort of common language, a master-tongue. Part of it was auditory, part pictorial, and there were smells and tastes and tactile sensations that were sometimes familiar and sometimes spiced with the absolutely alien. And it was chaotic.

Something like this, perhaps. . . .

"—Big Lizards getting too numerous this season— tame threvvars have the same eyes not on Callisto though—vacation soon—preferably galactic—solar system claustrophobic—byanding tomorrow if square rootola and upsliding three—"

But that was merely the word-symbolism. Subjectively, it was far more detailed and very frightening. Luckily, reflex had lifted Kelvin's fingers from the button almost instantly, and he stood there motionless, shivering slightly.

He was afraid now.

The robot said, "You should not have begun the rapport until I instructed you. Now there will be dan-

ger. Wait." His eye changed color. Yes . . . there is
. . . Tharn, yes. Beware of Tharn."

"I don't want any part of it," Kelvin said quickly.
"Here, take this thing back."

"Then you will be unprotected against Tharn. Keep
the device. It will, as I promised, insure your health,
fame and fortune, far more effectively than a—a horoscope."

"No, thanks. I don't know how you managed that
trick—subsonics, maybe, but I don't—"

"Wait," the robot said. "When you pressed that button, you were in the mind of someone who exists very
far in the future. It created a temporal rapport. You
can bring about that rapport any time you press the
button."

"Heaven forfend," Kelvin said, still sweating a little.

"Consider the opportunities. Suppose a troglodyte of
the far past had access to your brain? He could
achieve anything he wanted."

It had become important, somehow, to find a logical
rebuttal to the robot's arguments. Like St. Anthony—
or was it Luther?—arguing with the devil, Kelvin
thought dizzily. His headache was worse, and he sus-
pected he had drunk more than was good for him. But
he merely said: "How could a troglodyte understand
what's in my brain? He couldn't apply the knowledge
without the same conditioning I've had."

"Have you ever had sudden and apparently illogical
ideas? Compulsions? So that you seem forced to think
of certain things, count up to certain numbers, work
out particular problems? Well, the man in the future
on whom my device is focused doesn't know he's *en
rapport* with you, Kelvin. But he's vulnerable to com-
pusions. All you have to do is concentrate on a problem and then press the button. Your rapport will be
compelled—illogically, from his viewpoint—to solve
that problem. And you'll be reading his brain. You'll
find out how it works. There are limitations; you'll

learn those too. And the device will insure health, wealth and fame for you."

"It would insure anything, if it really worked that way. I could do anything. That's why I'm not buying!"

"I said there were limitations. As soon as you've successfully achieved health, fame and fortune, the device will become useless. I've taken care of that. But meanwhile you can use it to solve all your problems by tapping the brain of the more intelligent specimen in the future. The important point is to concentrate on your problems *before* you press the button. Otherwise you may get more than Tharn on your track."

"Tharn? What—"

"I think an—an android," the robot said, looking at nothing. "An artificial human . . . However, let us consider my own problem. I need a small amount of gold."

"So that's the kicker," Kelvin said, feeling oddly relieved. He said, "I haven't got any."

"Your watch."

Kelvin jerked his arm so that his wristwatch showed. "Oh, no. That watch cost plenty."

"All I need is the gold-plating," the robot said, shooting out a reddish gray from its eye. "Thank you." The watch was now dull gray metal.

"Hey!" Kelvin cried.

"If you use the rapport device, your health, fame and fortune will be assured," the robot said rapidly. "You will be as happy as any man of this era can be. It will solve all your problems—including Tharn. Wait a minute." The creature took a backward step and disappeared behind a hanging Oriental rug that had never been east of Peoria.

There was silence.

Kelvin looked from his altered watch to the flat, enigmatic object in his palm. It was about two inches by two inches, and no thicker than a woman's vanity-case, and there was a sunken push-button on its side.

He dropped it into his pocket and took a few steps forward. He looked behind the pseudo-Oriental rug, to find nothing except emptiness and a flapping slit cut in the canvas wall of the booth. The robot, it seemed, had taken a powder. Kelvin peered out through the slit. There was the light and sound of Ocean Park amusement pier, that was all. And the silvered, moving blackness of the Pacific Ocean, stretching to where small lights showed Malibu far up the invisible curve of the coastal cliffs.

So he came back inside the booth and looked around. A fat man in a swami's costume was unconscious behind the carved chest the robot had indicated. His breath, plus a process of deduction, told Kelvin that the man had been drinking.

Not knowing what else to do, Kelvin called on the Deity again. He found suddenly that he was thinking about someone or something called Tharn, who was an android.

Horomancy . . . time . . . rapport . . . *no!* Protective disbelief slid like plate armor around his mind. A practical robot couldn't be made. He knew that. He'd have heard—he was a reporter, wasn't he?

Sure he was.

Desiring noise and company, he went along to the shooting gallery and knocked down a few ducks. The flat case burned in his pocket. The dully burnished metal of his wristwatch burned in his memory. The remembrance of that drainage from his brain, and the immediate replacement, burned in his mind. Presently bar whiskey burned in his stomach.

He'd left Chicago because of sinusitis, recurrent and annoying. Ordinary sinusitis. Not schizophrenia or hallucinations or accusing voices coming from the walls. Not because he had been seeing bats or robots. That thing hadn't really been a robot. It all had a perfectly natural explanation. Oh, sure.

Health, fame and fortune. And if——

THARN!

The thought crashed with thunderbolt impact into his head.

And then another thought: I *am* going nuts!

A silent voice began to mutter insistently over and over. "Tharn—Tharn—Tharn—Tharn—"

And another voice, the voice of sanity and safety, answered it and drowned it out. Half aloud, Kelvin muttered: "I'm James Noel Kelvin. I'm a reporter—special features, legwork, rewrite. I'm thirty years old, unmarried, and I came to Los Angeles today and lost my baggage checks and—and I'm going to have another drink and find a hotel. Anyhow, the climate seems to be curing my sinusitis."

Tharn, the muffled drum-beat said almost below the threshold of realization. *Tharn, Tharn.*

Tharn.

He ordered another drink and reached in his pocket for a coin. His hand touched the metal case. And simultaneously he felt a light pressure on his shoulder.

Instinctively he glanced around. It was a seven-fingered, spidery hand tightening—hairless, without nails—and white as smooth ivory.

The one, overwhelming necessity that sprang into Kelvin's mind was a simple longing to place as much space as possible between himself and the owner of that disgusting hand. It was a vital requirement, but one difficult of fulfillment, a problem that excluded everything else from Kelvin's thoughts. He knew, vaguely, that he was gripping the flat case in his pocket as though that could save him, but all he was thinking about was: I've got to get away from here.

The monstrous, alien thoughts of someone in the future spun him insanely along their current. It could not have taken a moment while that skilled, competent, trained mind, wise in the lore of an unthinkable future, solved the random problem that had come so suddenly, with such curious compulsion.

Three methods of transportation were simultaneously clear to Kelvin. Two he discarded; motorplates were obviously inventions yet to come, and quirling—involving, as it did, a sensory coil-helmet—was beyond him. But the third method—

Already the memory was fading. And that hand was still tightening on his shoulder. He clutched at the vanishing ideas and desperately made his brain and his muscles move along the unlikely direction the future man had visualized.

And he was out in the open, a cold night wind blowing on him, still in a sitting position, but with nothing but empty air between his spine and the sidewalk.

He sat down suddenly.

Passers-by on the corner of Hollywood Boulevard and Cahuenga were not much surprised at the sight of a dark, lanky man sitting by the curb. Only one woman had noticed Kelvin's actual arrival, and she knew when she was well off. She went right on home.

Kelvin got up laughing with soft hysteria. "Teleportation," he said. "How did I work it? It's gone. . . . Hard to remember afterward, eh? I'll have to start carrying a notebook again."

And then— "But what about Tharn?"

He looked around, frightened. Reassurance came only after half an hour had passed without additional miracles. Kelvin walked along the Boulevard, keeping a sharp lookout. No Tharn, though.

Occasionally he slid a hand into his pocket and touched the cold metal of the case. Health, fame and fortune. Why, he could—

But he did not press the button. Too vivid was the memory of that shocking, alien disorientation he had felt. The mind, the experiences, the habit-patterns of the far future were uncomfortably strong.

He would use the little case again—oh, yes. But there was no hurry. First he'd have to work out a few angles.

His disbelief was completely gone.

Tharn showed up the next night and scared the daylights out of Kelvin again. Prior to that, the reporter had failed to find his baggage tickets, and was only consoled by the two hundred bucks in his wallet. He took a room—paying in advance—at a medium-good hotel, and began wondering how he might apply his pipeline to the future. Very sensibly, he decided to continue a normal life until something developed. At any rate, he'd have to make a few connections. He tried the *Times,* the *Examiner,* the *News,* and some others. But these things develop slowly, except in the movies. That night Kelvin was in his hotel room when his unwelcome guest appeared.

It was, of course, Tharn.

He wore a very large white turban, approximately twice the size of his head. He had a dapper black moustache, waxed downward at the tips like the moustache of a mandarin or a catfish. He stared urgently at Kelvin out of the bathroom mirror.

Kelvin had been wondering whether or not he needed a shave before going out to dinner. He was rubbing his chin thoughtfully at the moment Tharn put in an appearance, and there was a perceptible mental lag between occurrence and perception, so that to Kelvin it seemed that he himself had mysteriously sprouted a long moustache. He reached for his upper lip. It was smooth. But in the glass the black waxed hairs quivered as Tharn pushed his face up against the surface of the mirror.

It was so shockingly disorienting, somehow, that Kelvin was quite unable to think at all. He took a quick step backward. The edge of the bathtub caught him behind the knees and distracted him momentarily, fortunately for his sanity. When he looked again there was only his own appalled face reflected above the washbowl. But after a second or two the face seemed to develop a cloud of white turban, and mandarinlike whiskers began to form sketchily.

Kelvin clapped a hand to his eyes and spun away.

In about fifteen seconds he spread his fingers enough
to peep through them at the glass. He kept his palm
pressed desperately to his upper lip, in some wild hope
of inhibiting the sudden sprouting of a moustache.
What peeped back at him from the mirror looked like
himself. At least it had no turban, and it wore horn-
rimmed glasses. He risked snatching his hand away
from a quick look, and clapped it in place again just in
time to prevent Tharn from taking shape in the glass.

Still shielding his face, he went unsteadily into the
bedroom and took the flat case out of his coat pocket.
But he didn't press the button that would close a mental synapse between two incongruous eras. He didn't
want to do that again, he realized. More horrible,
somehow, than what was happening now was the
thought of reentering that *alien* brain.

He was standing before the bureau, and in the mirror one eye looked out at him between reflected fingers. It was a wild eye behind the gleaming spectacle-
lens, but it seemed to be his own. Tentatively he took
his hand away. . . .

This mirror showed more of Tharn. Kelvin wished it
hadn't. Tharn was wearing white knee-boots of some
glittering plastic. Between them and the turban he
wore nothing whatever except a minimum of loincloth,
also glittering plastic. Tharn was very thin, but he
looked active. He looked quite active enough to spring
right into the hotel room. His skin was whiter than his
turban, and his hands had seven fingers each, all right.

Kelvin abruptly turned away, but Tharn was re-
sourceful. The dark window made enough of a reflecting surface to show a lean, loinclothed figure. The feet
showed bare and they were less normal than Tharn's
hands. And the polished brass of a lamp base gave
back the picture of a small, distorted face not Kelvin's
own.

Kelvin found a corner without reflecting surfaces
and pushed into it, his hands shielding his face. He was
still holding the flat case.

Oh, fine, he thought bitterly. Everything's got a string on it. What good will this rapport gadget do me if Tharn's going to show up every day? Maybe I'm only crazy. I hope so.

Something would have to be done unless Kelvin was prepared to go through life with his face buried in his hands. The worst of it was that Tharn had a haunting look of familiarity. Kelvin discarded a dozen possibilities, from reincarnation to the *déjà vu* phenomenon, but—

He peeped through his hands, in time to see Tharn raising a cylindrical gadget of some sort and leveling it like a gun. That gesture formed Kelvin's decision. He'd *have* to do something, and fast. So, concentrating on the problem—*I want out!*—he pressed the button in the surface of the flat case.

And instantly the teleportation method he had forgotten was perfectly clear to him. Other matters, however, were obscure. The smells—someone was thinking —were adding up to a—there was no word for that, only a shocking visio-auditory ideation that was simply dizzying. Someone named Three Million and Ninety Pink had written a new flatch. And there was the physical sensation of licking a twenty-four-dollar stamp and sticking it on a postcard.

But, most important, the man in the future had had —or would have—a compulsion to think about the teleportation method, and as Kelvin snapped back into his own mind and time, he instantly used that method. . . .

He was falling.

Icy water attacked him hard. Miraculously he kept his grip on the flat case. He had a whirling vision of stars in a night sky, and the phosphorescent sheen of silvery light on a dark sea. Then brine stung his nostrils.

Kelvin had never learned how to swim.

As he went down for the last time, bubbling a scream, he literally clutched at the proverbial straw he was holding. His finger pushed the button down again. There was no need to concentrate on the problem; he couldn't think of anything else.

Mental chaos, fantastic images—and the answer.

It took concentration, and there wasn't much time left. Bubbles streamed up past his face. He felt them, but he couldn't see them. All around, pressing in avidly, was the horrible coldness of the salt water. . . .

But he did know the method now, and he knew how it worked. He thought along the lines the future mind had indicated. Something happened. Radiation—that was the nearest familiar term—poured out of his brain and did peculiar things to his lung-tissues. His blood cells adapted themselves. . . .

He was breathing water, and it was no longer strangling him.

But Kelvin had also learned that his emergency adaptation could not be maintained for very long. Teleportation was the answer to that. And surely he could remember the method now. He had actually used it to escape from Tharn only a few minutes ago.

Yet he could not remember. The memory was expunged cleanly from his mind. So there was nothing else to do but press the button again, and Kelvin did that, most reluctantly.

Dripping wet, he was standing on an unfamiliar street. It was no street he knew, but apparently it was in his own time and on his own planet. Luckily, teleportation seemed to have limitations. The wind was cold. Kelvin stood in a puddle that grew rapidly around his feet. He stared around.

He picked out a sign up the street that offered Turkish Baths, and headed moistly in that direction. His thoughts were mostly profane. . . .

He was in New Orleans, of all places. Presently he was drunk in New Orleans. His thoughts kept going around in circles, and Scotch was a fine palliative, an excellent brake. He needed to get control again. He had an almost miraculous power, and he wanted to be able to use it effectively before the unexpected happened again. Tharn . . .

He sat in a hotel room and swigged Scotch. Gotta be logical!

He sneezed.

The trouble was, of course, that there were so few points of contact between his own mind and that of the future-man. Moreover, he'd got the rapport only in times of crisis. Like having access to the Alexandrian Library, five seconds a day. In five seconds you couldn't even start translating. . . .

Health, fame and fortune. He sneezed again. The robot had been a liar. His health seemed to be going fast. What about that robot? How had he got involved anyway? He said he'd fallen into this era from the future, but robots are notorious liars. Gotta be logical.

Apparently the future was peopled by creatures not unlike the cast of a Frankenstein picture. Androids, robots, so-called men whose minds were shockingly different . . . *Sneeze*. Another drink.

The robot had said that the case would lose its power after Kelvin had achieved health, fame and fortune. Which was a distressing thought. Suppose he attained those enviable goals, found the little push-button useless, and *then* Tharn showed up? Oh, no. That called for another shot.

Sobriety was the wrong condition in which to approach a matter that in itself was as wild as delirium tremens, even though, Kelvin knew, the science he had stumbled on was all theoretically quite possible. But not in this day and age. *Sneeze*.

The trick would be to pose the right problem and use the case at some time when you weren't drowning or being menaced by the bewhiskered android with his seven-fingered hands and his ominous rodlike weapon. Find the problem.

But that future-mind was hideous.

And suddenly, with drunken clarity, Kelvin realized

that he was profoundly drawn to that dim, shadowy world of the future.

He could not see its complete pattern, but he sensed it somehow. He knew that it was *right,* a far better world and time than his. If he could *be* that unknown man who dwelt there, all would go well.

Man must needs love the highest, he thought wryly. Oh, well. He shook the bottle. How much had he absorbed? He felt fine.

Gotta be logical.

Outside the window street-lights blinked off and on. Neons traced goblin languages against the night. It seemed rather alien, too, but so did Kelvin's own body. He started to laugh, but a sneeze choked that off.

All I want, he thought, is health, fame and fortune. Then I'll settle down and live happily ever after, without a care or worry. I won't need this enchanted case after that. Happy ending.

On impulse he took out the box and examined it. He tried to pry it open and failed. His finger hovered over the button.

How can I—he thought, and his finger moved half an inch. . . .

It wasn't so alien now that he was drunk. The future man's name was Quarra Vee. Odd he had never realized that before, but how often does a man think of his own name? Quarra Vee was playing some sort of game vaguely reminiscent of chess, but his opponent was on a planet of Sirius, some distance away. The chessmen were all unfamiliar. Complicated, dizzying space-time gambits flashed through Quarra Vee's mind as Kelvin listened in. Then Kelvin's problem thrust through, the compulsion hit Quarra Vee, and—

It was all mixed up. There were two problems, really. How to cure a cold—coryza. And how to become healthy, rich and famous in a practically prehistoric era—for Quarra Vee.

A small problem, however, to Quarra Vee. He

solved it and went back to his game with the Sirian.

Kelvin was back in the hotel room in New Orleans.

He was very drunk or he wouldn't have risked it. The method involved using his brain to tune in on another brain in this present twentieth century that had exactly the wavelength he required. All sorts of factors would build up to the sum total of that wavelength— experience, opportunity, position, knowledge, imagination, honesty—but he found it at last, after hesitation among three totals that were all nearly right. Still, one was righter, to three decimal points. Still drunk as a lord, Kelvin clamped on a mental tight beam, turned on the teleportation, and rode the beam across America to a well-equipped laboratory, where a man sat reading.

The man was bald and had a bristling red moustache. He looked up sharply at some sound Kelvin made.

"Hey!" he said. "How did you get in here?"

"Ask Quarra Vee," Kelvin said.

"Who? *What?*" The man put down his book.

Kelvin called on his memory. It seemed to be slipping. He used the rapport case for an instant, and refreshed his mind. Not so unpleasant this time, either. He was beginning to understand Quarra Vee's world a little. He liked it. However, he supposed he'd forget that too.

"An improvement on Woodward's protein analogues," he told the red-moustached man. "Simple synthesis will do it."

"Who the devil are you?"

"Call me Jim," Kelvin said simply. "And shut up and listen." He began to explain, as to a small, stupid child. (The man before him was one of America's foremost chemists.) "Proteins are made of amino acids. There are about thirty-three amino acids—"

"There aren't."

"There are. Shut up. Their molecules can be arranged in lots of ways. So we get an almost infinite va-

riety of proteins. And all living things are forms of
protein. The absolute synthesis involves a chain of
amino acids long enough to recognize clearly as a protein molecule. That's been the trouble."

The man with the red moustache seemed quite interested. "Fischer assembled a chain of eighteen," he
said, blinking. "Abderhalden got up to nineteen, and
Woodward, of course, has made chains ten thousand
units long. But as for testing—"

"The complete protein molecule consists of complete sets of sequences. But if you test only one or two
sections of an analogue you can't be sure of the others.
Wait a minute." Kelvin used the rapport case again.
"Now I know. Well, you can make almost anything
out of synthesized protein. Silk, wool, hair—but the
main thing, of course," he said, sneezing, "is a cure for
coryza."

"Now look—" said the red-moustached man.

"Some of the viruses are chains of amino acids,
aren't they? Well, modify their structure. Make 'em
harmless. Bacteria, too. And synthesize antibiotics."

"I wish I could. However, Mr.—"

"Just call me Jim."

"Yes. However, all this is old stuff."

"Grab your pencil," Kelvin said. "From now on it'll
be solid, with riffs. The method of synthesizing and
testing is as follows—"

He explained, very thoroughly and clearly. He had
to use the rapport case only twice. And when he had
finished, the man with the red moustache laid down his
pencil and stared.

"This is incredible," he said. "If it works—"

"I want health, fame and fortune," Kelvin said stub-
bornly. "It'll work."

"Yes, but—my good man—"

However, Kelvin insisted. Luckily for himself, the
mental testing of the red-moustached man had included briefing for honesty and opportunity, and it
ended with the chemist agreeing to sign partnership pa-

pers with Kelvin. The commercial possibilities of the process were unbounded. Du Pont or GM would be glad to buy it.

"I want lots of money. A fortune."

"You'll make a million dollars," the red-moustached man said patiently.

"Then I want a receipt. Have to have this in black and white. Unless you want to give me my million now."

Frowning, the chemist shook his head. "I can't do that. I'll have to run tests, open negotiations—but don't worry about that. Your discovery is certainly worth a million. You'll be famous, too."

"And healthy?"

"There won't be any more disease, after a while," the chemist said quietly. "That's the real miracle."

"Write it down," Kelvin clamored.

"All right. We can have partnership papers drawn up tomorrow. This will do temporarily. Understand, the actual credit belongs to you."

"It's got to be in ink. A pencil won't do."

"Just a minute, then," the red-moustached man said, and went away in search of ink. Kelvin looked around the laboratory, beaming happily.

Tharn materialized three feet away. Tharn was holding the rod-weapon. He lifted it.

Kelvin instantly used the rapport case. Then he thumbed his nose at Tharn and teleported himself far away.

He was immediately in a cornfield, somewhere, but undistilled corn was not what Kelvin wanted. He tried again. This time he reached Seattle.

That was the beginning of Kelvin's monumental two-week combination binge and chase.

His thoughts weren't pleasant.

He had a frightful hangover, ten cents in his pocket, and an overdue hotel bill. A fortnight of keeping one jump ahead of Tharn, via teleportation, had frazzled his nerves so unendurably that only liquor had kept him going. Now even that stimulus was failing. The drink died in him and left what felt like a corpse.

Kelvin groaned and blinked miserably. He took off his glasses and cleaned them, but that didn't help.

What a fool.

He didn't even know the name of the chemist!

There was health, wealth and fame waiting for him just around the corner, but what corner? Someday he'd find out, probably, when the news of the new protein synthesis was publicized, but when would that be? In the meantime, what about Tharn?

Moreover, the chemist couldn't locate him, either. The man knew Kelvin only as Jim. Which had somehow seemed a good idea at the time, but not now.

Kelvin took out the rapport case and stared at it with red eyes. Quarra Vee, eh? He rather liked Quarra Vee now. Trouble was, a half hour after his rapport, at most, he could forget all the details.

This time he used the push-button almost as Tharn snapped into bodily existence a few feet away.

The teleportation angle again. He was sitting in the middle of a desert. Cactus and Joshua trees were all the scenery. There was a purple range of mountains far away.

No Tharn, though.

Kelvin began to be thirsty. Suppose the case stopped working now? Oh, this couldn't go on. A decision hanging fire for a week finally crystallized into a conclusion so obvious he felt like kicking himself. Perfectly obvious!

Why hadn't he thought of it at the very beginning?

He concentrated on the problem: How can I get rid of Tharn? He pushed the button. . . .

And a moment later, he knew the answer. It would be simple, really.

The pressing urgency was gone suddenly. That seemed to release a fresh flow of thought. Everything became quite clear.

He waited for Tharn.

He did not have to wait long. There was a tremor in the shimmering air, and the turbaned, pallid figure sprang into tangible reality.

The rod-weapon was poised.

Taking no chances, Kelvin posed his problem again, pressed the button, and instantly reassured himself as to the method. He simply thought in a very special and peculiar way—the way Quarra Vee had indicated.

Tharn was flung back a few feet. The moustached mouth gaped open as he uttered a cry.

"Don't!" the android cried. "I've been trying to—"

Kelvin focused harder on his thought. Mental energy, he felt, was pouring out toward the android.

Tharn croaked. "Trying—you didn't—give me—chance—"

And then Tharn was lying motionless on the hot sand, staring blindly up. The seven-fingered hands twitched once and were still. The artificial life that had animated the android was gone. It would not return.

Kelvin turned his back and drew a long, shuddering breath. He was safe. He closed his mind to all thoughts but one, all problems but one.

How can I find the red-moustached man?

He pressed the button.

This is the way the story starts:

Quarra Vee sat in the temporal warp with his android Tharn, and made sure everything was under control.

"How do I look?" he asked.

"You'll pass," Tharn said. "Nobody will be suspicious in the era you're going to. It didn't take long to synthesize the equipment."

"Not long. Clothes—they look enough like real wool and linen, I suppose. Wristwatch, money—everything in order. Wristwatch—that's odd, isn't it? Imagine people who need machinery to tell time!"

"Don't forget the spectacles," Tharn said.

Quarra Vee put them on. "Ugh. But I suppose—"

"It'll be safer. The optical properties in the lenses are a guard you may need against mental radiations. Don't take them off, or the robot may try some tricks."

"He'd better not," Quarra Vee said. "That so-and-so runaway robot! What's he up to, anyway, I wonder? He always was a malcontent, but at least he knew his place. I'm sorry I ever had him made. No telling what he'll do in a semi-prehistoric world if we don't catch him and bring him home."

"He's in that horomancy booth," Tharn said, leaning out of the time-warp. "Just arrived. You'll have to catch him by surprise. And you'll need your wits about you, too. Try not to go off into any more of those deep-thought compulsions you've been having. They could be dangerous. That robot will use some of his tricks if he gets the chance. I don't know what powers he's developed by himself, but I do know he's an expert at hypnosis and memory erasure already. If you aren't careful he'll snap your memory-track and substitute a false brain-pattern. Keep those glasses on. If anything should go wrong, I'll use the rehabilitation ray on you, eh?" And he held up a small rodlike projector.

Quarra Vee nodded. "Don't worry. I'll be back before you know it. I have an appointment with that Sirian to finish our game this evening."

It was an appointment he never kept.

Quarra Vee stepped out of the temporal warp and strolled along the boardwalk toward the booth. The clothing he wore felt tight, uncomfortable, rough. He wriggled a little in it. The booth stood before him now, with its painted sign.

He pushed aside the canvas curtain and something —a carelessly hung rope—swung down at his face, knocking the horn-rimmed glasses askew. Simultaneously a vivid bluish light blazed into his unprotected eyes. He felt a curious, sharp sensation of disorientation, a shifting motion that almost instantly was gone.

The robot said, "You are James Kelvin."